THE CIA AND THE MARSHALL PLAN

THE CIA
AND THE
MARSHALL
PLAN

Sallie Pisani

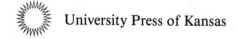 University Press of Kansas

Published by the University Press of Kansas (Lawrence, Kansas
66049), which was organized by the Kansas Board of Regents and is
operated and funded by Emporia State University, Fort Hays State
University, Kansas State University, Pittsburg State University,
the University of Kansas, and Wichita State University

Library of Congress Cataloging-in-Publication Data

Pisani, Sallie.
The CIA and the Marshall Plan / Sallie Pisani.
p.   cm.
Includes bibliographical references (p.   ) and index.
ISBN 0-7006-0502-9 (alk. paper)
1. Marshall Plan.   2. Reconstruction (1939–1951)   3. Europe—
Foreign economic relations—United States.   4. United States—
Foreign economic relations—Europe.   5. United States.   Central
Intelligence Agency.   I. Title.
HC240.P555   1992
338.9 '17304—dc20   91-16840

British Library Cataloguing in Publication Data is available.

Printed in the United States of America
10 9 8 7 6 5 4 3 2 1

The paper used in this publication meets the minimum requirements of
the American National Standard for Permanence of Paper for Printed
Library Materials Z39.48-1984.

FOR MY FAMILY

CONTENTS

Acknowledgments

ix

ONE

Introduction

1

TWO

A Grounding in American Interventionism

9

THREE

Uncoordinated Intervention

34

FOUR

Coordinated Intervention

58

FIVE

France: Fully Functioning Intervention

81

SIX

Italy-Iran: Interlocking Themes for Global Intervention

106

SEVEN

Interventionism and Presidential Transitions

128

Appendix

139

Notes

147

Bibliography
171
List of Abbreviations
179
Index
181

ACKNOWLEDGMENTS

I am pleased to have the opportunity to acknowledge the support, honesty, and friendship exhibited by my dissertation advisor, David M. Oshinsky. Lloyd Gardner and Philip Greven helped immeasurably—I have indeed been a fortunate student of history. Thanks also to my outside reader, John Leggett, for his challenging perspective.

At a critical juncture in this project, my friend George Sirgiovanni helped me restructure and clarify my ideas.

During my graduate years I benefited from the support of the Rutgers History Department, both financially and through the sharing of time and ideas. I would especially like to thank Samuel L. Baily, Mark Wasserman, John W. Chambers III, Allen Howard, and Michael Adas for suggestions long incorporated in this work.

I was fortunate enough to spend my graduate years at Rutgers in the company of Paula Baker and Kathleen Jones. Their ideas encouraged me to ask a different set of questions than would normally have been the case for a diplomatic historian.

During the last year of this project I have received scholarly support from my colleagues in the History Department at Monmouth College, particularly Thomas Pearson; financial support from the College Grants Committee; and administrative consideration from Dean Gloria Nemerowicz. The community at Monmouth has a way of collaborating to create an atmosphere conducive to scholarly endeavor.

As all historians know, particularly those of us in diplomatic history, archivists are a special breed. Everywhere I traveled they were there to help, especially the fine people at the Harry S. Truman Library, Dennis Bilger in particular. The Truman Library also honored me with a fellowship, allowing me to spend considerable time in Independence. Nancy Bressler and her assistants at Seeley Mudd Library at Princeton and Anne Newhall at the Ford Foundation all made my visits profitable. Special mention is fitting for the people at the National Archives. Understaffed and overworked though they may be, George Chalou and Ed Reece at Military Reference and Kathy NiCastro in the Diplomatic Branch always seemed to have the answers I needed. Ron Grele, the director of the Columbia Oral History Project, advised me on the legal aspects of oral history as well as directing me to valuable sources. In my case it is certainly true that this work would not have taken form without them all.

Special friends have not only been accepting of the vagaries of a social life with an academic but have read drafts and helped me contact sources. I have counted through the years on the friendship of Sally and Ted Thomas, Susan and Roger Cohen, Janet and Walter Dunsby, Mary-Lou and Bart Carhart, James Anderson and Glen Cowan, Tom and Maureen Deakin, Judith and John Fredericks, Peter Wegener and Saliba Sarsar.

My editor at Kansas, Mike Briggs, encouraged me throughout this project. His wit, wisdom, and extraordinary patience sustained me.

My greatest and fondest debt is to my family. My husband, Frank, my daughter, Aurora, and my son, Francis, abided it all with love and appreciation for my task. My mother, Martha Clayton Kremer, stayed proud that I was so engaged, even when I was less than attentive. My father-in-law, Frank Pisani, helped in ways that can't be measured. My brothers, Ward and Clayton Kremer, were always there when I needed them. My sister-in-law, Betty Kremer, became my sister. My father, Ward Kremer, left me the legacy of loving history. That is why this book is dedicated to them.

ONE
INTRODUCTION

I n August 1941 the two most powerful men in the Anglo-American world, Franklin Roosevelt and Winston Churchill, met aboard ship off the coast of Newfoundland to discuss the great crisis confronting their countries. Battered Britain had been fighting for its survival for nearly two years; the United States would soon join that country in the war against the Axis. Deeming "it right to make known certain common principles . . . [upon] which they based their hopes for a better future for the world," Roosevelt and Churchill drafted the Atlantic Charter. This document enunciated the moral basis for the Allied cause during World War II.

Of the charter's eight points, none was more idealistic, more liberally democratic, and more likely to trigger future conflict than Point Three. Here the signatories asserted the "right of all peoples to choose the form of government under which they will live" and their desire "to see sovereign rights and self-government restored to those who have been forcibly deprived of them." These lofty words, reaffirming President Woodrow Wilson's commitment to universal self-determination, reflected a fundamental American conviction about what nations would do if left to choose their own form of government: This process would always lead to democracy.

What Roosevelt and Churchill failed to see at the time was that idealistic obedience to this principle would set the stage for future conflict. The historian Gaddis Smith has suggested that an "irresolvable contradiction" lay within this idea. "How," he asked, "could the United States pledge to respect the right of every nation to determine its own way of life and at the same time insist that such a way of life imitate American ideals of human rights?" And if an existing government violated those rights, Smith queried, should "the United States abandon the principles of non-intervention and self-determination in order to rectify . . . that violation?"[1]

These important questions faced American policymakers once World War II was over, as American ideas about self-determination were challenged by political events in Europe. The devastated countries of Western Europe seemed ripe for the expansionist ambitions of the Soviet Union. American policymakers, though they wanted to intervene on a massive scale to remedy Europe's plight, also retained allegiance to the principles of the Atlantic Charter. Moreover, they found it difficult to imagine that other peoples, given a free choice, might reject Western-style democracy. Thus when the Soviet Union tried to influence the "self-determination" process in its own favor, U.S. policymakers were sure the outcome would be tainted.

The postwar threat to free choice in Europe seemed complicated and dangerous. The wartime Fascist assault on self-determination was military—obvious to everyone—making it easier to mobilize support for a credible opposition. Now the Soviets employed new, subtler tactics that were far more difficult to counteract. Using methods that American policymakers called "subversive," the Soviets marshaled their resources in an attempt to swing elections sharply to the left in several European nations. American policymakers responded by devising methods to ensure the goal of self-determination without having to build mass support on behalf of such a policy. They feared such a complex, long-term problem would be difficult to explain to a volatile American public unsophisticated about foreign policy issues. Instead, policymakers added a Cold War corollary to the principle of self-determination: massive infusion of U.S. aid would be required for war-torn Europe to reaffirm its democratic faith.

When even this expanded principle proved insufficient to the task at hand, the U.S. government found it difficult to publicly admit the extent to which intervention would be necessary to ensure that self-determination yielded the desired results. Accordingly, covert political activism gained acceptance as the best means of achieving those results without having to confront directly discordant realities. As such, the idealistic vision of self-determination rested upon a foundation of actions and methods that were wholly incompatible with self-determination itself.

Large-scale covert activity required wholesale changes in the U.S. bureaucracy, especially in the intelligence community. The notion of planning and implementing operations under the aegis of intelligence, rather than simply gathering information, was a new one. In addition, a trained professional elite was needed to carry out covert planning and operations. In fact, such an elite—endowed with all the experience, background, and training needed—already existed in the United States. This book concerns the men who developed the covert intervention policies of the early Cold War years and an organization to carry them out called the Office of Policy Coordination. These men acted in a spirit of shared idealism about self-determination, even as they recognized its limitations in the harsh reality of Cold War geopolitics. They saw their mission in postwar Europe as one of guiding the process of self-determination along a path leading to freedom, stability, and prosperity. Viewing themselves as part of a team of experts charged with a task vital to their country, they relished the opportunity to take on this challenge.

Crucial figures in this group include Richard M. Bissell, Jr., John A. Bross, Kermit Roosevelt, Lawrence Houston, and Franklin Lindsay, all self-described as covert political activists or "determined interventionists." The latter term is intriguing. By it they defined themselves as ardently and actively opposed to isolationism, a diplomatic posture they feared would reassert itself after World War II, to the great detriment of America's national security and long-term global influence. "Determined interventionists," as the name suggests, were willing and able to intervene actively in postwar world affairs, especially against what they perceived to be the growing might of the Soviet Union.

The label "determined interventionist" is not, as far as I have been able to ascertain, contemporary with the Marshall Plan. Bissell first used it in my November 1983 interview with him. The above definition of the term derives from my questions to him regarding its meaning. Subsequently, in interviews with the others, I mentioned the term to elicit their responses. They all expressed relish for it. What needs to be said is that they enjoyed it in the sense of bemusement, appreciating Bissell's use of the language. Some smiled, some chuckled rather wryly. This may be the place to note that these men never referred to themselves as spies, covert operators, or any of the more common terms of the trade. They did speak of covert operations and covert activism, discussed at length their activities in these arenas, but never defined themselves with those words.

In the course of analyzing the determined interventionists, it has occurred to me that understanding their functional relationship to policymaking may explain them somewhat more fully than their own self-definition. Finding the residence of power in covert operations is complicated. Harry Howe Ransom, in a discussion of the broader topic of intelligence and policymaking, has said that "policy making is not a simple static action. Rather it is a dynamic process. A key element in this process is the information available to the policy makers. The man, or group, controlling the information available to the policy makers does in fact play a major if indirect role in policy making."[2] Ransom added that the "long tenure of CIA people gives them added influence, especially on the NSC."[3] Bureaucratically the CIA has "great continuity" in NSC because "the military and other departments" follow a "policy of rotation" of their representatives attending NSC meetings.[4] Further, Ransom cited the CIA's power in a crisis situation where "intelligence agents . . . are believed to possess superior, authoritative knowledge."[5] Ransom even posited that the "CIA may become a third force in national policy making."[6]

Ransom's insights are useful in understanding policymaking in the covert sphere as well. Policymakers certainly set the goals and had a final outcome in mind. These goals and outcomes were then transmitted to the operatives, who provided a variety of plans for accomplishing the goals, including case scenarios for the future ripple effect of each plan. Because the operational plans contained the political biases and social persuasions of nonpolicymakers (affecting their choice regarding the range of suggested options), field personnel directly influenced decisionmaking and long-range political outcomes. And because, in this period, the determined interventionists were believed to be the only ones with the ability to get the job done, other options were not solicited. In the final analysis, however, the decision on which option to employ rested with the policymaker, either elected or appointed.

My goal is to explain why the United States began to use covert operations in peacetime. To do so I believe we must understand the men who created the new form of intervention as much as the institutions involved, because these men were the generators of a unique and far-reaching approach. Therefore, I will begin by explaining who they were, what their life experiences were, and what they believed, since it was those factors that provided the type of reaction to foreign policy events we are concerned with here. To accomplish this I think we should look at the problem topically rather than chronologically. Therefore the plan for this book is as follows: First we will look at their formative years of experience and their early government service during the Progressive years, the New Deal, and World War II. In the second chapter, I explore the factors linking them to one another. Those factors include their experience in government crisis management agencies, a developing world view including skeptical notions about mass democracy and fear of the Soviets, a sense that there was a corps of individuals who saw the world as they did, and a sense that the corps should and would act to respond to the new threat from abroad.

Our next task is to follow the determined interventionists during the years between the end of World War II and the acceptance of peacetime covert operations by the federal government. In this period the determined interventionists created an extensive network among individuals interested in private-channel covert activities. Their goal—to wage a vigorous battle against international Communism—neatly meshed with the views held by an emerging anti-Soviet foreign policy establishment in Washington.

In chapter three, I explain how the determined interventionists, relying heavily on the networks they were developing through occupations in the private sector, began a covert assault on Communist infiltration even as Washington policymakers were contemplating doing so themselves. Through a variety of missions and private foundations already primed to direct foreign economies and political systems, they applied their expertise to the new global problem presented by Communist action. But the expanding Cold War required substantially more funds than were available even from the most committed foundations. It became apparent that some sort of cooperative arrangement with the government would be necessary.

We must next understand the events that brought the private anti-Communist effort fully into the purview of the federal government. In chapter four, the determined interventionists are placed in the context of global politics and the new institutional demands for their expertise created by the Cold War. Against a background of increasing tension between the Soviet Union and the United States, the determined interventionists staffed a new covert organization called the Office of Policy Coordination (OPC). The OPC redirected the CIA, acted to coordinate foreign policy, and complemented America's first massive foreign economic aid program—the Marshall Plan. The agency's first major assignment was covert political assistance to the Marshall Plan. To understand their practical role, I have chosen France and Italy as case studies (chapters five and six).

Understanding the philosophical justification for peacetime covert operations is a more difficult task. By the early 1950s the CIA had become a vehicle for liberal policy elites at a time when domestic political considerations precluded the actions they considered necessary to thwart Soviet ambitions. The Washington climate was so anti-Communist that the policy of establishing a leftist, though non-Communist, labor union or government in a European country would have proved politically fatal. Policymakers and determined interventionists alike believed covert political activism was necessary, not only because of Soviet subversion of the Marshall Plan, but also because the domestic political climate prevented open pursuit of their goals.

Nevertheless, the bureaucratic apparatus they established in those critical years has become a standard weapon in the president's arsenal of options. Revelations of covert failures, beginning with the debacle at the Bay of Pigs, have caused many Americans to question the continued use of covert political action. Accordingly, literature on the subject of covert operations has most often emphasized its paramilitary aspects, as exemplified by the invasion of Cuba. Peter Wyden's *Bay of Pigs*, Richard Immerman's *The CIA in Guatemala*, and Stephen Schlesinger and Stephen Kinzer's book on Guatemala, *Bitter Fruit*, all subject individual paramilitary operations to intense scrutiny and provide important analysis.[7] Frank Snepp's *Decent Interval* gives us a chilling glimpse of the final days of the nation's most protracted paramilitary operation, that attached to the Vietnam War.[8] Moreover, we are beginning to get memoirs of those involved in recent paramilitary operations in Latin America, such as Arturo Cruz, Jr.'s soul-searching personal account in *Memoirs of a Counterrevolutionary*.[9]

It is, nevertheless, also true that this subject has always inflamed some hearts. *The Lawless State*, by Morton H. Halperin, and others, begins with the Allende affair and proceeds to examine the "criminality" of the intelligence community; Harry Rositzke has voiced concern that the "Me generation" would be more subject to KGB recruitment because of the lure of "money, recognition and adventure"; and Jonathan Kwitny, in *The Crimes of Patriots*, contends there is a connection between the CIA, big banking, and drug smuggling.[10]

Complaining that the "literature has been overwhelmingly preoccupied with exposés of individual operations," John Prados recently set out to fill "that gap by broadly surveying paramilitary actions rather than fastening on to single cases" in *President's Secret Wars*.[11] While I greatly admire Prados's book, my own is in some measure a reaction to his claim that "paramilitary operations are not the sole type of covert action, but they are the most significant and have the greatest potential for damaging American national interests."[12]

My claim is that the emphasis on paramilitary operations in the literature has led to a distorted picture of covert operations in their seminal period. In fact, a recreation of the predominant views within the OPC and the CIA in the early Cold War era, 1946–52, reveals that paramilitary operations were regarded as only one method on a spectrum of covert options. Indeed, paramilitary ventures were undertaken with reluctance and generally as a measure of last resort. More often the agency relied upon covert economic, political, and psychological operations because they suited the circumstances and were more difficult to detect than paramilitary operations.

Since it is my aim to clarify and add to the record information on the important question of the appropriateness of covert operations then and now, I have emphasized the formation and evolution of covert operations as an arm of United States foreign economic policy during the Marshall

Plan years. I argue that the preponderant attention to the paramilitary activities of the CIA, while certainly justified by the political and diplomatic importance of those activities, seriously misrepresents the thinking of the agency in those years. As I will show, in its early years the CIA believed in the effectiveness and acceptability of a broad range of nonmilitary forms of covert intervention in defense of American interests and ideals. Focusing on the paramilitary aspects has led to much vilification but less comprehension of the agency's actual modus operandi during its critical formative period.

TWO

A GROUNDING
IN AMERICAN INTERVENTIONISM

A merican foreign policy, in the words of one early Cold War covert operative, is very much the story of "a hands-on nation."[1] Throughout its history the United States has intervened in the affairs of other nations on behalf of its perceived self-interest. The means employed have included military action, economic coercion, and—in the present century especially—covert operations and complicated foreign aid schemes designed to enhance United States influence abroad. This chapter offers a brief overview of the country's interventionist history, coupled with an examination of the evolving world view of modern America's most "determined interventionists"— the covert political activists who built the private and official intelligence networks involved in so many important operations directed at America's friends and foes overseas.

In recent years "interventionism" has acquired very negative connotations with many Americans, who now equate the term with U.S. bombing raids on primitive villages and other acts of brutality against faraway, and often assumed to be less sophisticated, people. This is most ironic, given that America's leaders have repeatedly justified the nation's interventionist tendency as an effort to extend its democratic institutions abroad. An even greater irony, however, is that these ideals were too often betrayed by those most determined to advance them, leading to far-reaching and frequently tragic consequences for the peoples of the globe.

The tentative beginnings of America's interventionist spirit can be traced to Puritan times. In his classic essay "Errand into the Wilderness," historian Perry Miller described the Puritan mission as one in which these hardy New England settlers created a new society, a civic entity made perfect by its adherence to the laws of God.[2] But the Puritans' New World was also to be a "city upon a hill," an example to all people. In time, the Puritans expected that godless Europe would see the error of its ways and emulate the model society carved from the New England wilderness. To be sure, except for periodic skirmishes with neighboring Indians, the Puritans confined their interventionism to their own citizens in an effort to establish a sanctified society. Still, the notion—that their Puritan society was superior to all others and that the world would be infinitely better if only this were universally acknowledged—survived as an important taproot of American thought.

Over several generations Puritan New England shed its strict theocratic framework and developed into a more secular and commercial world. But colonial society did not entirely lose its "mission" of old; rather, this declension converted the Puritans' theocratic "errand" into a crusade to establish a secular model of stable, prosperous democracy for the rest of the world. As Thomas Paine proclaimed in his 1776 pamphlet *Common Sense*, "every spot of the old world is overrun with oppression. Freedom hath been hunted round the globe." Paine's words, implying that the fledgling United States had the task of sustaining some universal concept of freedom, would become an anthem for successive generations of Americans. Few would appreciate that their ideas on freedom would not necessarily fit the economic realities, cultural habits, or national aspirations of other peoples in the world.

From the start, America's leaders, imbued with a sense of the nation's mission, labored hard to enhance the vitality of what Benjamin Franklin called "our rising empire." To that end, Thomas Jefferson sought to acquire French-owned New Orleans, the port city from which thousands of profit-seeking western settlers transported their cotton and other goods to market. Believing any country that owned New Orleans would forever be America's "natural and habitual enemy," Jefferson informed his cabinet that if the French "refused our rights" of purchase, then he would seek an alliance with the British to force the sale.[3] When Napoleon surprised the administration with an offer to sell the entire Louisiana territory to the United States, Jefferson, fearing that Napoleon might change his mind, hurriedly agreed. Significantly, the president himself believed that he had overstepped his legitimate constitutional authority by concluding the transaction without informing Congress or the general citizenry. However, he justified his action on the grounds that overriding national self-interest compelled him to sidestep orderly procedure and the rule of law. Future presidents would often resort to the same rationale, not always with the same positive results that Jefferson achieved.

In the antebellum period, the United States embarked on a vigorous campaign of territorial and economic expansion. The War of 1812 was due partly to the desire of congressional "War Hawks" to annex Canada and partly to President James Madison's insistence on neutrals' rights on the high seas. Gen. Andrew Jackson, in hot pursuit of some raiding Seminoles in southern Georgia in 1818, invaded Spanish Florida with a force of 3,000 men, thereby strengthening Secretary of State John Quincy Adams's hand in negotiating the purchase of this strategic peninsula. In 1823 President Monroe boldly proclaimed his famous Doctrine, which served notice on Europe that the United States would not tolerate additional colonization efforts in the Americas. And throughout, Indian tribes were pushed steadily westward in a series of brutal campaigns, routinely justified as necessary for the advancement of civilization and progress.

In some administrations audacity easily coupled with America's sense of mission. James Knox Polk's war with Mexico in 1846 resulted in a triumph over the Mexicans that netted the United States undisputed control over Texas and extensive new holdings in the Southwest, including California. President Polk nearly went to war with Great Britain as well, over the disputed Oregon territory; however, a compromise was agreed upon that gave the United States a substantial portion of the Pacific Northwest. In the early 1850s, Millard Fillmore's administration sponsored Commodore Matthew C. Perry's Pacific expedition, which succeeded in opening Japan to American trade. In the spirit of the times, the ardently nationalistic "Young America" movement favored the expansion of America's democratic institutions throughout the world. Popular with some Democrats, the Young America movement inspired President Franklin Pierce to sanction several ill-considered attempts to acquire Cuba. In 1854 a secret U.S. diplomatic report, stating that if Spanish authorities refused to sell Cuba, "then, by every law, human and divine, we shall be justified in wresting it from Spain," was revealed to the public. A deeply embarrassed Pierce disavowed the "Ostend Manifesto," and the episode, as well as the existence of slavery in Cuba, was a contributing factor to the United States' failure to acquire this rich island prize.[4]

Notwithstanding this and other setbacks, many nineteenth-century Americans confidently assumed that the United States had been specially chosen by God to be a unique empire of freedom. In 1845 John L. O'Sullivan, a New York newspaper editor, memorably expressed this idea when he wrote that it was America's "manifest destiny to overspread and to possess the whole of the continent which Providence has given us for the development of the great experiment in liberty and federated self-government entrusted to us."[5] Over the decades, O'Sullivan's "manifest destiny" served as the most popular and convenient pretext for continental expansion of the United States as well as its even more ambitious interventionist ventures abroad.

By the 1880s and 1890s the United States had become powerful enough to venture diplomatically throughout the hemisphere, especially if a European power threatened to intrude. Even before the Spanish-American War broke out in 1898 there were tests of American determination to influence events in South America. The most important was a British-Venezuelan dispute over boundaries in British Guiana in 1895 that led President Grover Cleveland to offer America's services as an arbitrator. When Britain refused and proceeded to land troops in Nicaragua, popular protests rose to fever pitch. The American public supported its policymakers' determination to dominate the hemisphere. Cleveland's forceful Secretary of State Richard Olney, adding what came to be known as the Olney Corollary to the Monroe Doctrine, used the occasion to enunciate the fully matured rhetoric of determined interventionism: "The people of the United States have a vital interest in the cause of popular self-government. . . . They believe it to be for the healing of all nations, and that civilization must either advance or retrograde accordingly as its supremacy is extended or curtailed."[6] To be sure, Olney conceded that "the age of the Crusades has passed," and so Americans "are content with such assertion and defense of the right of popular self-government as their own security and welfare demand."[7] In short, self-interest and the defense of democracy would be permanently commingled by American diplomats, never separated and examined apart from one another. No determined interventionist of the subsequent Cold War era would have disagreed or could have stated Olney's assertion any better.

The war with Spain in 1898 was a watershed event in American history. Of all the factors that led to this conflict, none was more significant than the United States' considerable commercial interest in Cuba, then torn by revolution as Cuban nationalists struggled to free themselves from Spain. To protect their investments, the American business community naturally wanted an end to this turmoil on terms favorable to the United States. President William McKinley pressured Spain to give up her Caribbean colony; Spanish intransigence, followed by the mysterious destruction of the battleship *Maine*, emboldened an already jingoistic Congress and general public to action. The United States did not lose a single campaign, and victory came in three months' time. The spoils of war included the Philippines, which nicely augmented the recent acquisition of Hawaii in the Pacific. Filipino nationalistic uprisings were brutally crushed by Americans dismayed by the actions of a people who did not regard it a blessing to live under the U.S.-dominated economic and political order forced upon them. In the Caribbean, Spain ceded Puerto Rico to the United States, and of course the Spanish had to withdraw from Cuba, which became an American protectorate.

In a burst of imperialistic enthusiasm, the United States had become a world power, with vast new economic and territorial interests and responsibilities. Heady prospects, indeed! Doubters and dissenters were for the most part drowned out by men like Albert Beveridge of Indiana, who in his famous "March of the Flag" speech in September 1898, proudly declared, "We cannot fly from our world duties; it is ours to execute the purpose of a fate that has driven us to be greater than our small intentions. We cannot retreat from any soil where Providence has unfurled our banner; it is ours to save that soil for liberty and civilization."[8]

At the close of the nineteenth century the United States was firmly committed to a course of intervention on behalf of its commercial interests and democracy. Military strength and the power of the dollar were used to achieve American goals. From William McKinley to Woodrow Wilson, chief executives employed both methods, shifting from one to the other as circumstances warranted. McKinley and Roosevelt relied both on military intervention and diplomatic missions, while William Howard Taft resorted mainly to monetary pressure, or "dollar diplomacy."

McKinley's successor, Theodore Roosevelt, was an unabashed interventionist. His initial fame came from his spectacular charge up Kettle Hill in the 1898 war with Spain. While campaigning for the Republican vice presidency he asked voters to return his party to office "because now at the dawn of a new century we wish this giant of the West, the greatest republic upon which the sun has ever shone, to start fair in the race of national greatness."[9] As president he received the Nobel Peace Prize for his efforts in settling the war between Russia and Japan in 1904-5. But when Colombian authorities did not accept American terms for building the long-delayed trans-ocean passage, his administration encouraged and financed a successful Panamanian revolution against Colombia. U.S. recognition and naval protection was immediately granted to the new "republic" of Panama, whose leader immediately signed a treaty granting territory to the United States to build a canal. All this was accomplished without the direct knowledge of Congress and the American people. Roosevelt later justified his method by saying that if he had intervened through "traditional conservative methods," by which he meant Congress, the debate would have lasted forever. "But," he boasted, "I took the Canal Zone and let Congress debate, and while the debate goes on the canal does also."[10]

The canal was Roosevelt's most memorable foreign policy legacy, but the "corollary" that bears his name also had a lasting impact on U.S.-Caribbean affairs. When Venezuelan President Cipriano Castro reneged on debts to various European nations, Roosevelt claimed it as a U.S. prerogative to enforce good economic behavior on the societies to the south, thereby outflanking angry European creditors and preserving the Monroe Doctrine. Roosevelt informed aides that the United States was only doing "what a policeman has to do" and that intervention would "show these Dagos that they will have to behave decently."[11] Shortly thereafter, Roosevelt relied on his "corollary" to intervene in the Dominican Republic, where American investments seemed in jeopardy after the assassination of President Ulises Heureaux.

Taft, too, confronted the problem of debtor nations to the south. But rather than intervene militarily, he established several complicated financial protectorates to manage debts in the Central American states. Privately financed and closely supervised by the State Department, these protectorates were encouraged to replace European capital with American, thereby permanently eliminating the possibility of European intervention. Taft also hoped the infusion of American capital would discourage revolution. He enthusiastically promoted this new policy as "substituting dollars for bullets" and believed that it "appeals alike to idealistic humanitarian sentiments . . . and to legitimate commercial aims."[12] Admitting that his dollar diplomacy was "frankly directed to the increase of American trade," Taft proposed heavy investment in each targeted market country since "free opportunity in foreign markets [would] soon be indispensable to our prosperity." Outlining the components of his plan for South America, Taft asserted that America needed a merchant marine, "good American banks," coverage by American newspapers, a trained foreign service "systematically brought into direct contact with the industrial, manufacturing and exporting interests of each country." All of these precautions were to be taken so that "American business men may enter the foreign field with a clear perception of the exact conditions to be dealt with."[13] In short, Taft placed the U.S. government in service to America's commercial interests, providing financial infrastructure, publicity, and intelligence.

Despite Taft's determination to use dollar diplomacy to achieve diplomatic goals, he would learn that "if the use of force . . . has limitations, it also has legitimate capacities. Without force, the best intentions fail to stop destruction."[14] When the Nicaraguan government flaunted Washington's initiatives in 1912, Secretary of State Philander Knox ordered marines into Nicaragua to restore order. Still Taft had made an important realization: something other than military force was needed to blunt revolutionary tendencies and economic nationalism around the world. Woodrow Wilson and his successors would build upon this idea.

During the "watch" of Taft and Roosevelt before him, American society went through a period of significant transformation. Prompted largely by the changes and inequities brought about by the industrialization of the United States, a broad range of Americans came to believe that something had to be done to correct conditions stemming from these changes. In areas ranging from public health, education of new immigrants, control over public resources, and improvement in the industrial workplace, Americans sloughed off the notion that domestic intervention was pernicious. Moreover, they began to demand that government take a prominent role in alleviating deplorable conditions in society.[15] These ideas had a profound impact on foreign policy, particularly on the form of American intervention. But just as many progressive reforms—as they were called—did not bear fruit until the presidency of Woodrow Wilson, so too, with the exception of Taft's dollar diplomacy, did the progressive impulse in foreign policy await the former president of Princeton University. It is during the Wilson administration that we get our first glimpse of the sires of determined interventionism in the twentieth century.

The effect of the progressive impulse on foreign policy did not obscure military and monetary methods; rather, it added to them. Progressivism tended to shift interventionist tactics to reflect domestic social interventionism.[16] As such, intervention began to take the form of extensive programs of foreign aid attached to requisite programs for social and political modernization. Zealous interventionists proselytized for the democratic political system in the process of augmenting modernization programs. They were, as historian Arthur Link said, "fundamentally missionaries of democracy."[17] The new interventionism also required a cast of characters with special skills. As domestic progressivism produced and relied on a class of "highly trained, non-partisan experts" to manage the "complex task" of "governing a modern city," global intervention required a corps of experts to manage foreign policy programs.[18] Where once William McKinley had sent former Indian fighters—men with such contempt for dark skin they relished training their sights on the newest wave of "nigger" targets—to quell rebellion in the Philippines, Woodrow Wilson sent marines with prodigious modernizing skills to the Caribbean. A subtle shift, no doubt, for the marines were still quasi-occupational forces in the eyes of their "hosts." Yet, just as the overt power of Tammany Hall bosses lost currency in progressive eyes, the iron clad fist of Rooseveltian diplomacy gave way to a new, more subtly persuasive set of ideas about achieving foreign policy goals.

The First World War, the Russian Revolution, the Treaty of Versailles, and other global traumas forced successive administrations to reassess U.S. foreign policy. Increasingly, commercial trade came to be regarded as a means of "managing" foreign countries, intelligence and observation rose to prominence as a way of giving the United States an edge in global competition, and youthful experts—men such as William J. Donovan, Allen Welsh Dulles, W. Averell Harriman, and George Frost Kennan—were assigned to technical missions in various countries of economic importance to the United States. To advance the diverse interests of the United States, all four of these men dabbled in unorthodox warfare between the years of American involvement in World War I and the Wall Street crash of 1929. Yet only Donovan would have labeled it as such. The others came more slowly to the same conclusion, even as they developed methods that they and other "determined interventionists" would find useful in covert operations later. Significantly, all four shared a loathing for military engagement as they knew it—particularly trench warfare—and all believed that trouble lay ahead with the new USSR. In addition, all had a first-hand opportunity to gauge the ability of the United States to hold its own at the negotiating table, an intellectual delight in observation and analysis of a competitor, an ardent faith in bilateral and multilateral commercial enterprise as a mechanism for world order, and, above all, a Wilsonian belief that "efficient government could come only from 'an educated elite.' "[19]

The individual most interested in unorthodox warfare methods was William J. Donovan. Growing up in a large, poor upstate New York household, he attended a small Catholic men's college. Proving himself there, he transferred to Columbia and then on to the military, where he distinguished himself early as ambitious, driven, and requiring a great deal of his men. His first foray into unorthodox warfare was paramilitary activity in Mexico in 1915. Disconcerted by the constitutional crisis there, President Wilson ordered Gen. John "Blackjack" Pershing to command a regiment to stabilize Mexico and thereby secure American interests south of the border. Assigned to Pershing, Donovan got his first taste of military adventurism. It was what Donovan wanted—a chance for glory, promotion, and patriotic endeavor. Soon after the Veracruz mission Donovan was assigned overseas to the European war.

Donovan's experience with trench warfare deeply influenced his thinking. As commander of the "Fighting 69th," he led America's famed Irish contingent. He was sickened by the carnage he saw—waves of men leaping out of their trenches to be slaughtered by the occupants of the opposing trench; then a retreat, waiting until the enemy lept out of its trench to be massacred in turn. Donovan left the trenches to coordinate American actions with the activities of British intelligence, bringing him into contact with an established intelligence organization. Impressed, Donovan immediately became America's foremost advocate of unorthodox methods.

Donovan's interest in intelligence stemmed from another source as well. At the end of the war he was in Siberia observing American attempts to restore Russia, if not to the Czars, at least to the Kerensky coalition that had ruled briefly after the fall of the monarchy. In 1919 Donovan concluded that the Lenin regime was on a collision course with Western democracy. He predicted that this conflict would take the form of a "subversive" war and that in order to gain the "peace the world so badly needs" the United States would have to win.[20] Donovan's course was set. Americans, like all participants in World War I, had been disheartened by the trenches. And Donovan, like Wilson, was concerned with Soviet ideology. Donovan was rapidly acquiring experience and a network among those exploring alternative ways to exert global influence. His ultimate goal was an American intelligence organization to prevent future wars and thwart Soviet subversion.

Donovan was not alone in the belief that an overarching intelligence organization was needed. But before Pearl Harbor, intelligence in the United States tended to take the form of independent efforts prompted by American diplomatic personnel. Typical of these efforts was that of John A. Gade, a State Department representative in the Baltic countries and a naval attaché in Copenhagen in 1918 and 1919. Gade proposed a central intelligence organization in 1929. Touting, as had Donovan, the World War I intelligence units of the British and French, Gade thought the United States should establish a similar organization reporting directly to President Hoover. At that time, no one agreed with him.[21]

The lack of interest in intelligence reflected the dominant isolationist mood of the 1920s. Foreign policy was not a high priority in the administrations of Warren Harding or Calvin Coolidge. And as for Herbert Hoover, his Secretary of State, Henry Stimson, is said to have had "fewer worries about American foreign relations than almost any of his predecessors."[22] In 1929 no U.S. agency conducted clandestine foreign operations abroad and "no U.S. agency had foreign intelligence as its primary interest or activity, though several were collecting information and intelligence abroad."[23]

Peacetime intelligence was collected overtly through the "attaché system." Borrowing on the State Department's long history of overt collection through diplomatic sources abroad, the navy set up its own system of naval attachés under the Office of Naval Intelligence (ONI). The navy had begun using the attaché system in the 1880s because it was concerned about the impact of the switch from wood hulls to steel and from sail power to steam. In peacetime the navy wanted to know the character of foreign navies, especially the size, power, and other capabilities of foreign shipping and naval armaments. They were less interested in the movement and intentions of peacetime foreign navies. The ONI pioneered what would later be called national estimates, the craft of estimating the various capabilities of foreign governments. But the navy did not see its role as analytical. They collected information and made it available; evaluation was left to the "ultimate consumer," at that time the secretary of the navy, or the cabinet level officer in charge of the department, not the president. Attachés from other U.S. government departments received assignments to overseas posts to advance the perspective of their departments in diplomatic decisionmaking. The Treasury Department installed attachés to keep a record of smuggling, collection of consular fees, and drug traffic. Commerce, Agriculture, and Interior departments created national estimates pertinent to their areas of interest.

Early peacetime collection was overt, and a strict code prevented "dubious methods." Honor was important to one's career, particularly in the navy. Crudely duplicitous methods were cause for stern reproach. When Secretary Stimson discovered that the State Department had funded a War Department effort to break codes, he closed the Manhattan "Black Chamber" offices, calling the plan a "blow for gentlemanliness in foreign affairs."[24] Sensitivity to this code prompted George Kennan to deny that Riga, the blossoming school for Sovietologists, was an intelligence outpost.

Other young interventionists continued to cling to even more traditional diplomacy. Young men on the move in the State Department went to Versailles to help arrange a lasting peace; Allen Dulles was among them. A member of the Boundary Commission, he and his co-worker Charles Seymour, the future president of Yale University, were literally engaged in "redrawing the map of Europe."[25] Dulles was just as ambitious as Donovan. As the nephew of Wilson's Secretary of State, Robert Lansing, Dulles had little trouble gaining entry into the State Department. Dulles expected power. Privilege, connections, and his State Department lineage granted him an opportunity; he had little doubt he would gain from it. Yet even without a patron, Dulles's background and Princeton associations assured an easy compatibility with the other young men at Versailles. They, too, were appalled by the recent carnage, and by the present spectacle of American diplomats trying to maneuver amidst the wiles of European diplomacy as practiced by the victorious Allied foreign ministers. Dulles and his young colleagues fretted about their country's inability to prevail in the diplomatic arena, convinced that there had to be a better way to secure American global influence. Dulles became an activist at Versailles. His experience there provided him with a goal: finding a successful means for advancing U.S. interests around the world.

Some young interventionists believed that commerce offered the surest way to exert U.S. influence. Trusting, as President Taft had, in the strength of the American dollar as diplomatic leverage, businessmen such as Averell Harriman expanded that notion to include vast commercial arrangements between private American concerns and foreign governments. These ventures were profitable, and they helped modernize the cosigning nation. Coming from the private sector, they promised minimal U.S. government intervention, satisfying old prejudices against such intrusion. International commerce, Harriman reasoned, could even be a way to protect the peace, for who would wage war against a major trading partner? Indeed, perhaps this would even be true of Russia.

Harriman's family had a tradition of introducing modern technology into nations with which it did business. Averell's father, E. H. Harriman, dropped out of school at age 14, borrowed three thousand dollars, and bought himself a seat on the New York Stock Exchange. By the time of Averell's birth, E. H. was one of the richest men in the United States. In the 1920s Averell was coming into his own in a family of American industrialists in which "great wealth" was seen as an "obligation and responsibility" that "must work for the country."[26] Averell had a vision of a "worldwide transportation empire." In 1922 he founded the Deutsch-Russische Transport Company, a jointly owned shipping operation. Through a complicated scheme with the Germans, Harriman was able to extend credit to the Soviet Union. Although the State Department protested, Harriman insisted that it benefited American business interests while ending the economic isolation of the Soviet Union. He contended that "trade and credit could be used as levers" in international relations.

In 1924 he obtained a concession from the Soviets to operate manganese mines in Soviet Georgia. This valuable element, essential for steel production, would be hauled away in railroads built with Harriman family money. Harriman confidently believed that forging commercial ties with the Soviets would help ease the USSR into the global economy, thereby achieving the international stability desired by everyone. Harriman marshalled his family's considerable resources behind numerous other commercial agreements with the USSR and other countries. These agreements would ensure Harriman's, and America's, continued influence overseas.

As the Soviet Union became somewhat more important in foreign policy affairs in the 1920s, other Americans developed a keen interest in this imposing political and economic competitor. Foremost among the intellectuals concerned with the USSR and its potential global influence was George Kennan, a career State Department official. Part of a new contingent of career diplomats, he was one of the first to attend a school for Soviet studies the State Department had set up at Riga. There, instructors—mostly White Russian émigrés escaping the "new" Russia—tutored Kennan and his fellow State Department scholars in Russian history, culture, languages, and nuance. In this way the State Department developed the cohort of experts who would, it was hoped, help make intelligent decisions relating to the USSR. Kennan excelled and has been called the "chief ideologue" of the early Riga School. Throughout his early career he "attached himself as . . . an explicator to men of power" and rose rapidly within the ranks of the Sovietologists who would turn observation and analysis into useful intelligence for foreign policymakers in Washington.[27]

While these four men, who would become pivotal to interventionism during the Cold War, were starting their careers, important transformations in American foreign policy were under way. As historian Joan Hoff Wilson has explained, the late Progressive era resulted in a greater appreciation among American businessmen of the economic benefits of foreign trade. After World War I especially, they came to equate America's domestic prosperity with its capacity for moral and economic leadership in the world. Businessmen increasingly regarded America's role in assisting corrupt and warring Europe as proof of the fundamental superiority of the U.S. system. Business ethos at the time contained a vision of the "American mission" as serving "as an example at home and abroad of social justice and democratic strength."[28] As Wilson put it, "They rhetorically equated their own self-interest and economic achievements with the notion not only that they were serving their country through their endeavors, but that what they did was a 'glorious service to all humanity'."[29]

Of course, these men had a corporate agenda as well as a personal one. They wanted closer business-government cooperation to gain assistance "in the form of legislation promoting business combinations in foreign trade."[30] They also thought the war had "removed the last remnants of economic nationalism and that economic interdependence had become the rule rather than the exception in international relations."[31] This view led them to believe that the "most important practical and humanitarian responsibility of United States diplomacy was to take the lead in the economic reconstruction of war-torn Europe" to create a "new world community among industrialized nations."[32]

Yet there lay within this rhetoric an elitist agenda not immediately apparent in their words. This agenda explained and justified their predominant role in the new world order. U.S. businessmen believed that only the "best upper class men in business are really genuine in their belief [of service] and are consistent in its practice."[33] Thus it became fashionable for businessmen to offer their expertise to Washington on a "dollar-a-year" basis. This practice, while doubtless of much benefit to many government agencies, reinforced the growing assumptions about the need for businessmen to have a prominent place in international diplomacy. Interestingly, this was in some respects a more secularized view of American leadership in the early days of the Republic. The historian Gordon Wood has argued that early Americans often thought of leadership in highly moral terms. The natural leader was one whose virtue—in the Young Republic it was called "public virtue"—brought him inevitably, though often reluctantly, to public service.[34] In the 1920s, businessmen and others often linked expertise and financial success with public virtue. They served because the new criteria for leadership tapped them as the natural leaders of the time. Moreover, the idea soon occurred to American businessmen that modernizing poor but potentially consumer-oriented lands around the globe was as useful as revitalizing Europe itself.

A mong the earliest attempts to lend business expertise for this purpose was the Millspaugh mission to Iran in the 1920s. Arthur C. Millspaugh, an economic advisor in the State Department, was employed by the Iranian government in 1922. His mission was to bring "American engineers and agricultural and financial experts . . . to assist in the huge task of westernization."[35] Millspaugh stayed the full five years of his contract, despite "considerable opposition" from some sectors in Iran.[36] He was given "complete power to reorganize and centralize the nation's finances."[37] By 1925 he had "provided for the first time clear budget allocations for capital expenditure," a goal he accomplished by organizing the data so that Iran's budget could be published for the first time. Millspaugh's efforts helped cut the public debt, enabling the savings to be used elsewhere.[38] Most of what Millspaugh salvaged through efficient government procedures was credited to modernization efforts. Mines, agriculture, and industries were funded, and roads, railroads, harbors, irrigation channels, public buildings, and other infrastructure were built. Millspaugh also worked on a massive famine prevention program that dovetailed with the road-building project. Roads were constructed and trucks were purchased so that food could be transported to needy rural areas. In response to international demand, Millspaugh also devised a plan for reducing opium cultivation in Iran.

Millspaugh's first mission ended in 1927 with some rancor. Apparently, Reza Shah Pahlavi, father of Shah Mohammed Reza, at first cooperated with Millspaugh; naturally the shah was eager for modernization and westernization. But they parted ways when Millspaugh insisted that money "found" as a result of efficiency in government be used for additional public works, while the shah insisted that it be used to strengthen his military forces. Not for the last time would Americans be confronted with such a dilemma.[39] But at the time Americans were optimistic that their foreign aid largesse would produce progressive trends. The problems inherent in America's long-range global planning would not be obvious for some time.

Given the tenor of businessmen's attitudes toward public service, government, and foreign policy in the 1920s, it is not surprising that the generation of future determined interventionists who entered college in the late twenties and early thirties was greatly influenced by a vision of optimism and American commercial strength abroad. But this perspective was badly shaken by the economic crisis that followed the Wall Street crash of October 1929. Of course, the Depression revealed a pressing need to "intervene" in the domestic sector to restabilize the American economy. During Herbert Hoover's presidency that effort mainly entailed a voluntary, cooperative effort between business and government. Hoover disliked the idea of heavy-handed government intervention, preferring private ventures on the model of his massive relief efforts to aid the Soviets in their famine years of the early 1920s, supplemented by government assistance. President Franklin Roosevelt took a different approach—massive government intervention in the economy. "Economic depression and New Deal activism," stated Michael Hogan, "led spokesmen for the capital-intensive bloc and great investment banks to redefine New Era formulations in a way that left more room for organized labor, conceded a larger role for the state, and included Keynesian strategies of aggregate economic management."[40]

In many ways Roosevelt's approach was a blueprint for the post–Second World War reconstruction plan for Europe, the Marshall Plan. FDR's New Deal relied on an elite cadre of bureaucratic experts, much as progressive reform had. In the 1930s Washington became a mecca for highly-trained men and women whose mission was to restore the economic capacity of the United States. Some even harbored the hope that a broader social agenda could be successfully pursued, by an administration determined to use executive power to intervene directly in the lives of citizens on an unprecedented scale. They were an idealistic group and, as Gaddis has reminded us, it is important not to "downplay . . . the role of ideals in American foreign policy" or "underrate the role of distinctive individuals in history."[41]

Many who might be called "distinctive individuals" of the early Cold War years were in college in the late twenties and early New Deal era. Richard M. Bissell, Jr., was at Yale; John A. Bross, Kermit Roosevelt, Lawrence Houston, and Paul Nitze at Harvard; Franklin Lindsay at Stanford; Frank Wisner at the University of Virginia. In these formative years, they found themselves swept up in the concerns of the time. "It is hard for me even now," said Bissell, "to understand the impact of the depression on me."[42] It certainly had a direct impact on their curricula. Yale, for instance, began in 1930 to reorganize its course offerings in economics and government to reflect the need for new skills to meet the domestic crisis. Course offerings such as Public Utilities and Valuation, Modern Problems of Taxation, Agencies in International Relations, Public Administration, and Municipal Government demonstrated a trend toward the specific problems Yale students in economics and government would face after graduating.[43] Yale also created an international relations department out of the economics and government departments, in response to the business community's growing belief in world economic interdependence.

Indeed, much of what Joan Hoff Wilson has called the "independent internationalism" of the Hoover era remained after 1933, including a vision of the American system that equated capitalism with democracy and a need to apply it universally.[44] Michael Hogan has added that "to the open and competitive international system envisioned in classical theory—American leaders would add new mechanisms of economic planning, new institutions of coordination and control, and new partnerships between public and private elites in the collective administration of world trade and development."[45] No doubt the evolving concerns and attitudes affecting the curricula at Yale influenced similar modifications at universities attended by other determined interventionists as well.

For the older determined interventionists, the 1930s brought about a hardening of attitudes toward the Soviets. Kennan, still at Riga, made a specialty of Soviet ideology. Harriman left the USSR in 1928, and in 1932 he supported the candidacy of Franklin Roosevelt, whom Harriman served as an official in the National Recovery Administration and as chairman of the Business Advisory Council. For Allen Dulles it was a slack time, with no opportunity for the espionage activities he so cherished. He fretted about his inability to afford to do it on his own and saw his regular occupation as drudgery. The main problem for Dulles was politics—he was a highly recognizable Republican. Donovan, now a successful Wall Street lawyer, continued to lobby for an American intelligence agency. But Roosevelt was a hard man to convince, preferring personal emissaries such as his friend, the socialite Jacob Astor. Donovan also had tough competition from the Rockefeller Foundation.

The Rockefeller Foundation operated in South America much as the Economic Recovery Program would function later in Europe. Its aim was to modernize South America, improving living standards by training middle-range personnel to emulate American models, then sending them out to upgrade their villages. Through subsidiaries such as the Latin American Agricultural Program and International Basic Economy Corporation, a closely held corporation owned by Nelson Rockefeller and his brothers, the foundation directed its activities in Mexico, Colombia, and Chile. When government officials told Rockefeller that the Mexican corn crop was in peril, the foundation began an agricultural program, choosing strains of corn that were progressively more hybrid and educating farmers who were resistant to change. After corn development, the foundation went on to wheat and beans. The foundation also targeted the Mexican family for potential development. "To this end," claimed the director of the Latin American program, "women are being introduced to better methods of homemaking and living. Back in their community they are expected to share their new knowledge." Obviously, the foundation needed government cooperation, from Washington as well as the recipient locale. In Washington foundation officials were careful to have State Department approval for their targeted geographic regions. In the field they were able to report that "in each country in which the Foundation is operating its local office is organized as a semi-official agency of the local government. . . . The head of our Mexican operation has official status in the Mexican government."[46] With its strategic presence in South America, the foundation regularly provided Washington with intelligence on the region. The last thing the foundation wanted was an official American intelligence organization on its turf.[47]

T oward the end of the decade, as the younger men graduated from college, Europe was again at war. Senior men such as Dulles drifted toward internationalism. After the Japanese bombed Pearl Harbor, Donovan finally succeeded in con-

vincing Roosevelt of the need for an American intelligence agency, the
Office of Strategic Services. Kennan continued to rise in the diplomatic
service, with important postings in Moscow and Berlin. Harriman
brought his experience to bear in a number of official and quasi-official
posts, often on monetary issues such as the Lend-Lease program. Junior
men first tried to establish careers, but world events intruded. Nitze and
Bissell joined the war effort early. Bissell—after attending Groton, Yale,
and the London School of Economics—was teaching and further revising
the curriculum of the economics department at Yale. Originally an
America Firster, Bissell soon converted and became "a zealous anti-iso-
lationist."[48] He left Yale in the summer of 1941 to join the War Shipping
Administration in Washington. Nitze had signed on with an investment
banking company, Dillon, Read, two weeks before the 1929 crash. There
he met James Forrestal. After a family trip to Germany in 1937, where he
was frightened and disturbed by a variety of experiences with Hitler's
tactics, including the imprisonment of a Jewish friend and client, Nitze
took a leave of absence from Dillon, Read. During that year he became
an America Firster and then an ardent anti-Soviet after the Nazi-Soviet
Pact in 1939. He returned to Dillon, Read anti-Soviet but pro-Roosevelt,
particularly supportive of the New Deal version of Keynesian economics.
Forrestal recruited Nitze into government in 1940 to work as his aide.
Forrestal was one of a group known as the "Silent Six," wartime advisors
to President Roosevelt.[49] Nitze recalled that Dillon, Read paid his salary
and Forrestal housed him and that the arrangement was "totally illegal
and improper." His assignment was to work with John Galbraith and
George Ball on a strategic bombing survey.[50]

World War II dramatically changed American ideas of war to include
what Bradley Smith has termed "shadow warfare." The Nazis employed
guerrilla attacks, sabotage, and secret intelligence, which "revolutionized
the rules of war."[51] The opening assaults on the Low Countries relied
heavily on the use of fifth column units and subversion. The Nazis were
said to have swept through Europe by trickery, dressing their troops in
Dutch uniforms to slip by. Many concluded that the Nazis were winning
because there was a "conspiratorial, centrally directed, Fascist underground."[52] Rumors of parachutists dressed as nuns, false papers, snipers,

and mysterious explosions helped explain to terrified European populations and their Allies the suddenness of the Führer's overwhelming victories. Some of these rumors were true, but more to the point was the excellent intelligence network established by the Germans. Nevertheless, these stories found their way to the United States and were believed.

American anxieties were further fueled by British intelligence expert William Stephenson. The British Secret Service set up a propaganda office in Manhattan's Rockefeller Center to build sympathy among Americans for the plight of England. Part of Stephenson's argument was that Hitler never could have blitzed Europe without subversion, and therefore the long-term security of the United States was in jeopardy, too. In June 1940 Frank Knox responded to the threat by sending Donovan to Britain to coordinate the ONI operations with the British effort. Donovan's trip led to some early collaboration, but the British soon concluded that the United States had nothing to offer and squeezed Donovan out.

After his return to the United States, Donovan published a series of articles called "Fifth Column Lessons for America," which claimed that no amount of genius could have produced German victories; rather, it was the two hundred million dollars the Germans put into their fifth-column activities. He warned that the United States might find itself "crippled by . . . civilized inhibitions."[53] Yet Donovan did not get his way until the Japanese bombed Pearl Harbor on 7 December 1941. Not only were Americans infuriated by the surprise attack, they saw it as a result of subversive activity. Japanese pilots were rumored to have had help on the ground. Pilots were said to have been supplied with maps of Honolulu showing the location of the base. Agricultural workers purportedly cut arrows in pineapple fields giving directions to the military installation. Fifth-column activity was suspected everywhere. All this was consistent with warnings from Donovan.

As a result of Donovan's prompting, President Roosevelt inaugurated the Office of Coordinator of Information in the summer of 1941, with Donovan as its chief. The COI collected and analyzed information garnered from other agencies, sending its reports directly to the executive office. A year later, after Pearl Harbor, Franklin Roosevelt expanded and renamed the wartime intelligence unit. The Office of Strategic Services

(OSS), also led by Donovan, functioned in areas such as research and analysis; secret intelligence and its protector, counterespionage; special operations units for sabotage and resistance aid; morale operations for covert propaganda; operational groups for guerrilla operations; and maritime units for aquatic sabotage.[54] Naturally there was considerable bureaucratic scrambling for the new unit, but the famous OSS finally emerged as an independent outfit, with Donovan as its chief. Dulles headed its European headquarters, located in Bern, Switzerland. The new and very glamorous unit quickly drew recruits.

Among the earliest recruits was Kermit Roosevelt, grandson of the early twentieth-century interventionist Theodore Roosevelt. After studying at Groton and Harvard, Roosevelt went to Berkeley to pursue a doctorate in history. He wrote a dissertation on covert operations during the British Civil War. In 1941 he gave a copy to his uncle, Washington columnist Joseph Alsop, who told him "Kermit, don't publish this. Show it to my friend Bill Donovan."[55] Roosevelt did so and became one of Donovan's first employees in the new OSS.

Many future determined interventionists worked in the wartime OSS. Lawrence Houston went to the Judge Advocate's Corps after graduating from Harvard and was recruited as an attorney for the OSS. He served in the Mediterranean theater—Caserta, Athens, and Cairo—returning to Washington in November of 1945 as counsel to the special services unit of the OSS. John Bross, also an attorney, went from Wall Street to the OSS in London. Frank Wisner and Frank Lindsay became OSS field operatives, working for Robert Joyce, a Californian who had graduated from Yale in 1926 and had gone into the Foreign Service in 1928. The OSS connection would prove important, because when Dulles began to think about retaining a cohort of covert specialists after the war, he drew heavily from among former OSS men. The Joyce connection from OSS days would have considerable bearing as well. Joyce stayed on in the State Department, becoming the crucial liaison with the new covert organization. Perhaps coincidentally, OSS men who had served under Joyce were awarded key positions in the new Office of Policy Coordination.

Moreover, social connections helped solidify this developing network of determined interventionists. Bissell knew Harriman and Dulles.

Roosevelt was related to Alsop, who was a friend to Donovan. Some of the men had known each other in college: Bissell knew Tracey Barnes, another operative in the OSS and the OPC, when they were at Yale; and Bissell, Bross, and Barnes were at Groton together. Such connections were significant. But of course, the exigencies of war necessitated a broad spectrum of activists. As Roosevelt said, it was hard to keep up with "Achesonian elitism" when you needed "men with talent."[56] Bissell, too, insisted that the so-called "old boy network" came into existence during the war and that it was thoroughly integrated with labor leaders and others whose social standing would not have recommended them if there had been no other criteria.[57] During the war they got to know one another, learned how to maneuver within the sprawling Washington bureaucracy, becoming good friends in the process.

Thus, while there seems to have been a "tightly knit group of men" coming together at the end of the war who avowed interventionism to restore Europe, the source of their determination was not merely social class. As journalists Isaacson and Thomas have noted, "for many more of the gentry" their sense of class "bred complacency and idleness"; yet for "those who did choose public service . . . it was not just the United States they sought to serve but, in a broader sense, the culture and civilization of the West." When these men, who would create and implement the Marshall Plan, "came of age," the United States was "vibrant and raw, poised to touch more of the globe with its power than any nation ever." Yet, it was isolationist and self-absorbed. What these men wanted was "to restore Europe, not change it," by supplying the capital and tools. As Isaacson and Thomas have summarized it, their vision was spectacularly bold; it "demanded a reshaping of America's traditional role in the world and a restructuring of the global balance of power. By seeking change in order to preserve, these men were, in their own way, revolutionaries in the cause of order. . . . Almost four decades later, the creators of the Pax Americana remain partially obscure figures, semiprivate men who preferred to exercise power discreetly and shunned the glare and tumult of politics."[58]

World War II brought the determined interventionists together, and the Cold War kept them together. They had lived through and triumphed over the Depression and a world war. But now there was a new threat, greater than either because it was more subtle—an amorphous, intangible struggle for "the minds of men." But they were ready. Collectively, they had experienced all the threats the Soviets could muster, and they had the methods to counteract them. The war had created the OSS and a strong covert capability. Truman never meant to obliterate the covert function, and his official disbanding of the OSS in 1945 was really a partitioning. No units were scrapped, and all found new bureaucratic homes.

What the president wanted was a peacetime covert organization. Where the OSS was primarily a military unit, the new organization would be a complement to a foreign aid program. Hence, the paramilitary covert capability would be low-key, while economic and political capabilities—hardly used in wartime—would dominate. Because the new struggle was essentially ideological and economic, postwar covert activists tended to come from backgrounds in economics, management, advertising, filmmaking, law, and academia. The Cold War would be an intellectual's struggle. Thus, the OPC drew from a wider set of skills: Harriman's multi-lateral treaties and business combines, Kennan's analysis, Dulles's sophisticated use of indigenous personnel, all coalesced by Donovan's organizational framework. Among the younger men, Bissell added sophisticated Keynesian analysis; Houston brought legal expertise. Paramilitary and political operations came with Lindsay and Roosevelt, administrative skills with Bross.

Many of OPC's methods and operations were not new. The complicated transactions represented by Deutsch-Russische—so beneficial to the Soviets in the 1920s—had been overtly undertaken at that time. But in the early Cold War, Soviet propaganda attributed evil design to American programs, forcing them underground. In France, for example, actions once considered benevolent were suddenly portrayed as strangling and oppressive.

Men who engineered these transactions continued to do so, frequently becoming covert operators themselves. Evidence shows their awareness of the momentous transition, but never for a moment did Averell Harriman, for example, believe what had been good business and good patriotism in 1920 had ceased to be so in 1948. For this reason he developed duplicate funding procedures to obfuscate American foreign aid procedures. For his part Dulles was quite pleased, for the United States had found a way to succeed in the international arena and he was at the hub of it all. Bissell, Nitze, and the younger generation emulated their elders with zeal, bringing new technical skills and wartime connections to bear on the problem of Soviet subversion. Only Kennan seemed unsure. But his uncertainty may have been more in hindsight, for at the time he was one of the strongest advocates of a peacetime covert organization—either within or outside of the government. Political circumstances, and a lot of hard work by the determined interventionists, would bring this goal to fruition.

THREE

UNCOORDINATED INTERVENTION

V -E Day, May 1945, should have signaled the start of a bright new era in Europe. Hitler was dead, the war was over, Western Europe was free again. But keen observers knew that all was not well. The destruction and chaos left by the conflict to end right-wing totalitarianism had provided a breeding ground for leftist tyranny. John Bross, a Wall Street lawyer who served in the London headquarters of the Office of Strategic Services, sensed it within a few days of the glorious celebration of Allied victory. On V-E Day he flew to Paris to join in the festivities. Upon arrival he was informed by the officer in charge that there was not a room in the entire city. Undeterred, Bross asked for a jeep. He had a sister living in Biarritz at the time, and reasoned that he could find a billet with her. Nothing could have prepared Bross for what he saw as he drove through the French countryside. In each small village French citizens flew the Russian "hammer and sickle"; crowds in the streets chanted "Vive Stalin." As Bross recalled it years later, he "knew there was going to be trouble."

Frank Lindsay saw trouble ahead, too. As part of an OSS political advisory team trying to wrap up the war in the Balkans, Lindsay had firsthand experience with Soviet intransigence. The Allies needed emergency airfields for evacuation and repair of damaged aircraft. The Soviets allocated landing strips and then refused to let Allied planes take off after they landed for fuel and repair. In a desire to get at the root of the problem, Lindsay and a colleague planned an evening sortie to one of the landing fields. A naive young Soviet officer on late night shift handed Lindsay his orders. Once they were translated, it appeared that the snag originated in Moscow, for the orders said that no Allied planes were to be permitted to leave the airfield.

What Lindsay experienced would not have surprised the highest levels of Allied command. They were used to Russian demands. All through the war the Grand Alliance was strained by squabbling over such important issues as the timing of the Allied invasion of Europe, the Italian surrender, the fate of Poland, and reparations. At wartime conferences in Teheran and Yalta, Churchill and Roosevelt had studiously avoided commitment to the Soviets on reparations, and the issue of a protective cordon in Eastern Europe was clouded by Rooseveltian vagueness. But few at the highest levels realized what Bross had seen, that huge numbers of Europeans were attracted by Communism and were being assiduously wooed by the Soviets, facts that would endanger the U.S. plan for reconstruction of Europe. It would take several years before the West would comprehend the extent and nature of Soviet efforts, and it would take even longer to develop a coordinated counteroffensive to this threat.

A llied leaders regarded the alleviation of the physical, economic, and social plight of Europe as their first priority. Yet nothing could have prepared them for what they saw, felt, heard, and smelled in Berlin just before the Potsdam conference. Churchill, wandering aimlessly around Hitler's bunker, was "captured" by "the grisly aftermath in Berlin of heavy Allied bombing."[1] Charles M. W. Moran "felt a sense of nausea . . . it was like the first time I saw a surgeon open a belly and the intestines gushed out."[2] President Truman was "thankful that the United States had been spared the unbelievable devastation of this war." Robert Murphy, an American diplomat, said "the odor of death was everywhere . . . the canals were choked with bodies and refuse." Gen. Lucius Clay summed up the stunning experience: "It was like a city of the dead."[3] Reading such accounts, one senses deep chagrin during what should have been a glorious moment in these leaders' lives. Their recognition of the magnitude of the calamity would propel the Western governments to immediate remediation. We find no such ruminations from Stalin. Doubtless, the twenty million Russian dead enabled him to look at Berlin with aplomb, thinking only of reparations.

Berlin was the focus for early Cold War antagonism among the wartime Allies. Little agreement existed, nor had there been long-range Allied planning, regarding Germany's future. For their part the Americans were considering several alternatives for postwar Germany: among them dismemberment or pastoralization—a scheme to remove industrial might and recreate a harmless, agrarian German society. The French were sensitive to the possibility of a "new" Germany, preferring to protect themselves against future military assault. The Soviets, who had suffered grievously during the war, were determined to take reparations and were thus especially rankled by Allied refusal to determine reparation rates. Consequently, as the victorious armies converged on the conquered city, tensions rose quickly. American leaders already harbored doubts about the compatibility of capitalism and Communism. The Soviet's determination to institute their own reparations scheme—dismantling and removing everything of value in their sector and transporting it east—did nothing to alleviate this apprehension.

Because of growing East-West tensions, American policymakers rapidly "came to believe" that a revitalized and de-Nazified Germany was essential to rebuilding Europe and staving off Communist intrusion.[4] Before long, American leaders, if not European leaders, were committed to the task of bringing Germany rapidly back into the fold as a democratic buffer on the eastern boundary of Western Europe. But as a temporary political solution, the Allies elected to divide Berlin into four zones, each to be governed by one of the conquering nations. The idea that four powers could peacefully govern the decimated city seems almost silly in the hindsight of Cold War experience. But at the time it was the best that could be done in a deadly game precipitated by fundamentally antagonistic powers confronting each other over the spoils of war.

American leaders were concerned about the intrusion of Communist ideas on the domestic front as well. Their dismay was grounded in their fear that the postwar economy would be so weak that the United States might return to the Depression conditions of the thirties. Since American policymakers believed the crucial prerequisite for Communism was economic malaise, they suspected the United States might be at risk.

Determined interventionists had no faith in the loyalty of the American people, no notion that Americans could sustain further economic distress. As Thomas K. Finletter warned, although "the American people are as politically mature as any," they have "recently gone through a decade of depression and misery and they do not intend to repeat the experience. Substantially full employment and social security are not mere campaign catchwords. They are living demands which the American people intend to see achieved—or else. Any government which does not substantially solve these problems will be repudiated."[5]

Finletter, after all, had the specter of Nazi Germany in recent memory. Hadn't the Germans turned to a dictator under economic stress? Hence, Finletter warned, "if our government in its present form fails to meet their demands, the people will almost certainly destroy it and set up a totalitarian government in its stead."[6] As Washington wisdom held at that time, totalitarian governments of either extreme were equally possible.

At least one group in Washington, those at the Office of War Mobilization and Reconversion, such as Richard M. Bissell, Jr., Cord Meyer, and William Remington, thought there was already a drift to the left among American labor unions.[7] The Office of War Mobilization was instituted during the Second World War as a civilian war agency with statutory basis, serving the executive with broad powers.[8] After the war it became the Office of War Mobilization and Reconversion, its duty to convert wartime industries for peacetime use and develop housing and jobs for returning GIs. Bissell saw it as a "miniature Marshall Plan for the United States" and liked the fact that "it produced order."[9] The OWMR suspected that depression fears had created a vulnerability to leftist propaganda among laborers. They agreed with Finletter's prescription that "violent fluctuations in the economy" must be eliminated and that "full and steady employment" must be provided.[10]

But the OWMR was subject to flux. Truman annoyed liberals by appointing Missouri banker John W. Snyder to replace Fred Vinson as chief. The new director took the offensive against economic controls and lifted restrictions on building materials, "shifting construction emphasis from family housing to commercial—resorts, race tracks and cocktail lounges."[11] Executive administration actions combined with betrayal of liberal goals on unemployment compensation brought howls of protest from liberal administrators such as Chester Bowles.[12]

As is often the case in transition periods, a new office—Temporary Controls—combined many wartime agencies "as a way of winding down the control period."[13] The OWMR was liquidated, but the functions and projects remained in place under the Director, who became assistant to the president.[14] Interestingly, Richard E. Neustadt, who served the Truman White House in the Bureau of the Budget from 1946 to 1950, explained that the former OWMR Director John Steelman actually worked on labor relations problems, "lumped in with the coordinating role carried over from OWMR. But the specific, pressing . . . labor problems naturally took precedence over the vaguer stuff of coordinating operations."[15] Little wonder that Richard Bissell described this period as having a lot of charm because it was so fluid, with a good deal of latitude.[16]

Utilizing the fluidity of the postwar bureaucracy, determined interventionists within the OWMR developed a two-phased plan for recapturing American labor: they would purge domestic unions of leaders they thought unfit and develop plans for private industry guaranteed to create upward mobility for workers and prosperity for management. One labor leader they had in mind was Philip Murray, president of the Steelworkers Union and the Congress of Industrial Organizations (CIO).[17] Murray, not looking for friends in any camp but his own, challenged wage controls and steel management at the same time and even demanded a two dollar a day pay increase. By January 1946 President Truman was obliged to instruct labor and industry to settle their differences. Benjamin Fairless, president of U.S. Steel, requested time to check with other producers, to which Murray agreed.[18]

Meanwhile, Price Administrator Chester Bowles and OWMR chief John Snyder engaged in a blazing war over the level of price increase steel should be allowed. Price control advocate Bowles suggested $2.50 a ton; Snyder, eager to ease wartime restrictions on the economy, urged $4. Steel countered by demanding $7.[19]

On 18 January "agitator" Murray accepted the president's suggestion of an 18.5 cent an hour raise. Since Fairless was disgusted by Bowles' and even Snyder's paltry suggestions on tonnage rates, he used the 18.5 cent increase offered steelworkers as leverage and rejected the agreement between Truman and Murray. Murray countered with a strike.[20] In February the government capitulated, offering steel at five dollars a ton. Fairless accepted and Murray called off the strike.[21] It seemed obvious that price controls were not working and equally obvious that labor would not be the winner in economic disputes. Bowles quit.

Simultaneously, Bissell developed a pilot plan for U.S. Steel, hoping to remedy the effects of economic fluctuation in this industry always hard hit by periodic layoffs. Operating on the premise that workers not guaranteed a steady and rising annual wage could become restive and disillusioned, Bissell envisioned a system whereby workers could bank overtime hours for withdrawal as paychecks during slack periods. To convince workers that upward mobility was possible in the postwar world, Bissell also proposed a 2 percent annual pay increase. Although these ideas were not subject to debate as part of the public agenda, economic planners associated with the OWMR were convinced that economic stability, a rising standard of living, and the removal of leftist labor "agitators" were as essential in the United States as in Europe in the immediate aftermath of the war.[22]

There is a strange irony in all this suspicion regarding American labor leaders. As the Marshall Plan/OPC collaboration unfolds in chapters five and six, we will find that policymakers relied on American labor to swing the sympathies of their European counterparts. Whether Marshall Plan personnel believed they needed a purged and purified labor force to do that job or whether they really feared Communism in American labor is hard to determine. But perhaps there was another reason.

It could be that Philip Murray and others were considered too aggressive in their determination to influence Marshall Plan goals and strategy. Murray, for instance, wrote the president on 14 November 1947 regarding his view of what he called the "Basic Principles Which must govern Foreign Aid Programs." Murray proposed three objectives: first, take care of the destitute; second, help them raise their standard of living and have the maximum trade with the United States; and third, permit all nations to solve their problems in a democratic fashion. All this, Murray insisted, should be given without political or economic strings attached.[23]

George Meany also had strong opinions. Writing to Robert LaFollette of the Harriman Committee on 5 November 1947, Meany, too, called for stronger language on democracy in the Marshall Plan legislation, the de-emphasis of that Marshall Plan darling, monetary reform, and taking out all Latin phrases. A cynic might conclude that leftist leanings were acceptable if subservient to elite control, but calling the policy shots was too much to expect.[24]

A merican leaders and planners of the immediate postwar pe-riod were ardent exponents of capitalism, not only for the United States, but as a modernization scheme for other na-tions. They were mindful, certainly, of the benefits to the United States if capitalism became the principal strategy, or model, for global recovery. In fact, most U.S. leaders saw the extension of the capi-talist order as a necessity. But the most important stimulus to their activ-ism was the belief that capitalism brought freedom from want and would therefore assure the peace. Nothing about this view separated the deter-mined interventionists from American public opinion; what set them apart was their activism. Having been trained as expert capitalists, they believed they had both the ability and the duty to apply their skills in the struggle against Communism. The confrontation would be dual, fought in both public and private arenas. The public confrontation centered on events in Berlin, postwar ministerial conferences, and massive relief pro-grams. The private confrontation addressed the problems beneath the surface, particularly the apparent disaffection many Europeans felt with the West, as observed by Bross and others. Unarmed (in the orthodox sense), determined interventionists began to battle Communism by means of councils, groups, missions, and foundations. Functioning out-side of official government channels, they applied their expertise, money, and personal connections to a variety of problems facing Europe before desperate people turned to Moscow for help. As such, the determination to intervene in Europe between 1945 and 1948 was fragmented, uncoor-dinated. The goals, and sometimes the personnel, of the public and pri-vate sectors were shared, but the means employed were quite different.

The private confrontation launched two types of assaults on Communism: missions and foundation efforts. Missions, although often resorting to private sector personnel—thus retaining the aura of consultantships—were usually launched at the request of the federal government. Their aim was to improve a specific geographic area economically and, in the process, socially, to provide intelligence and coordinate economic and social reorganization with military or paramilitary action. As such, men with covert experience often played key roles in the missions. Foundations focused on a specific remedial approach, such as the behavioral sciences and modernization schemes, in their efforts to restructure a society. They were particularly useful in areas where official U.S. government intrusion would have been suspect. Having dual personnel, individuals with foundation and government credentials, was often essential in these efforts because of the need for men who were trusted with operations important in government circles.

Coordination of public and private efforts was achieved by using the Council on Foreign Relations (CFR) as a clearing house for projects. A foreign policy association with considerable funds available for research, the council was prestigious enough to draw heads of state for intimate monthly dinners and "off the record" after-dinner speeches at its elegant physical plant on Manhattan's Park Avenue. It had a closely held membership list of individuals with impressive diplomatic credentials in Washington. The determined interventionists, seeing an opportunity to lobby against a return to isolationism, were anxious to gain access to this forum. Allen Dulles "persistently sponsored" new members who were "activists in International relations."[25] They in turn proposed others, until a substantial cohort of covert political activists had gained entrance.

CFR contacts provided the determined interventionists with access to power, the friendship of like-minded men, and interaction with people who made policy on both sides of the Atlantic. Here they could exchange ideas, methods, research, and experience with something approaching academic standards. The council provided research facilities for State Department planners during the Second World War, and Marshall Plan administrators hoped they would do the same for the European Recovery

Program.[26] Council minutes for this period show that determined interventionists wore CFR and MP hats and were not shy about pressing their
point. And all members were propagandized because the council received
important reports from George Kennan of the State Department's Policy
Planning Staff concerning the Soviet political drive in Europe.[27] The material was apparently so secret and revelatory that the CFR worried about
leaks, deciding that only a digest of their meetings would be available in
council reports. And, because some of the projects contemplated by
these activists were so sensitive, the council was not always a suitable discussion place. In those instances, the council was instrumental in finding
other private sector sponsors.

Eventually, of course, the private and public sector anti-Communist effort merged. Reasons for collaborative effort were both
pragmatic and personal. Extreme civil disturbance, as in
Greece, and the tremendous financial commitments needed to
rebuild Europe required more resources than the private sector could
muster. On the personal level, combining the skills of private experts and
funding from the federal government was psychologically satisfying to
the determined interventionists because control and planning, already
firmly housed in the private sector through their foundation experience,
would give them the upper hand in the partnership. Moreover, suspicious
of the ineptitude of government bureaucracy, they felt assured of the outcome of their efforts if control could be retained.

The United States sanctioned and financed "missions" to troubled regions closely tied to the U.S. Cold War effort. They were called economic
missions but were also designed as intelligence-gathering posts and command centers for Communist activity. Financial sponsorship came from
the government through special grants. Mission directors were appointed
by Congress or the State Department. Representative of this type of project was the American Economic Mission to Greece, popularly known as
the Griswold Mission.

American policymakers were prompted to unravel the complex political picture in Greece because they were sure the Yugoslav-backed Com-

munist National Liberation Front threatened a civil war.[28] The State Department asked Dwight P. Griswold to lead the mission. Griswold had served in the OSS, was the former governor of Nebraska, and at the time of his appointment to Greece was the director of the Division of Internal Affairs and Communications, under the military government of Germany. The analysis of the Griswold Mission provided pivotal information for American foreign policymakers in the Cold War era.

Before asking Congress to authorize and fund Truman Doctrine aid to Greece, the president needed to know what the prospects were for that country. He needed information about the emerging civil war, the depth of the National Liberation Front's connections to Yugoslavia's prime minister, Josip Broz Tito, the extent to which Tito acted on his own or on orders from Moscow, and the likely ramifications of a Greek civil war for U.S. interests. The British were in Greece, but they were so financially weak they would soon have to pull out. Moreover, it was clear in Washington that British and American interests in this region, while superficially harmonious, were fundamentally competitive.

But the Griswold Mission was more than an intelligence gathering post. Griswold's overt task was the coordination of economic recovery. The drachma had to be stabilized, inflation stemmed, food shortages eliminated. A panoply of postwar crises had to be confronted by the American experts. Yet Griswold's correspondence with his superiors reveals a curious mixture of economic policy and antiguerrilla activity, for Griswold also directed the military effort against the Communist insurgents in Greece. He "programmed" the entire U.S. economic and paramilitary involvement in the Greek civil war.

Griswold also made long-term political assessments. In a communiqué just after the Czechoslovakian coup in 1948, he analyzed its political consequences for Greece. Like policymakers in Washington, Griswold was worried about a Communist victory in the Italian elections scheduled for April 1948. But he was out of tune with contemporary Washington thinking, while strangely prescient of opinions that would later emerge regarding the so-called Third World. Griswold reported that the Greeks were indeed concerned about the Czech coup, but only because they saw a possible parallel in U.S. efforts to exert pressure in the Italian election. They feared that Greece, too, might become a pawn in the Cold War between the United States and the Soviet Union.[29] As conditions worsened in Greece, Griswold's powers increased. By April 1948 he asked for and received broad powers to oversee Greek problems. By 1948 the Truman Doctrine was augmented by the more expansive Marshall Plan. Although not originally contemplated as Marshall Plan countries, after the importuning of Franklin Lindsay, Greece and Turkey were added to the list, bringing them into the newly coordinated private and public effort envisioned in the plan.

Since the Marshall Plan sanctioned a covert complement, the use of the mission for counter-subversive activities expanded.[30] To clear the way for action, Robert Lovett, the under-secretary of state, informed Paul Hoffman, administrator of the Economic Cooperation Administration, that Griswold would be in charge "for the time being." Normally in Marshall Plan countries the Marshall Plan station chief, reporting to Hoffman, would have final say. Circumstances took the power out of the hands of normal Marshall Plan channels. Greece was deemed crucial to Mediterranean and Balkan security and was considered very much at risk; therefore special arrangements were made, largely because of guerrilla activity. Lovett followed up these instructions by issuing the same decree to Secretary of War Kenneth Royall, whom he informed that Griswold had tactical control of methods and techniques for countering subversion. Not only were Marshall Plan administrators supplanted by Griswold, but the American ambassador to Greece was recalled as well, so that Griswold would have the appearance of absolute authority.

In Greece, U.S. objectives were to stop the guerrillas, stabilize the currency and stem inflation, manage foreign aid so that food was equitably distributed, and gather intelligence. Griswold integrated and prioritized problems, placing antiguerrilla actions in the forefront. He used economic policy as leverage to achieve political goals. Crudely stated, if Greeks wanted food, the Greek government would have to fight guerrillas. As such, the Griswold Mission provided the model for further coordination between the public and private sectors in international efforts.

Permanent collaboration was necessary because the proposed reconstruction of Europe under the Marshall Plan was an immense task, in terms of expertise and funding. After an arduous publicity campaign, the American public in general supported the plan.[31] But it took considerable effort to persuade individual segments of American society to back the Marshall Plan effort. George Marshall's speech at Harvard was not enough. A committed group proselytized for the plan and followed it through the legislative process, making sure that key congressmen and senators came to see the wisdom of the expensive undertaking and voted accordingly. Allen Dulles, for example, spoke at the Export Managers Club of New York City, stressing the Marshall Plan's benefits to American exporters.[32] It was common for proponents such as Dulles to stress the theme of Europe as "our best market." Paul G. Hoffman told the National Foreign Trade Convention that the Foreign Assistance Act "gave formal recognition to the interdependence of the United States economy and the economy of Western Europe." He predicted that "their most brilliant era [was] in front of them" because "the 270 million people of the Marshall Plan nations are essentially good people. That must be obvious, because they are your ancestors and mine."[33] The Marshall Plan's administrative office even published booklets informing small businessmen of ways the plan could help them. And there were countless "how to" pamphlets for potential American entrepreneurs who might want to trade with Marshall Plan countries. Academics with an interest in foreign relations were also helpful in selling the Marshall Plan. Yale President Charles Seymour was called upon when important votes came up in Congress. Seymour agreed to lobby key legislators, to convince them to vote for the plan.[34] The die had been cast in Greece. The United States was going to pursue a multifaceted policy of economic aid, military presence, organizational expertise, planning, propaganda—whatever it took to defeat Communism.

A nother important order of business was the international political organization necessary to bring the fundamentally exhausted European governments to life.[35] Averell Harriman, secretary of commerce and chairman of the president's Committee on Foreign Aid, wanted the Europeans to take the initiative, determine goals, and formulate their own plans. After that the United States would assist. Men such as Sir Oliver Franks, leader of the Organization for European Economic Cooperation, gave stature to an organization that had to develop nuts and bolts plans for European revitalization.

At the working level—that is, the men who actually supervised the hammering out of the plans—were the determined interventionists. Frank Lindsay, formerly of the OSS, was in Paris as a consultant to the American group, helping to write the plans for each country. Leading committees working in Washington on specific problems such as railroad reconstruction, steel, and coal were: Max Milliken of the War Shipping Department, research and analysis at the State Department, MIT, and the Ford Foundation; William Remington of the War Production Board and the War Reconversion Board; Samuel Van Hyning of the War Shipping Board and research and analysis at the OSS; Herman Liebert of research and analysis at the OSS; John Tuthill and Thomas Geiger of the State Department; Richard M. Bissell of War Reconversion, the Ford Foundation, and the Economic Cooperation Administration (ECA); and his brother-in-law Hector Prud'homme.[36] It was an enormous task, but one faced with enthusiasm by former New Dealers and wartime agency personnel. It was an opportunity to show the organizational skills of the new partnership between the private and public sectors.

Even at that, the extraordinary amalgamation of domestic proselytization, international political and economic planning, and organizational expertise was not enough. A new element had been added to the problem: political subversion orchestrated by the Cominform. American leaders found that they needed another mode of offense. The tactics they decided to use, covert political operations, had not been previously contemplated by the United States in peacetime and were carefully hidden from the public, both American and European.

The shift to covert operations suggests a frustration with the uncoordinated effort described thus far. U.S. policymakers saw that they would have to form a covert organization and began to do so. But this did not mean the exclusion of private sector activity against Communism. Because it was often necessary to act fast, and sensitive covert operations often required careful, time-consuming preparations, policy planners retained contact with private agencies that had done such planning and were willing and able to help. The Ford Foundation is an excellent case in point.

The Ford Foundation was established on the principle that the behavioral sciences provided a scientific basis for experts to help the citizens of underdeveloped nations improve their standard of living. They poured millions into their projects. For a brief period in the early Cold War years, the foundation's view meshed with that of the determined interventionists. Perhaps the best description of the mesh in objectives was provided by Milton Katz. Katz said that the foundation had "a view of foreign policy which identified the primary sources of trouble as poverty, illness, disease and human misfortune. . . . If one would deal with these things, people would straighten themselves out and have a peaceful world."[37] The foundation thought that the behavioral sciences could provide the answer to these problems. Once people were taught how to live right, they could mend their own lives.

How could a private foundation hope to effect these changes? How did it approach the problem? Katz described the process:

> I began by trying to identify the essential problems of American foreign policy, as they would appear to the U.S. government. After the officers (of the foundation) as a group agreed to take certain problems of American foreign policy as our point of departure, we came to question number two which was: what can private individuals and groups do about them? That quickly took a narrower form as question three: what can private groups do with money—that is, money to be spent in lawful ways—as distinct from other forms of private activity?[38]

Ford had decided to intervene in the Third World nations on behalf of American foreign policy. The goal was to provide developmental assistance, often through establishing a qualified middle range of bureaucratic personnel. In the beginning Ford employed a full roster of experts in early Cold War planning and management—Marshall Plan personnel, Griswold Mission people, former OSS men and women. By the late 1950s the process had become more institutionalized with the establishment of the Council of Applied Economic Resources at Stanford University, funded by the Ford Foundation to create an exchange program to train Indian students in banking and finance.

Ford people were convinced that the creation of a qualified bureaucracy would modernize their country of special concern—India. An example of this type of thinking was the effort to help India nationalize its banking system. Ford Foundation personnel believed in the creation of a class of small, independent farmers and businessmen in India. One way to achieve that goal was to nationalize the banks, placing control of the loan process in the hands of the government rather than a landed aristocracy that was less inclined to ease credit policy. Ford viewed America's success as linked to that class of small businessmen inclined to support the government. Accordingly, they attempted to recreate America, as they imagined it, in foreign lands. This type of mythological handling of whole classes of individuals appeared in Marshall Plan efforts in Europe, where the European laborer took on something of the aura of Jefferson's yeoman farmer.

Although foundation members were not trying to become an "ersatz Department of State," they did see themselves as an arm of public policy.[39] They believed that in sensitive times there was less fear of private foundations than of government. This gave foundation people a latitude governments did not have. It also provided a special opportunity for coordinated public and private efforts in the foreign policy sphere. But Katz and others at Ford saw the limitations of this type of joint action. They knew it was wise to keep away from "tension points like Berlin and Trieste"; it was important that they not permit themselves to become "over-zealous at this sort of thing."[40]

One might wonder how the federal government viewed foundation activities in the Third World. There seems to have been no disagreement between the parties. Ford and the Rockefeller Foundation checked their projects with the State Department. John D. Rockefeller III attended the Policy Planning Staff (PPS) meeting on 15 June 1948 to say that his foundation was getting ready to embark on a new project either in Africa or Southeast Asia and that he "wanted to know which one the PPS preferred." The PPS decided that "from the standpoint of U.S. national interest, Africa should have priority." Paul Nitze disagreed, arguing for Southeast Asia.[41]

It seems safe to assume that similar collaboration existed between Ford and the federal government, or at least Ford was careful to employ a great number of people with government connections. Whatever the method, relations went smoothly. An interviewer asked Milton Katz, "Did you have any trouble dealing with federal agencies, perhaps the CIA?" Katz replied, "No, I had been an officer in naval intelligence and worked in the OSS in World War II. I also worked with Ferdinand Eberstadt on the chapter of his report proposing a CIA."[42]

By 1952 Ford's board members began to experience some disenchantment, however, because of the determined interventionism of Katz, Richard M. Bissell, Jr., and others. W. H. Ferry told an interviewer that "Bissell wanted to make the foundation mainly into . . . a sort of officially, well-financed arm of American foreign policy."[43] Board member Edwin H. Land expanded on this theme. In the beginning, Land felt, there was

> a sense of freedom and playfulness . . . in the sense that you could explore ideas, even initiate quite daring undertakings in the interest of the country. A good deal of that playfulness has gone as we made the transition from being the trustees of an organization for which we were responsible to trustees of an organization which in a strange sort of way we were monitoring, an organization that somehow is not the creature of the founders or the trustees, but a servant . . . of the national governmental organization.[44]

An example of the type of determined interventionism that caused this friction between board and expert may well have been something called the "Defector Program" or "Kennan proposal" discussed at a meeting on 3 April 1951. The meeting was attended by CIA Director Walter Bedell Smith, Allen Dulles, Paul Hoffman, and others. The government men were worried because defectors from the Soviet bloc did not receive

proper attention and support from the West and had a tendency to rede-
fect. Since Western policymakers felt there was a dearth of intelligence
on the Eastern Bloc, they were anxious to make the most of Soviet defectors. What they wanted was a long-range rehabilitation and placement
program, handled with private funding. They wanted international publicity, directed by the CIA. The agency wanted to house some defectors in
Washington to get intelligence. Dulles and James Hunt of the CIA would
be in charge. Paul Hoffman, the administrator of the Marshall Plan, was
skeptical from the first.[45]

At the same meeting Dulles made a corollary proposal. He wanted to
establish a "beach-head university" in Strasbourg to house and employ
educated refugees from Eastern Europe. Dulles thought they would start
modestly—20 professors, 100 students, at a cost of $500,000 for the first
year. The goal, of course, was the same as that of the Kennan proposal—
more and better intelligence.[46]

Board members divided into two camps. It is fairly accurate to say that
those with experience in intelligence and covert political activism were in
favor of the stepped-up activism of the foundation, while those without
experience were against it. John Howard, assistant to Dwight Griswold in
Greece, pressed Rowan Gaither, the president of the foundation, on the
question of acting as a CIA channel. Howard argued that the board
avoid a decision in principle and decide instead on each specific case as it
arose, and "in which all other channels have been exhausted and it is in
the national interest that the Foundation act as a channel."[47]

Hans Speier wrote Gaither in May of 1951 that there were organizations in West Germany providing valuable support for the United States
in the Cold War but that it was embarrassing for the High Commissioner
to support them in view of the constraints of the occupational statutes.
At the time the High Commissioner and the State Department were co-
operating with the CIA in channelling covert funds to these organizations, and both strongly preferred that "private initiative" play a more
conspicuous role.[48]

Some foundation board members were very uneasy about these proposals. Gaither flew to the foundation's Pasadena office, polled the staff,
and later reported to board member Bernard Gladieux that the Pasadena

staff was opposed "as a matter of policy." Board member Dyke Brown condemned the elitist nature of the refugee groups and complained about the price tag. When George Kennan asked for an annual bequest of $110,000 plus clerical and building expenses of $86,000 to fund an exile group, Brown quipped: "I can't believe this [much money] is necessary to get whatever information ten refugees have to give."[49]

But the determined interventionists did not let up. Other proposals surfaced, making it apparent that they hoped to interest the Ford Foundation in a broad range of covert operations. In-house memos indicated that Ford was being urged by its own experts to initiate conferences with the State Department, Defense, and the CIA on "the whole range of potential political warfare activities," or what Hans Speier and Don G. Marquis called the "Kennan study on political warfare—psychological, fifth column, etc.."[50]

The board continued to resist, but in November 1951 a handwritten, undated lament signed "D" in Rowan Gaither's correspondence read: "Rowan—I do not know . . . I am, as you know, entirely against any further efforts on the refugee problem as such. I assume my memo on this circulated after leaving here to PH, MK and RH, but have heard nothing further on the subject. Would you think I might raise this in my talks on Program 1 and see how many officers are pro and con?"[51] The evidence indicates that "D" was probably overwhelmed. On 7 November 1951 Joseph McDaniels wrote to Bernard Gladieux regarding the refugee problem, saying:

> This will confirm our conversation this date to the effect that the New York Office, on request of Pasadena, will continue its study of the refugee program, devoting its attentions primarily to identifying the agencies which are now working in this field, ascertaining their effectiveness, and finally, recommending which in your judgment the Foundation could possibly use with some certainty that any grant made it or them would insure a good job being done.[52]

It would be easy now to say that the Ford Foundation was duped by the determined interventionists, who used it as a home for covert political activism. However, that is not the case. Some board members were very much against the specific projects surrounding the "Kennan proposal," but others were not. More importantly, they all concurred in the hiring of Richard M. Bissell, Jr., and others who they knew were activists. The correspondence surrounding Bissell's hiring is instructive. A great deal of negotiations took place. The board wanted someone with an interest in economic problems, with a research orientation. Bissell made it very clear to the recruiters that he wanted action projects, not research, and that many of the projects he was interested in were not primarily economic. He said he would spend considerable time in Washington trying to improve policy formulation and the procedure by which policies were carried into action. He told Ford recruiters he might be in slight disagreement with them as to the type of projects an economic institute ought to undertake. He also said his definition of economic action projects was broader than that of Paul Hoffman, the director of the ECA.[53]

Despite Bissell's caveats, Ford Foundation hired him in July 1951. He left in March of 1953. President Eisenhower wanted him for a special assignment, one that Milton Katz speculated with Rowan Gaither "might be a matter of high priority and classification."[54] (Bissell went to the CIA.) But throughout the early 1950s, the Ford Foundation continued to be courted for covert political operations. A foundation representative met with State Department officials on 11 January 1952. A memo to President Truman on the meeting indicated that "his [the foundation man's] main concern was the need for demonstrating that the Ford contribution would be separate from the U.S. Government and that the program was an emergency one which could not be handled by the Government." According to the memo, the Ford representative acquiesced when assured that it was an emergency and that "the assistance of the voluntary agencies was indispensable to the success of the program."[55] Apparently there were still reluctant board members, though, because the Ford representative indicated "the real test would come when the State Department put their plan on paper and submitted it to Mr. Gladieux in New York."[56]

Clearly the conflict between the determined interventionists and the Ford Foundation was not about goals, but methods. Ford was in the mainstream of American foreign policy and definitely not "soft" on Communism, yet there was the matter of the foundation's charter. Board of Trustee members—no matter how loyal to the government, how fearful of the Soviets, and how politically astute they were—simply did not believe that the actions proposed by the determined interventionists jibed with the foundation's charter. Given the secrecy requirements of determined interventionism, activism within a foundation with antagonistic board members would eventually have been self-defeating.

Where could a determined interventionist go when frustrated in this manner? If one had an activist frame of mind, believed in the planned application of expertise in economics, politics, and propaganda? If one believed, having had experience in the OSS, the missions, the Marshall Plan, and the foundations, in joining the organizational and financial strengths of the public and private sectors? And, if one strongly believed Communism represented the greatest challenge Western democracy had ever faced, and therefore could condone the idea of covert operations to meet covert operations? There was a place. A new organization that combined all these ideas and approaches and that paid well was attracting many people who had been bound to each other professionally and socially for years. Determined interventionists went to the CIA, the new institutional darling of Cold War Washington.

Curiously, they faced conflict at the CIA as well. In some sense they were an invasionary force. The CIA also was predicated on the application of expertise, but it was a different kind of expertise with entirely different aims and methods. It was not interventionist; it was a classic spying organization. It gathered information. The CIA was formed in 1947 under the National Security Act because, as Harry S. Truman said: "The President ought to have a source of information that covers the whole world and the only way to get it is to have an intelligence agency of his own which will keep him informed of what goes on." It collected and analyzed information and forwarded it to the executive.[57] It was not an activist agency. Its personnel had expertise in what was called clandestine collection. Others had experience in the wartime Special Operations group of OSS, the sabotage unit.[58] But under their 1947 charter they had no directive enabling them to politically or economically affect conditions anywhere. To make matters worse, peacetime intelligence was a new concept in the United States and had met with considerable resistance. After the war, despite Donovan's lobbying, Truman disbanded the OSS. Certain of its branches were transferred to the departments. Research and Analysis, the analytical branch of the OSS went to the State Department. Secret Intelligence and Counterespionage went to the War Department. Secret Intelligence clandestinely collected intelligence within other countries while the Counterespionage branch protected those intelligence operations by keeping tabs on enemy intelligence operations, hence the nickname "spy's spies." Little is known of what became of the other branches: the Church Committee concluded in 1975 that "although it is impossible to determine conclusively, there is no evidence that OSS subversion and sabotage operations continued after the war."

The idea of a coordinated intelligence service was not dead, however. It surfaced repeatedly, in different forms. Some felt intelligence should remain with the various departments—War, Army, Navy, and State—while others believed an independent service was necessary. Ferdinand Eberstadt, who chaired the committee on intelligence for the 1947 executive reorganization effort, proposed a centralized agency. But the Central Intelligence Group, as it was called, would be just a coordinator of information provided by other intelligence-gathering agencies; it would not produce intelligence itself. That put the new agency in a very weak position bureaucratically, and its survival probably stemmed from the fact that two of its four early directors were men of power in the policymaking bureaucracy in the early Cold War years.

The functional evolution of the CIA from a coordinating agency to a producing agency came about because of the personal and political strength of CIA Director Hoyt Vandenberg, the nephew of Arthur Vandenberg, ranking Republican on the Senate Foreign Relations Committee. Despite the resistance of the departments to civilian involvement in intelligence and a new organization with direct access to the president, Vandenberg was able to get an independent research and analysis function into the agency, which made it a producer of intelligence. It could now compete because its intelligence was not as narrow as the other departments. The range of the new agency's interests would be far broader than, say, army or navy intelligence.

In 1946 Vandenberg added to the agency's strength. He acquired the former Special Services Unit, which had been shunted off to the War Department in 1945 when the OSS was disbanded. Special Services was responsible for clandestine collection in foreign lands. Vandenberg brought the unit into the CIA, renaming it the Office for Special Operations. This gave the agency additional personnel and a few field stations.

In 1947 the National Security Act created the Central Intelligence Agency out of the Central Intelligence Group. But the new agency was not very powerful. Its main function was to issue a report, called *The Daily*, on intelligence gathered from other agencies. The consumers of this intelligence, senior-level policymakers, were far from satisfied. What they wanted were "national estimates," as suggested by the Dulles-Jackson-Corea Report of 1948. National estimates are reports on a variety of factors in important countries—agricultural production, industrial capacity, resource levels. Between 1948 and 1950 the agency struggled to develop that capacity and to gain a voice in Washington. Because political analysis was firmly entrenched at the State Department at that time, the CIA zeroed in on national estimates, or economic analysis. This decision was wise because the CIA's consumer list suddenly burgeoned. With the acquisition of sophisticated economic analysts such as MIT's Max Milliken, the agency was able to provide competent economic analysis of Soviet bloc countries. With the onset of the Korean conflict this skill probably provided the edge for survival against departmental jealousy and rivalry for supremacy at National Security Council meetings.

Even so, the nascent intelligence agency did not have an easy time of it. And to make matters worse—or better, depending on perspective—a new element had to be considered. Probably as a result of Soviet recalcitrance in leaving Azerbaijan in 1946, and the Greek civil war, cabinet officials began to consider covert operations. It seemed quite possible that the organizational structure for covert operations would end up at the CIA, but there was some conflict over the location. In 1946 Robert Patterson,

the secretary of war, suggested to James V. Forrestal that covert psychological warfare be considered. A State-War-Navy Coordinating Committee (SWNCC) meeting decided that the covert assault should limit itself
to psychological warfare. In peacetime it would be directed by the
SWNCC, but during war it would report directly to the president. After
some debate it was decided, in June 1947, that covert psychological activities should be undertaken. Admiral Roscoe H. Hillenkoetter, who replaced Vandenberg as director of Central Intelligence in May 1947, did
not want these operations nestled in the CIA. The organizational debate
proceeded, and finally on 4 November 1947 Truman approved the State
Department as the home for psychological warfare. By the twenty-fourth
he had rescinded the order after strenuous objections by George C. Marshall, the secretary of state. Marshall wanted a covert function very
much, and subject to his guidance, but he did not want to risk tarring
State by "quartering" the new unit.

On 14 December 1947 Truman signed NSC 4/A authorizing covert psychological approaches for Eastern and Central Europe. An office to
carry them out, the Special Procedures Group, was established within the
Office of Special Operations, the clandestine collection outfit at the
CIA. The anomaly of having an activist group within a clandestine collection group would lead to difficulties, but at the time it seemed the only
place to go. One-third of CIA personnel was former OSS, the agency had
overseas stations, although not many, and they had the unvouchered
funds essential for secrecy.

Covert operations started as psychological warfare in 1947, and their
first efforts were modest and "amateurish." But by May 1948 men like
Kennan and Marshall were proposing full-scale covert political action.
The subject was common at PPS meetings. Kennan would have been
willing to house these operations at the State Department, but in the end
they too went to the CIA, replacing the Special Procedures Group, as we
will see in the next chapter.

For the present we should consider the two groups of experts. To a
clandestine collection man trying to gain credibility and recognition for
efforts in the Washington bureaucracy, the subtle but indicative shift to
covert operations was less than pleasing. Barely was a foothold gained

than expertise was eclipsed. The shift also created a monumental personality conflict. Clandestine collection is a quiet, long-term affair, with little fanfare and even less bravado. But by 1948 ranks were swelling with hordes of "civilians" with no concept of cover, a sense of themselves as having all the answers, and a desire to take action, daring action, to stem the tide of Communism.

Among the new covert men there was a sense that something could be done, that it was time to stop studying these matters and take action. There was a need for a bureaucratic home, but little tolerance for the current occupants and their painstaking techniques. It was the same challenge they had faced in the foundations. But this time the charters were on their side; policymakers were ready to take action and the determined interventionists were expert activists. To be sure, the determined interventionists would have to fight for their place in the agency, but they were holding all the cards. Soviet covert subversion made their techniques seem necessary. Although the participants may not have sensed it at the time, the battle for the CIA was over before it began.

As he disbanded the wartime Office of Strategic Services in the fall of 1945, Harry S. Truman claimed he was "concerned about 'building up a gestapo.'"[1] Later, as president emeritus, he claimed that "the CIA was set up by me for the sole purpose of getting all the available information to the President. It was not intended to operate as an international agency engaged in strange activities."[2] Historians have read his statement as meaning that he detested the idea of an American intelligence organization and of covert operations. On the contrary, Truman was angered because, he believed, existing intelligence-gathering operations were not sharing their data with him. Moreover, he and his advisors feared Soviet subversion in Europe and thought the United States should have a covert capability.[3] As Truman expressed it to University of North Carolina President Gordon Gray, "It is hardly an exaggeration to say that the policy of averting a third world war may depend upon the strength and effectiveness of our efforts in the field of psychological warfare."[4]

Truman also wanted an intelligence organization that was strictly secret, and the activities of the OSS had become a matter of considerable public interest. Ironically, what had caused the loss of secrecy about the OSS was its success and the efforts of its chief, William Donovan, to keep it alive. Donovan embarked on a self-congratulatory media campaign with that aim in mind. Doing the circuit of business and civic organizations, he spread stories about the successess of the OSS in wartime Europe. Typically Donovan would plant an OSS agent in the audience, then recount his tale of adventure, and finish by saying: "And here, right in our audience is Agent X, the hero of our story." Nothing could have been less to the liking of the intelligence community, whose members began to regard even their hero Donovan as something of an outsider.[5]

Truman acted to remedy some of these problems. Under the National Security Act of 1947 he created a new intelligence organization, the Central Intelligence Agency, but it was not empowered to undertake covert operations. As events began to recommend a covert capability, the president was forced to create a new covert organization. Authorized in 1948 by National Security Council directive 10/2, the new organization was called the Office of Policy Coordination. Despite presidential rhetoric, Truman's actions show his intention to provide the United States with secret capabilities.

A complex set of factors, including existing belief systems, global political events, prior experiences of covert political activists, domestic political considerations, and institutional requirements, caused Truman to create a covert capability. Equating the totalitarianism of the Fascist and Soviet regimes—"I don't care what you call them, Nazi, Communist or Fascist," Truman said—he believed tactics that were useful against one might be useful against the other.[6] When a political coup toppled the Czechoslovakian government in February 1948, top policymakers— James Forrestal, George Marshall, George Kennan, Allen Dulles, Averell Harriman—immediately reassessed their strategy and sanctioned a covert initiative. They drew on the experience of former OSS operatives and the cohort of determined interventionists. Because there was a sense of haste and because of the expertise of the cohort, the organization Truman authorized allowed tremendous flexibility and initiative by its personnel.

Although there was a backdrop of anticommunism in America against which the global political events of 1948 were viewed, Truman's decision was nonetheless colored by his desire to retain executive control and to ensure complete secrecy by avoiding congressional involvement as much as possible. Truman and his advisors believed the complex factors influencing his decision would be difficult to resolve, because the Cold War required a range of actions that could not be taken openly in a democracy.[7] From this decision came the doctrine of plausible denial—that is, that actions undertaken covertly could be plausibly denied by the government if they were exposed. Sanctioning the view that overt techniques were not sufficient, Truman took the responsibility for finding alternative methods.

Intense fear prompted authorization of covert political action. Until 1947 Communism created a malaise, a sense that something was going

wrong. But by 1947, as a result of Soviet actions in Greece, Iran, and Turkey, Truman decided to take the initiative. In a rousing speech before a
joint session of Congress, he alerted the American people to the dangers
of Soviet political manipulation and offered assistance to any people "re-
sisting attempted subjugation." His plan, the Truman Doctrine, offered
military assistance and was aimed primarily at Turkey and Greece.

The Truman Doctrine was a specific response to the Mediterranean situation, but it led rapidly to the Marshall Plan, a generalized version of
Truman's determination to resist political subversion. By May 1947 drafting of the Marshall Plan was in progress and Washington's top policymakers were proselytizing for it. The compelling force behind the plan was
American fear that the dislocations of World War II would cause the
"collapse" of "modern civilization" in Europe. As George Marshall told
a Harvard commencement audience, "Europe's requirements for the next
three or four years . . . are so much greater than her present ability to
pay that she must have substantial additional help or face economic, social and political deterioration of a very grave character." The purpose of
the Marshall Plan "should be the revival of a working economy in the
world so as to permit the emergence of political and social conditions in
which free institutions can exist."[8]

While the nationwide campaign to promote the Marshall Plan proceeded, men at the "working level"—generally those just below the top
posts—were in Washington. Richard M. Bissell, Jr., assisted W. Averell
Harriman, the secretary of commerce and chairman of the President's
Committee on Foreign Aid. With the exception of Harriman, committee
members were not officeholders but distinguished private citizens who
were to review the situation in Europe and render a judgment as to what
U.S. responsibility ought to be. They worked feverishly for four months,
not always agreeing. One night after the formal meeting had dispersed,
Senator Arthur Vandenberg, chairman of the Foreign Relations Committee, called Bissell to say he needed the legislation immediately—the time
was right to present it to the Senate. Vandenberg decided independently
that the promotional effort had peaked. Bissell wrote all night, taking
the document to Harriman the next morning. Fifty to one hundred copies were delivered for press review, but the full committee never saw it.

The next day the press commended the plan. The tenor of their remarks indicated they thought it was about time America used its immense wealth for world stability.[9] The Senate got the go ahead, and the committee relaxed. Seeing almost universal support for the legislation, the formal committee kept quiet about the conditions of the drafting.[10] It would have been impossible to gather the formal committee and write a coherent draft on such short notice. The men at the working level—during this period they were often determined interventionists—got the job done.

Over in the House it was the same. Franklin Lindsay, the former OSS demolitions expert, was involved in the effort to gain Congressional approval of the Marshall Plan. Congressman Christian Herter of Massachusetts, whose foreign policy experience went back to his service with Allen Dulles at Versailles, was the chairman of the House Select Committee on Foreign Aid. Herter was determined to win over the strong isolationists in Congress. He and Lindsay organized a group of congressmen, including first-termer Richard M. Nixon, and took them to Florina in northern Greece, almost on the Yugoslav border, to gain an appreciation of the circumstances in the region. They hoped a first-hand look at the Greek civil war would convince the congressmen that conditions in Greece warranted American aid. Florina was as close to the civil strife as anyone would want to get, since Tito had not yet split with Moscow and the northern border of Greece (Macedonia) was a safe haven for Communist guerrillas. When the congressional mission returned to Washington, the members all voted for the Marshall Plan and "took two or three with them," Lindsay recalled.[11]

Policymakers had political and economic expectations for the Marshall Plan. It was to provide the revitalizing force for the European economy because, as Allen Dulles said, "democracy requires a reasonable standard of living. . . . It is impossible in areas of want." Not many people in Washington would have disagreed with Dulles when he told the Brown alumni in June 1947 that the "communists won't need guns if there is economic chaos."[12] It was expected that the Marshall Plan would help stabilize Europe politically by maintaining a forum for Big Three cooperation. Political cooperation would not only speed up economic recovery, but ensure the direction the recovery would take. Policymakers did not expect the Soviets to contribute to the Marshall Plan but they did expect them to acquiesce.[13]

Some historians have taken the view that American diplomatic manipulation forced the Soviet veto of the Marshall Plan. But for those policymakers whose greatest concern was open markets and prevention of the nationalization trend, the retention of the Big Three was a logical step. Arguing that the United States pushed the Soviets into the veto makes an assumption that all policy elites wanted estrangement. The evidence does not bear that out. In particular the determined interventionists wanted free trade with the Eastern bloc, and in fact Marshall Plan records indicate that even after the Soviet walk out, a variety of accords were reached with individual Eastern countries. Marshall Plan personnel, for instance, helped gain approval for an agreement between the Italians and the Soviets.

While there may always be disagreement as to the importance of U.S. trade with the countries of Eastern Europe before the war, the authors of the Marshall Plan considered it an important factor, noting that "Eastern Europe has been effectively diverted from its normal channels of trade to the great loss of the west."[14] And in May of 1948, determined interventionists Allen Dulles and Franklin Lindsay told the House Select Committee on Foreign Aid that "before the war Eastern European countries had far closer ties (trade) with western Europe than they did with each other. . . . There was little unity among them."[15] Whatever the realities of prewar trade, it seems difficult to assume that American postwar economic strategy would have intentionally excluded a substantial block of potential customers. But whatever the intentions of the determined interventionists, the Soviets walked out of the Paris conference on the Marshall Plan in July of 1947, taking Poland and Czechoslovakia with them.

Because policymakers still hoped for a positive turn in East-West relations before the momentous events of the spring of 1948, their response to political events in Europe was fragmented; it lacked cohesion. They still hoped that some accommodation could be reached with the Soviets through diplomatic and economic channels. Allen Dulles's ideas are instructive on the evolution of attitudes toward the Soviets during this period.

Dulles was the chief of the OSS in Bern during World War II. He returned home convinced that covert operations were useful, largely because his office had been instrumental in orchestrating the surrender of the German army in northern Italy. He was also concerned about Communist political action in Europe and received regular correspondence, beginning in the summer of 1945, from former OSS contacts in Europe who were attempting to form cohorts to resist Communism.[16]

While it might be tempting to say that Dulles was an ardent anti-Soviet from some time in prehistory, that was not the case. His former OSS superior, Gen. William J. Donovan, certainly was. In 1919 Donovan visited Siberia. A diary entry from that year suggests he thought conflict with the Soviet Union was inevitable and that he was sure covert action could prevent such a war. In Donovan's words, "We can prevent a shooting war if we take the initiative to win the subversive war."[17] But Dulles, while suspicious of the Soviets, found the fear of a Nazi resurgence more worrisome. Reflecting the thinking of policymakers at the time, Dulles favored the formation of a non-Communist left as the best way to counter that trend. As he told his frequent correspondent Vera M. Dean of the Foreign Policy Association, "We should welcome a liberal and leftist oriented Germany," because it was there and in the labor unions that the "sturdiest anti-Nazi elements" were to be found.[18]

Regarding the Soviets, Dulles adopted a wait-and-see attitude. In 1946 he addressed the Princeton University Bicentennial Conference on Development of International Society. He cautioned his audience that Czechoslovakia was "an experiment, a point where the two powers and their policies meet and must try to work out a settlement which would leave the people concerned the freedom to work out their own way of life, government and social system." Dulles admitted it was too early to tell whether it would work. Would the experiment build up what he called an insulating zone between two fundamentally divergent and dynamic systems, or would it open a way toward mutual understanding and create the basis for a peaceful system?[19] Yet despite his caution, optimism was evident in his most private ruminations. In a tiny notebook where he had scribbled thoughts on the speech promoting the Marshall Plan to be delivered at the Brown commencement, the final line is "Russians inherently peaceful."[20]

Torn between accommodation and suspicion, Dulles acted to maintain a covert capability in case a need arose. He retained an extensive network of contacts with old OSS friends in Europe, who kept him informed of political conditions and Communist activities. He and his sister, Eleanor Lansing Dulles, provided a social milieu in which determined interventionists could get to know one another and exchange views. And Dulles persistently sponsored determined interventionists—Tracy Barnes, William H. Jackson, Frank Wisner, Cord Meyer, men who would later become significant covert political activists—to the Council on Foreign Relations.[21]

Because Dulles thought an activist stance might be necessary to counter Soviet subversion, he wanted to keep the cohort of activists together. By 1948 Dulles appeared to be correct. Policymakers, like Dulles, had adopted a cautious attitude, particularly in countries with parliamentary governments, such as Czechoslovakia. That is why Dulles referred to Czechoslovakia, "that point where the power of the Western Democracies touches the power and policies of Russia," as an experiment. If parliamentary governments worked—and to them a successful government meant that even with a Communist minority represented, the door would still be open to Western trade and influence—so much the better. Before 1948 they retained the belief that such an accommodation might be possible.

The fall of Czechoslovakia in February 1948 caused a change and hardening in American attitude. Before that, individuals who were fearful of the Soviets found a voice in George Kennan, whose Long Telegram warned of the protracted struggle he envisioned against the Soviets. Many others in Washington were alarmed by the escalation of Soviet-backed propaganda in Europe. But the Czech crisis seemed to "crystalize the problem."[22] Before that time policymakers believed open elections leading to pluralistic governments were possible, safe, and desirable. They were unprepared for the fact that parliamentary governments could be manipulated and overthrown by the acquisition of certain key ministerial posts such as the Interior (state police) or Agriculture (food distribution and land use) departments.[23]

In Czechoslovakia a crisis ensued when moderate parliamentarians protested the reorganization of security police by handing in their resignations to President Eduard Benes. After some delay Benes accepted the resignations, permitting the Communist leader of the coalition government, Clement Gottwald, to form a new government. The newly organized government was Communist controlled. In the midst of the crisis, Jan Masaryk—the Czech foreign minister and "one of the foremost diplomatic figures in Europe"—died, either a suicide or victim of political murder.[24]

Events in Czechoslovakia crystallized the problem for the American public as well as for policymakers. Americans saw the Czech coup as "Munich all over again." Reactions were extreme, as shown by a *Newsweek* poll indicating there were those who called for a "preventive atomic strike against the Soviet Union." And a Gallup poll showed that by July, 69 percent of those questioned thought American policy was too soft toward Russia.[25]

Policymakers were probably cautious in assessing this change in American public opinion. As John Lewis Gaddis has noted, at the time Truman announced the aid program for Greece and Turkey, "although most Americans supported the Administration's determination to take a firm stand, few seemed willing to make the sacrifices necessary to implement this policy. Pressure for instant demobilization continued, raising doubts as to whether the Pentagon could maintain the military strength necessary to back up a tougher diplomatic strategy."[26] Marshall planners probably had not forgotten that less than one year before "popular demands for the abolition of wartime taxes and economic controls made it clear that the government would have difficulty in financing aid to nations threatened by communism."[27]

That explains why policymakers echoed—and probably spurred— strong public reaction. Secretary of Commerce Harriman told a Congressional committee that "there are aggressive forces in the world coming from the Soviet Union which are just as destructive in their effect on the world and our own way of life as Hitler." George C. Marshall described the Czech situation as a "reign of terror." Lucius Clay telegraphed Washington from Berlin that war might come "with dramatic suddenness." Harry S. Truman called for quick passage of the European Recovery Program and Universal Military Training.[28]

After the Czech coup, policymakers—primarily Marshall, Harriman, Kennan, and Forrestal—decided to change their tactics. They moved fast because April elections were scheduled in Italy and they were determined not to allow a repeat of the Czech situation. The Communist party was strong in Italy. *New York Times* Rome correspondent Emmet Hughes told a group in James Forrestal's office that he took "a gloomy view of the Italian situation." That the "Communists may have 45% of the vote . . . which would mean that they would have to be taken into the government. If they do not win . . . there is an even chance [they] will resort to force."[29] The feeling in Washington was that no matter what the numerical outcome, a Communist presence would make Italy ungovernable.

Concern about tactics received attention at the CFR as well. In 1947, the U.S. foreign policy group, led by Thomas Finletter, proposed that the United States needed CIA "special executive agents."[30] The following year, on the day of the Czech coup, a meeting of the political group heard America's UN delegate, Porter McKeever, say that the "Marshall Plan was a dynamic concept which lent itself well to . . . propaganda efforts," which he thought "ought to be primarily through the operation of political, economic and social groups in western Europe." He recommended the use of European and American labor groups and émigrés from Eastern Europe to transmit this type of propaganda. The use of "indigenous democratic elements" for propaganda purposes had been on the docket at the council since the inception of the political group in December of 1947. Members of the group favored the formation of a committee at the State Department to "centralize" propaganda "in one high official."

By March, Bryce Wood, the secretary of the Rockefeller Foundation, noted privately that "the events of the past two weeks and imminence of the Italian elections makes me wonder whether the . . . United States should endeavor to influence the Italian electoral campaign by techniques such as the giving of financial aid to non-communist parties for use in their pre-election propaganda?" Correspondence among CFR staff members indicates they did not think it was "worth discussing." Nevertheless, at the regular meeting on 10 March, Wood proposed making "dollars available to the non-communist elements for use in the election."[31]

James Forrestal, the secretary of defense, was particularly concerned about the Italian elections. While others discussed and fretted, he personally raised money from private sources in New York, "East Coast money," and funneled it to the Christian Democrats.[32] He tried to engage the new CIA and was turned down because the legislation establishing the agency did not provide for political action.

Forrestal acted in this solitary fashion because he believed there was a crisis, found the existing institutions inadequate to meet the crisis, and saw no other way to proceed. But he was not operating against the wishes of Washington policymakers. At the same time Forrestal was maneuvering to influence the elections in Italy, policymakers and the Policy Planning Staff of the State Department were working to institutionalize the type of operation Forrestal initiated. Forrestal, in the meantime, had connections in Wall Street among people who would willingly contribute substantial funds to ensure a non-Communist victory in Italy. He tapped his sources and funded the election.

Forrestal's initiative signalled an end to the notion that redemocratizing European countries could be accomplished simply by regenerating their economies. With the institutionalization of the covert method, the United States admitted as much and added a new, permanent component to their strategy in "defense of democracy." The institutional response to the Czech coup was the formation of a new covert political organization, the Office of Policy Coordination (OPC). It was formed because policymakers believed that the existing institution for European reconstruction, the Marshall Plan, did not have the functional mechanisms to get the job done. The Economic Cooperation Administration was not properly equipped to counter the subversive activities of the Communists in the form of manipulating elections, propagandizing labor and student organizations and the type of postelection maneuvering seen in the Czech incident. What policymakers wanted was a flexible organization with additional functions and freedom from the meddling of a sedentary bureaucracy. As George Marshall said, they wanted to be able to act quickly in an emergency. They wanted an organization with the capability to act as Forrestal had in Italy. Primarily it would exert influence through private and governmental channels. The new bureaucratic apparatus would work alongside existing institutions, sharing personnel and resources, but would remain free from them; it would be guided by the same policy directives but retain flexibility of action. Existing institutions would be free of the new organization as well, a crucial requirement since the new initiative required unorthodox methods not authorized by the directives of existing departments and agencies. In common parlance what Truman authorized was an organization to carry out covert operations. The OPC was America's first peacetime covert organization. But no one in Washington, including the president, thought 1948 was peacetime.

The OPC acted as a complement to the Marshall Plan, providing functions that could not be performed by the CIA or through diplomatic channels. And yet to use the term complementary in some way diminishes the sense of peril policymakers felt at the time. As they saw it, the Marshall Plan was falling short because it had no political functions. The CIA had no political capability, and diplomatic channels were so tradition-bound they were sterile. And there was no recourse to arms—the House had rejected universal military training. To make matters worse, the Cold War provided the additional challenge of "subversion"—a new type of political warfare. How could a democracy combat this type of threat?

Policymakers relied on men with experience and expertise, many of them from the OSS, as they rushed to create a new organization. But they knew this war was different. They would not be able to mobilize public opinion and create a climate tolerant of the means they would employ. The new organization would not gain public acclaim, as the OSS had. There would be no plaudits. The concept of plausible denial signalled admission of that fact and a belief that it was necessary.

James Forrestal added momentum to the formation of the OPC. In the spring of 1948, before taking action on his own, Forrestal tried the CIA. At the time, Admiral Roscoe H. Hillenkoetter—a man with impres-

sive years of sea duty and little experience with intelligence operations—
was the director of Central Intelligence. After one NSC meeting Forrestal
approached Hillenkoetter to see if the CIA could provide the necessary
support. Hillenkoetter asked for an opinion from Lawrence Houston,
general counsel of the CIA. Houston informed Hillenkoetter that the
National Security Act did not provide statutory authorization to engage
in covert operations. Hillenkoetter persisted, claiming that section 5 of
the National Security Act gave the CIA authority. Houston was ada-
mant, insisting that the National Security Act provided for intelligence
only and that covert operations might depend on intelligence but were
not part of it. But Houston did tell Hillenkoetter that if the CIA could
get a proper directive from the executive and funds from Congress, the
agency had the ability to carry out the supporting functions contemplated by Forrestal.[33]

The reticence shown by the agency is explained by the fact that the
CIA directive of 1947 was limited to intelligence gathering, espionage,
and counterespionage, all of which involve the clandestine collection of
information about foreign governments. What Forrestal wanted was to
change the nature of the CIA from passive to active by creating a function for covert activities including political, economic, psychological,
and paramilitary action. The agency had not engaged in covert activities
and had little or no capacity for them, its personnel being equipped for
the long-term, deep-cover function of traditional espionage.[34] Forrestal
did not wait. But his encounter with Hillenkoetter began the process of
legitimizing covert methods.

Forrestal was not the only one contemplating covert operations.
Prompted by doubts about the Italian elections, the State Department
also began to agitate for covert political activism. On 9 April, there were
two meetings of the PPS, one at 11:30 a.m., the other at 1 p.m. During
April, May, and June, when covert operations were discussed, this became the pattern. In the morning the limited PPS would convene, in the
afternoon they were joined by others with special expertise. On 9 April,
the staff discussed the establishment of Freedom Committees about
which they had "many serious questions . . . as to the practicability and
advisability of undertaking the covert activities envisaged."[35]

The final recommendation was prepared on 3 May 1948. At 11 a.m. the staff met as usual. At the afternoon meeting, between 3 and 4 p.m., George V. Allen, Charles Bohlen, Loy Henderson, Raymond Murphy, Francis Stevens, and Llewelyn Thompson joined as consultants on political warfare.[36] There was a discussion of a memo prepared by the staff on 30 April 1948 regarding "the inauguration of organized political warfare." The paper was "generally approved" and Kennan was to "present it tomorrow for discussion at a meeting of NSC consultants."[37]

George Kennan, the head of the State Department's Policy Planning Staff, submitted the plan for a permanent State Department agency to act covertly to counter Soviet subversion in Eastern Europe. Kennan, who was "a strong activist at the time," thought that "in the unusual circumstances prevailing. . . there was occasional need for actions by the United States Government that did not fit into its overt operations and for which it could not accept formal responsibility."[38] At the NSC meeting, he probably did not meet with any disagreement. At a meeting on 11 March, George C. Marshall stated that "he was very concerned about the lack of financial resources . . . to do things quickly, particularly when it is desirable that the actions not be documented." Marshall felt there was "an urgent necessity for concealed funds which should probably be appropriated to the CIA."[39]

Despite the fact that policymakers such as Forrestal, Kennan, Marshall, and Allen Dulles believed the situation required a covert response, there was considerable debate regarding the nature of covert activities and where they would be bureaucratically housed. Keeping the State Department from involvement was important, as was creating a funding mechanism that would invite minimal congressional scrutiny.[40] Secrecy required an institutional home which allowed flexibility, yet coordination with foreign policy objectives was imperative. And a sense of urgency permeated the entire debate.

Action came quickly. On 18 June 1948, the NSC approved a top secret document numbered NSC 10/2 establishing a covert arm within the existing CIA.[41] The new covert organization was soon named the Office of Policy Coordination. From its creation in 1948 until 1952 when the Marshall Plan was terminated, the OPC operated as the plan's complement.

Its actions were meant to be and remain covert so that they could be plausibly denied by the government.

By August 1948 the director of Central Intelligence had nominated Frank Wisner as director, Office of Special Projects, the first name given the covert organization. Wisner, the former deputy to the assistant secretary of state for occupied areas, had just returned from Europe. Traveling with Under-Secretary of the Army William Draper under the cover that they were in Europe to discuss CARE packages, Wisner in fact visited British Foreign Secretary Ernest Bevin, French Foreign Minister Georges Bidault, Secretary of Commerce Averell Harriman, who held a special roving ambassadorship as the Marshall Plan's special representative in Paris, Lucius Clay, the American military commander in Germany, and his political advisor, Robert Murphy. We can probably draw the inference that Wisner was being introduced around, briefed at the highest levels.[42]

At the same time, former CIA Director Sidney Souers reported to the NSC that, as provided in NSC 10/2, the secretary of state had designated "Mr. George Frost Kennan as his representative for NSC 10/2 affairs and the Secretary of Defense had designated Colonel Ivan D. Yeaton both as his and the Joint Chief of Staff's representatives. . . . The method of operation has been agreed upon by the representatives of the secretaries of State, the Joint Chiefs of Staff and the Director of Central Intelligence with respect to the initial procedures of the Office of Special Projects."[43] In fact Kennan very rapidly came to rely on Robert Joyce, whom OPC men thought of as their contact at State, as the man who gave him policy guidance. Joyce, one of the six members of the PS at the State Department, had what he called a "special relationship with OPC."[44] Joyce himself was a special liaison for OPC, having been in the Foreign Service since 1928. He had extensive experience in covert political activism, particularly as an OSS officer in the Yugoslavian campaign during the Second World War, where he was Frank Lindsay's contact man. As the State Department liaison between the Marshall Plan and the OPC, coordinating operations was to be his task. Joyce's office was at the agency so that the State Department did not have to have much knowledge of what was going on, but clearly they were interested.[45]

Although the goals of the OPC were the same as the Marshall Plan, the methods were different. The OPC copied the Marshall Plan's geographic divisions, positioning its representatives similarly in American embassies. OPC men were usually second in command at the embassy. They were registered with intelligence in the country where they were stationed, unless it was a particularly unstable government. Their job was to befriend heads of state and cultivate networks of informal meetings on a regular basis. Usually they were men of some prominence in the United States, were not regular civil service, and were outside the foreign service network. Therefore, they were not always welcome by the embassy staff because their purpose was to circumvent diplomatic channels, which were perceived to be inefficient because of their formalistic traditions.[46] The OPC was clearly a separate, covert organization. Its funds were unvouchered, and its personnel unknown, reporting only to the director of OPC, Frank Wisner. There was no organizational line incorporating it into the CIA or the State or Defense departments, although the CIA gave the OPC "quarters and rations" and nominally approved the OPC director, and State and Defense offered policy guidance.[47]

The relationship between the OPC and the Marshall Plan came about because the legislation for the ECA, PL 472, 1948, had duplicate funding and administrative cost procedures that could be allocated for special projects. The Marshall Plan tried special projects on its own but the results were not satisfying. It would take covert specialists to carry them out successfully. The OPC inherited these fledgling operations, mostly labor projects, funded them through Marshall Plan administrative expenses, and provided experts to carry them out.[48] Richard Bissell, the deputy administrator of ECA, explained the procedure, which bears repeating at length because he was the person in charge of the funds and one of the few people in a position to know:

> The OPC was formed right after the Marshall Plan, but there was no connection for some months. It was a complementary operation to secure Western Europe. Harriman, Foster, and Katz knew about it.[49] But I doubt that the Marshall Plan people knew or were double per-

sonnel. [That is, were employed by both organizations.][50] Some people Wisner may have had under ECA cover.[51] But Hoffman would have resisted that as he was thoroughly committed to economic measures.[52]

Wisner got counterpart funds for the OPC from the Marshall Plan. Recipient governments had to deposit 100 percent of the value of their received aid in their own banks. Five or ten percent went to the U.S. government for administrative—State Department—expenses. Five percent in each country was tapped privately. Hoffman probably knew but didn't like it. Didn't want to know. But he had been told by higher authority it was approved use. It was probably known in the planning community after the Italian elections. I became aware of it when Frank Lindsay left the ECA to go to the OPC. When I was dep- uty adminstrator of the Marshall Plan, counterpart funds were fun- neled to the OPC. Wisner came for the funds but said I didn't have to know what for. My feeling was that we needed this procedure because we needed a political action arm."[53]

At a later interview, Bissell noted that Averell Harriman had conceived of the plan and mechanism to assist the OPC with Marshall Plan funds. But it is clear from the statements of George Marshall and the actions of George Kennan and James Forrestal that many contemplated "emer- gency funding procedures" such as this one.[54]

It was clear that policymakers thought a political action arm was nec- essary, but the sense of crisis did not allow careful decisions about the type of action. There was a great deal of disagreement regarding tactics. Some favored political and economic warfare. Those who favored psy- chological warfare, known as the psy-warriors, were particularly ada- mant. Each specialist appears to have advocated his own area of expertise.

One explanation for this apparent competitiveness was that Frank Wisner favored the development of a theme for handling subversion in each country. Wisner himself was a psy-warrior. Accordingly, he was cha- grined that the Soviets could orchestrate mass demonstrations in the ma- jor cities of Europe. When that happened he would lean toward psycho- logical warfare as the theme for a country. He believed that when the

Soviets mounted demonstrations, pro-West counterdemonstrations could help roll back the Iron Curtain. Bissell disagreed. He believed psy-warrior tactics relegated American policy to gimmickry, probably because he favored economic tactics. Yet when he argued this point he became permanently estranged from one psy-warrior who happened to be an old friend, Nelson Rockefeller.[55]

Frank Lindsay's role in the new initiative was in the realm of paramilitary activity. He was to establish stay-behind nets and a core of resistance in Eastern Europe. Believing that the Soviets were capable of marching across Europe to the Atlantic, OPC defense strategy relied on organized resistance groups to prevent a potential Soviet drive. Lindsay was a logical choice to lead this type of action because of his experience in the Balkans as the senior U.S. field man in the wartime OSS.[56]

In practice it proved difficult to carry out the plan. The OPC directive called for a defense concept called "retardation," which meant blowing up bridges, railroads, and similar aids to access so that enemy forces could be pushed into pockets where the army could find and destroy them. A demolitions man, Lindsay had led this type of operation in Yugoslavia. The problem was the lack of resistance organizations to carry out the final assaults. A conflict arose between the army and the OPC when the latter could not develop resistance organizations.[57] Still, the field men were urged on by policymakers in Washington, even when field experience did not square with the view held in the capital. Washington exerted a great deal of pressure to get things done. Frank Wisner had been told he had a year to prepare for field operations, but that was forgotten in a matter of weeks. As Lindsay says, "If you expect war in six months you do a lot of things you don't do if you were going to take time. We didn't say no enough."[58]

The problem for Lindsay and other field operators was the conflict between the political aims of the policymakers and the feasibility of action in the field. Even given the flexibility of the new organization and the considerable expertise of its personnel, some actions were no longer possible in Eastern Europe. And to make matters worse, cooperation among the various institutions responsible for carrying out U.S. foreign policy was sometimes lacking.

Even within the OPC, cooperation was elusive. The OPC adopted a "project" system—refugee programs, labor activities, media development, political actions—rather than policy objectives.[59] Kermit Roosevelt remembered that "from overseas you could write a project in brief and vague language, funding was easily obtainable."[60] Project orientation tended to place the initiative with field personnel. It also generated competition, because "an individual within OPC judged his own performance and was judged by others, on the importance and number of projects he initiated."[61] Much later the Church Committee blamed project orientation and competition for what appeared to be a centrifugal tendency in OPC. But others, such as Bissell, maintain that the problem was rapid growth and an increasing delegation of authority.

On paper the OPC was organized as follows: field personnel were stationed overseas, and headquarters personnel were stationed in Washington. According to the Church Committee Report, the headquarters personnel in Washington were split into four staffs reflecting the four specialities of covert operations: political, psychological and economic warfare, and paramilitary operations. Bissell says otherwise, that even in early OPC days the functional staffs were covert actions, secret intelligence, counterintelligence, international organizations, and paramilitary operations. The real working units, Bissell claims, were covert actions and secret intelligence.[62] Both sources agree that the geographic area to be served was split into six divisions.

Originally headquarters personnel in Washington were to "retain close control over the initiation and implementation of projects to insure close policy coordination with the State and Defense Departments."[63] The men and women in the field were to be "standing mechanisms" for each covert action, but assignments would come from Washington. The functional groups were to design projects, with guidance from the NSC, and turn them over to the geographic divisions. The geographic divisions would then assign the project to the correct station overseas and provide instructions and personnel to carry it out.

Competition developed almost immediately. Functional staffs only reluctantly turned over control to the geographic divisions, especially on pet projects. Functional staffs and geographic divisions became competitors in initiating and administering projects. But Bissell maintains that the functional staffs very rapidly became just "staff." The real power resided in the geographic division heads and senior station chiefs. Division chiefs "as a collegium" had the greatest competence and power, and had direct access to Allen Dulles, a powerful man in intelligence, even before he formally joined the agency in 1950.[64] Station chiefs in important posts, such as Berlin and Paris, usually were superseded by no one. Critical to success in this bureaucratic conflict were the field men, most of whom were seasoned by World War II OSS experience, on familiar terms with heads of state in his assigned country, knowledgeable about the culture and politics of his area of expertise, disgusted with the inefficiency of bureaucracy, and comfortable with exerting authority.

The men of OPC had considerable personal power beyond the agency and the bureaucracy. Director Frank Wisner relied on this factor to maintain independence and exert influence in the bureaucratic tangle of Washington. Personal power combined with organizational flexibility led to what Stewart Alsop called a spirit of "derring-do, a willingness to take risks." Alsop, a longtime friend and spiritual colleague of many of the determined interventionists, credited their ascent to a "weakness of the State Department" causing "a vacuum which the Bold Easterners rather gleefully filled—Dulles, Wisner, Bissell, and company had no compunctions," Alsop claimed, "about involving themselves in matters of high policy."[65]

But as conflict developed within the organizational structure of the OPC, causing field operatives to step in and take the initiative, there was a blurring of the distinction between policymaker and operative.[66] Success in an organization such as the OPC became more directly related to the competence and imagination of field personnel. Coordinating political action and policy depended more and more on the willingness of field personnel to clear projects at headquarters. Occasionally, Kermit Roosevelt says, people were appointed who should not have had anything to do with an organization like OPC because they did not clear their projects with Washington.

Roosevelt referred in particular to Carmel Offie, whom he called the "wild man" in Italy, "one of Frank Wisner's occasional blindspots."

Wild man or not, Offie was very successful for a while. Arriving in Italy in June 1944, Offie ingratiated himself with Harold Macmillan. In the beginning Offie was only a peripheral character, showing up at dinners and on plane trips in the company of U.S. Ambassador Alexander C. Kirk. But by early 1945, at the peak of a crisis involving the Soviets in Trieste, MacMillan noted in his diary that "there was a meeting of the leading people, Alexander, McNarney, Offie and myself."[67] Offie was so entrenched that when the State Department tried to transfer him to Japan, Ambassador Kirk said he was "quite prepared to take the consequences of my refusal to continue as head of AMPOLAD office if Offie is removed."[68]

Offie had an "irrepressible" side that often caused headaches for Macmillan and the State Department. An inveterate collector of luxurious things, Offie often turned up in exotic ports, without papers, on buying sprees. State Department files show considerable chagrin on the part of the official diplomatic corps due to Offie's lack of respect for procedure. When the transfer to Japan was in the air, Offie apparently shipped an automobile to Japan for his use there, later disavowing it when he was not reassigned and State Department officials wanted to know what to do with the car.[69] While Lawrence Houston never mentioned Carmel Offie, his comment that "control got dicey" because of the fragmented responsibility for the organization may have been triggered by the "wild man" in Italy.[70] Harry Howe Ransom addressed the issue directly: "Beyond a certain point the secret agent, whether spy, secret propagandist, or guerrilla warrior cannot be controlled. To set loose expensive networks of secret agents is to open a Pandora's box of potential blunders, misfortunes, and uncontrollable events. To pack off a secret agent with a satchel of money to intervene . . . and expect to maintain tight operational control of him is a dubious expectation."[71]

The Carmel Offie story has a rather interesting conclusion. He was recalled to Washington, where he was picked up in a park and charged with homosexual activity. Interestingly enough, the agency had always been aware of Offie's proclivities, as he had made no secret of them. Offie argued his case before the agency, saying that because he was a known homosexual, blackmail would not be a possibility. According to Kermit

Roosevelt, the agency seriously considered keeping him. However, shortly after his arrest he was killed in the crash of a small airplane.[72]

American tactics in Europe had taken a decidedly covert turn. And, by 1950, the defense and institutional needs of the Korean War strengthened and changed the OPC. The economic, psychological, and political aspects of the OPC, predominant in Europe, receded after the beginning of the Korean War. The military requirements of the Far Eastern arena necessitated complementary paramilitary operations, although the tendency to retain civilian control and unvouchered funding remained the same. Early covert operators believed that the lessons of free enterprise might well be learned by government. Even when their primary concern was fighting Communist subversion, their secondary aim was to show bureaucracies how it might be done efficiently and cheaply. Acquiring a civilian airline, for instance, to move refugees and provide air support for anti-Mao forces in China, the OPC set up a cover that included an airplane service station. Awarded contracts from an unknowing Air Force, the OPC turned over a $30 million profit to the American government when they liquidated the airline in 1973.[73]

The Korean War also brought about changes in the institutional character of the OPC. Walter Bedell Smith, the new director of Central Intelligence, either decided or was instructed to bring OPC "into the fold." He informed Frank Wisner that henceforth the OPC director would report to him. Lawrence Houston speculated that Smith must have gone to the "top" and to the State Department and must have really done his homework to get this accomplished. Even so, as Bissell recalls, "it took Smith two years to fully integrate OPC down to the country desk level."[74]

Curiously, this integration process resulted in the domination of the CIA by the covert organization it aimed to control. Several factors led to OPC dominance over their clandestine collection rivals. For one thing they had a favored position with the State and Defense departments. The OPC received policy guidance from both and was, as Lindsay says, "the underside of State and Defense's responsibility." Also, project orientation promised faster and more visible results than clandestine collection. The OPC offered an alternative—taking the initiative. And OPC anticipated NSC 68, a major articulation of Cold War policy, written in 1950. NSC 68 called for a "non-military counter-offensive including economic, political and psychological warfare to stir up unrest and revolt in the satellite countries."[75] The OPC had been in business for two years and had added another function, paramilitary operations.

Probably the most important reason for OPC dominance was that the men of the OPC quickly rose to leadership positions within the CIA. Allen Dulles was appointed deputy director of plans—the head of covert operations. He was to supervise both the clandestine collection arm and the covert political activists. The animosity between the two was long-lived—or as Bissell says, "the clandestine group still viewed full merger as being absorbed by their own worst enemy."[76] In 1952, the year the ECA was scheduled to terminate, the bureaucratic merger was reportedly complete and Frank Wisner, former director of OPC, took over Dulles's job as director of plans. Dulles rose to the position of deputy director of the agency. This institutional shuffle in the early 1950s put covert political activists in control of the covert sector of the agency and the deputy directorship. Soon Dulles became the director, and when Wisner retired Richard M. Bissell, Jr., former deputy adminstrator of the Marshall Plan, was chosen to lead the covert section of the agency.

The CIA took a new direction. What had once been an agency for clandestine collection became largely an agency for covert action. There were compelling institutional reasons for the shift. Covert action was not mandated under the National Security Act of 1947, which established the CIA. And yet NSC 68 called for a Cold War offensive that included a strong covert capability in three of the four areas in which the OPC was already operating. The Korean War had further strengthened the OPC. As the Church Committee reported "in concept, manpower, budget, and scope of activities, OPC simply skyrocketed."[77] If the CIA meant to fulfill the requirements of NSC 68 and remain a prominent component of Cold War defense, it needed a covert complement much as the Marshall Plan needed one. The merger process integrated OPC personnel into the agency at the highest levels. The incorporation of the covert initiative represented by OPC ensured the supremacy of the CIA in the Cold War bureaucracy.

n a December 1963 letter to Clark Clifford about covert operations authorized by the 1948 NSC directive 10/2, Allen Dulles said, "This program was really Harry S. Truman's baby or at least his adopted child."[78] Adoption is a good word to describe Truman's decision to authorize covert operations. As military and political considerations played against a backdrop of anti-Communism in Washington, Truman and his policy advisors felt increasingly determined to take action. The Truman Doctrine and the Marshall Plan were concrete initiatives, but policymakers felt Soviet subversion, exemplified by the Czech coup, presented a problem not easily solved by orthodox means. Constraints of secrecy plus the institutional needs of the existing intelligence agency further complicated Truman's decision. But the shift to covert activities seemed logical because the Soviet threat took the form of covert subversion of Europe's political institutions.

Truman and his advisors believed that meeting a subversive threat placed a democracy at a disadvantage. They knew a cohort of American covert political activists were available to staff a new organization. Truman was committed enough to supplement that cohort by personally recruiting members, through his appointments secretary, Matthew Connelly.[79] Truman and his policymakers thought that congressional scrutiny was not compatible with solving the crisis presented by the Czech coup because secrecy requirements could not be met if everyone on Capitol Hill knew about the OPC. As Truman put it, "When the members of Congress got their noses into the private affairs of the President the set up ceased to function for the President."[80] Truman adopted covert operations as a technique because he thought it would get the job done. For a while he was satisfied. There were no more Czech-type coups in Europe during his administration.

FIVE

FRANCE: FULLY
FUNCTIONING INTERVENTION

A
ccording to Dean Acheson, Allied leaders in 1945 were convinced that "something new had to be created" from the rubble of Europe.[1] Acheson thought the role of the United States was "to help fashion what would come after the destruction of the old world," meaning that U.S. policymakers would restructure the war-damaged world in such a way that rebuilt nations would have a predilection toward the United States.[2] The primary agent of this policy was to be the Marshall Plan. Since a main assumption of American policymakers was that a high standard of living fostered democratic governments, the goal of the Marshall Plan was sweeping economic revitalization. Thus Congress declared that

> recognizing the intimate economic and other relationships between the United States and the nations of Europe . . . Congress finds that the existing situation in Europe endangers the establishment of a lasting peace, the general welfare and national interest of the United States. . . . The restoration or maintenance in European countries of principles of individual liberty, free institutions, and genuine independence rests largely upon the establishment of sound economic conditions; stable international economic relationships.[3]

But there were political and propaganda problems as well—Soviet political strength and propaganda drives in countries with large Communist constituencies, such as France. What policymakers wanted was a way to coordinate the solutions to those problems, which they termed "beneath the surface," with the Marshall Plan effort. To do so they created what they thought would be a temporary apparatus—the Office of Policy Coordination. In the Marshall Plan years, policymakers found that the various means available to them through the use of covert methods could be

useful in coordinating the Marshall Plan. Covert political activists identified and helped solve political problems inherent in the larger Marshall
Plan agenda. As such, the complementary efforts of the Marshall Plan
and the OPC afford a first view of fully integrated interventionism in the
Cold War; that is, the first attempt to fully integrate economic aid and
covert political activism.

Of major concern to the United States were those countries
with a history of Communist strength—France and Italy.
Thus, it was no accident that the European headquarters
for Marshall Plan activity was in Paris. W. Averell Harriman, given special ambassadorial status, established the Office of the
Special Representative, which was in charge of the entire Marshall Plan
program in Europe.

France provided a special set of problems, not the least of which was a
strong Communist party, the Parti Communiste Français (PCF). The
PCF was formed in 1920, the result of acceptance by the French Socialist
party of the "conditions" of the Communist International. Its strength
resided in the working-class unions of Paris and its suburbs. Maurice
Thorez, who would become the general secretary in 1930, brought his
own union of miners into the fold. They were joined by rural socialists of
the "peasant class," a group characterized by strong anti-establishment
and anticlerical sentiments. In general it can be said that the rise and fall
of French Communism depended throughout ensuing decades, as it did
in 1920, on the level of acceptance among indigenous socialist unions for
the international Communist agenda.

Until the rise of Fascism in Europe, French Communism was in peril,
its leaders persecuted and jailed. Membership declined from 109,000 in
1921 to 28,000 in 1933.[4] But in response to the political crisis of the
1930s, "all men of goodwill" joined in the united effort against Fascism.
The Popular Front electoral alliance of Socialists, Radicals and Communists won in 1936. Within this coalition, the Communist vote alone was
1.5 million, 15 percent of the total polled. In Parliament, Communist
representation increased from twelve seats to seventy-two. As in the

United States, many leading intellectuals believed that Communism offered an effective means to combat Fascism and promote social justice. In France, Stalin's support for the Republican government in Spain was particularly compelling.

Naturally, the Nazi-Soviet Non-Aggression Pact in 1939 stunned rank-and-file Communists and disgraced their leadership in France. Despite what has been called an "almost lethal blow" to the party, Communists regained their good reputation through the heroic and well-organized role they played as Resistance fighters after 1941. After the war, Thorez, who had been in Moscow, returned to France and entered de Gaulle's provisional government. He urged resistance fighters to disarm, Communist ministers to adhere loyally to the government, and workers not to strike. All of this he counseled during the peak period of party membership, a staggering 800,000 in 1946; in November 1946, 5.5 million Frenchmen voted Communist, 28.6 percent of the total vote.

Postwar policymakers worried about French Communism, to be sure, but there was a broader range of complaints against the French. Some policymakers had a tendency to assess the moral character of the nation, to ascribe national characteristics. Allen Dulles thought that France suffered from a "spiritual breakdown, a moral sadness, because they did not fill their historic role."[5] Dulles no doubt was referring to their early and decisive defeat at the hands of the Nazis as well as their collaboration after capitulation. State Department reports noted the "skeptical and individualistic character of the French."[6] One ECA official thought that "France has all the elements of prosperity except character and leadership."[7] Even Léon Blum was disappointed in his countrymen, especially "the exasperating individualism of the French people, their weakness for rackets—in a word, their display of 'Balkan' traits, . . . a corrupt state of mind spreading throughout every class of society, and despair because of it."[8]

When State Department personnel described the French as skeptical and individualistic, they were drawing on a perceived anticlerical and anti-establishment history. That "anarchistic" tendency permeated French Communism, which some policymakers regarded as a way of showing dissatisfaction in a Catholic country where radicalism was believed to have a strong anti-Catholic flavor. As Raymond Aron of *Figaro* told the CFR, "It is no coincidence that the largest Communist parties of western Europe are found in France and Italy."[9] French unions, with their Communist influence, were seen less as a vehicle for improving the economic position of the worker and more "as an organization for expressing and institutionalizing his social and political attitudes. Foremost among these . . . is the undercurrent of radical individualism."[10] But Arnold Wolfers struck another note when he told a discussion group at the CFR that the strength of the Communist party in France "is principally a result of the nationalistic tendency of the French Communists and of a tendency in France to lean towards Russia for protection against a feared U.S.-British-German coalition." Wolfers added ominously that the primary aim of the Soviet Union was to take France out of the Western camp.[11]

These tendencies in the French character inclined many in France to avoid the "mainstream," or American, view of modernization and industrialization. That was the reason they were attracted to Communism. They were apt to be cantankerous, not inherently leftist or fundamentally opposed to liberal democracy. The American theme for revitalization of France would have to include some hard lessons in accepting the realities of the modern industrial world. Policymakers insisted on efficiency and modernization in France because they feared that France would slip into the Soviet orbit unless it were able to solve its economic problems and raise the standard of living among working people. Policymakers believed that the French could solve their problem by copying American manufacturing methods and procedures.

Individuals employed by the European Recovery Program thought the French should manufacture heavy goods and modernize their plants as rapidly as possible. They were disgruntled that the French continued to produce what American planners thought of as luxury items, such as, wine and lingerie. In some ways French manufacturing choices reinforced a prevalent view of the French national character writ large: they were living beyond their means.[12] The French were believed to have outdated plants controlled by family networks who cared more for service and continuity than for competition. There was the perception that they made useless goods and sold them to their colonies and that they were antimodern, inefficient, indolent, and pigheaded.

In addition to the U.S. perception of the French national character, the French had some very substantive problems. They had huge trade deficits left over from World War II. According to State Department reports, much of this debt was owed to their overseas territories. Before the war, French trade with their territories had been offset by their ability to supply manufactures. The war stopped that, creating the deficit, as Vichy France continued to receive imports.[13] The handling of this deficit caused considerable friction, especially in the early stages of Marshall Plan activity. Thomas Geiger and Franklin Lindsay wrote Richard M. Bissell, Jr., in April of 1948 that "ECA dollars . . . should not be made available to settle outstanding growing deficits."[14] In May they stated in a memo that "U.S. dollars will not be used to settle debts . . . prior to ERP."[15]

Apparently not everyone agreed, because reports from the military attaché in Paris indicated that in July 1949 the ECA released 20 billion francs to retire the public debt.[16] This action did not escape the attention of the legislative branch in Washington. At a Senate hearing held in executive session, Senator Alexander Wiley of the Committee on Foreign Relations stopped the hearing saying, "I was told not longer than an hour ago that France and England both were using these counterparts for application on their national debt. . . . Is that true?" An ECA official admitted the fact, adding that this was "pursuant to the recommendation of the Civil Administration Committee."[17]

Both France and the United States also worried about the loss of French overseas territories. The French obviously wanted to retain them, but for the United States this posed a dilemma. The Atlantic Charter advocated an end to colonialism, but the need to retain French support in the European reconstruction, as well as keeping them strongly anti-Communist, created strong political reasons to make an exception on the matter of their colonies. OSS reports indicated that the "metropole," as the European parent nation was called, struggled in 1946 to restore a brisk trade with its colonies.[18] Even before the war the colonies were sending food and industrial raw materials to the metropole, and in 1937 the metropole had a deficit based on import of commodities from the colonies of $16.4 million. The war exacerbated the problem, driving exports down and imports up. By 1945 the import deficit was $866 million. Although the OSS report noted optimistically that colonial trade was the first to recover after the war, "recovery" meant 48 percent of the metropole's prewar level of exports to the colonies, mostly in the form of industrial equipment and manufactured goods. The OSS claimed that "this sale to the colonies of finished products needed domestically resulted in part from colonial pressure to receive some goods in return for its large exports to metropolitan France and in part from the urgent desire of the metropole to preserve its colonial markets."

Although the French could, and did, use regular program funds for development in Africa, Harry Bayard Price has noted that in this complex scenario, "ECA's contribution to . . . development in these areas [Africa] took three forms: 1. assistance, through grants and loans, for road and railway construction, river and port improvement, reclamation and irrigation projects, power plants, and other projects designed to help accelerate basic economic development . . . 2. assistance for strategic material development . . . 3. technical assistance."[19] Price has indicated that this was no paltry effort, since the total expenditure between 1948 and 1952 was $61.5 million for category one; $47.6 million for category two; and $1.04 million for category three. Typical of these times, "negotiations pertaining to aid" to develop African nations along the lines of the Tennessee Valley Authority were "conducted with the European governments concerned."[20] There is, at least, no mention of participation by the recipient nations.

The French were operating under a considerable handicap. They were unable to provide the coveted manufactures immediately, because of war damage at manufacturing sites. In addition, the European Recovery Program gave instructions as to what the French ought to manufacture, then backed up the suggestions with the threat of withholding Marshall Plan counterpart funds. And the French had competition from the United States, or at least they saw it that way. French policymakers believed the United States was dumping products in North Africa, trying to drive a wedge between the territories and the metropole. There were rumors that every village chief was driving a made-in-Detroit automobile.[21] How, the French asked, were they to compete?

Congressional leaders had strong feelings on the matter as well. Senator Wiley addressed the issue of the French colonial empire in North Africa with considerable anger. He knew the purpose of the counterpart funds was to help France rebuild so that the value of their currency would be restored. But he did not like the French attitudes, particularly toward U.S. trade with the colonies. Wiley claimed that "right now the French are building tariff barriers against our business in Morocco. They have shut out production of things from my own State, and that is the thanks we get for trying to put them on their feet."[22]

Despite such difficulties, if there was one thing policymakers agreed on about France, it was the danger of Communism in labor. State Department reports from Ambassador Jefferson Caffery in Paris gave studious attention to every move the Communists made to entice the French working class. Labor activists counted every pro-West rally a victory. CIA reports confirmed the difficulty of the task, given Communist strength in French unions. But the earliest warnings of instability in France came from the OSS. Even before the war's end there were signs of danger. On 24 February 1945 forty thousand people crowded into a sports arena for a meeting to protest food shortages. The mass protest, sponsored by the Paris Committee of Liberation, attracted a "predominantly working class" audience "with a large proportion of housewives." The speakers, mostly Socialists, held the crowd's attention for three hours with demands for more food and an end to the "Vichy-ridden administrations."[23]

At the same time, the Communists decided to suspend their traditional feud with the Socialists and join forces. The Socialists had worked hard for unity since 1940, according to the OSS, but the Communists had balked. The Socialists wanted Communist support for their nationalization program, although they were reticent about the Communist attachment to Moscow. Even after the liberation of Paris, the Communists continued to hold off the Socialists, keeping them out of offices in the Paris

Committee of Liberation and out of "positions of influence in the CGT [Confédération Générale du Travail]," the Communist Union. But suddenly in November 1944 the Communist party changed its position and proposed unity at the Socialist national congress. As the OSS reported, Socialists questioned Communist sincerity but needed the extra strength the Communists could give.[24]

Socialist and Communist strength in the labor unions facilitated their desire to remove Vichy influence from industry, producing a backdoor approach to nationalization of industry. In March 1945 the French government prosecuted a truck manufacturer named Berliet for his "very active collaboration with the enemy." As a result the factory functioned under a Comité de Gestion, or management committee. Subcommittees comprised of representatives of workers, supervisory personnel, engineers, and technical people administered the plant. As the OSS report indicated, this arrangement in no sense "constituted a nationalization of definitive character." It was simply an ad hoc measure, but "the functioning of the Berliet factories has been so profoundly changed that it is impossible to be mistaken about the effects. The concern is practically nationalized."[25] And the Berliet case was not the only one.

At times even industrialists called for nationalization as a way to save industry with Western help.[26] Nationalization worked because the French government, after receiving Marshall Plan funds, gave better interest rates on loans to nationalized industries. For instance Renault, a nationalized industry, got a 3 percent interest rate, while private companies were charged 8 to 9 percent interest.[27] Other government steps taken at this time also strengthened labor's hand. To help minimize any handicap in bargaining with representatives of management, the government established an educational program for the labor members of the French Worker-Management Committee. Course offerings included editing and style to assist self-expression, and accounting, so that workers would understand industrial bookkeeping and "not be overwhelmed by the management's use of technical accounting terms."[28]

But the postwar chaos also offered opportunity for Communist labor. By December 1945 the Communist party was trying to find "militant members with outstanding qualifications for posts in ministries controlled by the Communists."[29] It seemed to the OSS as though the Communists were organizing to insert leading party functionaries in government positions, a possible precursor to government takeover. This was a very real threat because many former Resistance heroes were important in the Communist party, and the political clout of the Resistance made them a key factor in any new government.[30] The Communists, however, did not see themselves as having an easy time with French labor, either. Jean Duret, a political economist and officer in the CGT, noted that the working classes were angry about salary levels and food shortages. That anger could be turned on the Communists as well as any other group. Duret himself had been warned that he would be given "an extremely cold reception" on a proposed tour of factories. Duret thought the unions would not resort to strikes at that time because of the war effort. But, he added, even the CGT and the Resistance were under attack from disgruntled labor, where he felt the complaints of the Trotskyites were "falling on fertile ground."[31]

As the war's end neared, Communist activism increased. In addition to the more common propaganda assault on the indolence of the American people, their ignorance of the suffering of poor nations, and the inability of a democracy to do more than provide a temporarily high standard of living, the Communists hit hard on U.S. incompetence in handling the problem of de-Nazification. In the particularly turbulent Riviera district, a Communist whose Resistance name was "Simon" said that Americans were incapable of reeducating the Germans because they had no creed of their own. He claimed that it would take a long time to reeducate the Germans, "but we Russians have already successfully carried out a similar experience. We have an ideal to offer that some of them have already understood; moreover, we have the means of imposing it on the coming generation."[32]

The Soviets were not averse to hinting broadly that the United States planned to colonize France, a propaganda line that was partially successful in playing upon French pride and fears. OSS reports show that the "fundamental reasons for anti-American feeling in informed circles . . . is the interference of the United States Government in French politics."[33] The OSS further indicated that there was a great deal of worry among the French populace about massive American imports and even the American presence in France itself.[34] The French believed that the United States wanted de Gaulle out of the way so that a "more amenable figure," or one more easily persuaded by American policymakers, would gain control. They also believed that the Americans practiced a kind of blackmail with food and equipment to get desired results.[35]

Of course, in the immediate postwar period the Soviets were careful to maintain the appearance of an alliance with the West. Publications attributable to the Communist party always described Communist-sponsored rallies as "pro-Ally." But the main purpose of such events was to tout the verities of only one French ally, "Comrade Stalin."[36] The OSS maintained a careful watch on these activities in the summer of 1945, particularly in Marseilles, where the Soviets maintained a military mission.[37] The mission included a political section, "a center of activity of the Soviet Consulate and of Soviet political activity for southern France," housed in the Hotel Splendide. It was constantly being expanded, mostly with officers coming in from Russia bearing the insignia of the secret police, "NKVD."[38] The district was particularly unstable. Reports of brutality by American soldiers against French people came in from Nice and Cannes, as did reports of ill-treatment at the hands of the Russians.

The Soviets were astute in their choice of propaganda issues. Not unexpectedly, they charged the United States with domestic racism. But, adding a new wrinkle, they also condemned the use of black American troops in the Marseilles area. Their line of reasoning: the Americans care nothing for you; they have stationed their hated black troops in your country; and violence against French people is being perpetrated by these troops. The European Recovery Program countered by publishing and distributing a booklet entitled "The Negro in American Life." A liberal piece, indeed; instead of emphasizing famous "Negroes," it portrayed African-Americans as mainstream and middle class—wives in aprons sending kids off to school, blue-collar dads off to the factory with their lunch pails. It has a truly Betty Crocker flavor.

All of this activity prompted Philip Horton, chief of the Special Intelligence Branch of OSS in Paris, to write Washington suggesting the establishment of a "permanent, independent and completely clandestine intelligence service on the Continent."[39] But in the meantime OSS reports continued. Following the procedure established during the war by Arthur Goldberg's OSS Labor Division, close tabs were kept on each political party, dossiers maintained on their personnel, leaders in the provinces and small villages were contacted to judge their level of tolerance for the Communists, and the increasing Communist strength in the French army was monitored closely.[40] The OSS sent a strong signal to Washington that Communists were taking advantage of war-caused upheaval in French society.

Once ECA funding was approved, Congress came to see the wisdom of Horton's suggestion on intelligence. At a Senate Foreign Relations Committee hearing, Senator Wiley stressed his approval of the use of Marshall Plan counterpart funds for propaganda purposes. Wiley expressed appreciation for the "fine work" ECA was doing but added that the crisis in Italy and France indicated money should be spent "to get out the truth in certain ways." In Wiley's opinion, the United States was "selling something besides our goods and merchandise."[41]

Wiley became quite specific on the use of counterpart funds. Saying that "practical stability in the world depends upon who wins the psychological warfare," he urged approval of up to twenty million dollars for that purpose. An ECA official indicated that from seven to nine million dollars had been spent on psychological warfare the previous year and that there were plans to increase the use of counterpart funds for this purpose. To clear up the matter of ECA discretion in this arena, Wiley asked the ECA representative whether "distribution would be available for some kind of this [sic] psychological warfare I am talking about . . . without any legislation." When he received an affirmative answer, Wiley closed the discussion by remarking that he would be glad to see more counterpart funds used for "this kind of impact upon the thinking of Europe."[42]

But Marshall Plan personnel were quite aware that the French were reluctant to have American ways forced upon them. Barry Bingham of the Paris Mission told Congress that "The French are allergic to propaganda. They often confuse what we call information with what they call propaganda."[43] Washington policymakers agreed, stating that "overt American propaganda . . . arouses a degree of suspicion, disbelief, and sometimes animosity, on the part of Europeans" because of their years of exposure to Nazi propaganda.[44] Therefore ECA "has chosen to push across its message whenever possible by working closely and quietly through indigenous groups."[45] The United States wanted to influence the direction of European reconstruction; to do so a climate favorable to American politics and commerce had to be created. Using the concept of indirection—that is, acting covertly—Marshall Plan personnel developed a plan to influence Europe without their actions being attributed to the United States. ECA defined indirection as the ability to "get across the ECA and U.S. Government foreign policy point of view, without either ECA or the U.S. Government being identified as the source of the material." The covert agenda had limitations, however. It was to be a political, economic, and psychological campaign. No paramilitary operations were considered. ECA "observed the practice of engaging only in those indirect activities which would neither endanger the lives of persons involved nor in any way jeopardize American prestige."[46] The primary tools of indirection were manipulation of the counterpart funds used to settle the French debt, formation of conduits to sponsor radio networks, production and distribution of films and publications through commercial organizations or other outlets, and assistance to governments and trade unions.

B y mid-1948, the European Recovery Program was operational, with its "Policy toward France" committed to paper. According to the ECA policy document, there were "only two possible courses of action for avoiding economic collapse and a Communist coup d'etat." The first was to continue supporting the middle parties, but Marshall Plan officials were already concerned that "the middle parties which have governed France since the liberation are no longer capable of pursuing a realistic economic policy which can bring about French recovery." The second was to make "as good a deal as possible with de Gaulle." Marshall Plan people were not pleased with that option because they found it "extremely difficult and unpleasant to work with him." But the ECA saw Communism as the alternative to de Gaulle. Therefore, they decided to continue center party support and to begin secret, high-level conversations with Le Grand Charles.

ECA personnel attributed much of their difficulty in France to the Cominform. By October of 1948 memos entitled "The French Crisis" were circulating at ECA. They saw the entire European recovery program as threatened by the situation in France because that "unhealthy" situation "has undesirable economic and psychological repercussions on the other participating countries." The undesirable effect was that France was receiving large amounts of assistance from the United States and the other participating countries, "far in excess of an amount which could be justified upon basic economic considerations." It was taking far too much money to get very little accomplished. The Cominform was blamed because ECA officials believed it was "undoubtedly centering its efforts to disrupt ERP in France." Therefore, reducing ECA assistance to France would be risky. In short, the ECA was caught in a bind.

Soon ECA officials decided upon a show of strength. Realizing the enormous impact withholding of funds would have, they began to bargain with the French. ECA would release money if the French complied with instructions. At first the U.S. government insisted on monthly accountings. Counterpart funds would be released if the "corresponding commitments made by the French Government" were carried out. Gradually they shifted to quarterly accountings. As ECA officers knew, the policy of using dollars for leverage was risky. Harlan Cleveland wrote Paul Hoffman that "we are learning the unhappy truth," that commitments could be elicited by "the use of so potent a weapon as counterpart." On the other hand it was difficult to decide whether to actually withhold funds if the French did not meet their commitments.[47] With the French government so unstable, they could cause a downfall or force the French into deficit financing. Cleveland concluded that rather than a complete cut-off, "bargaining with monthly counterpart releases is less dangerous because the bomb we are using will be less potent in the event that it goes off in our hands." He thought that a refusal to release counterpart funds at least once might "provide the necessary shock treatment" to the French government.

The subject of using counterpart funds as leverage came up at the CFR as well. Langbourne Williams of ECA's Industry Division in Paris told a study group that the United States "cannot stop its aid or even prevent the counterpart funds being used to balance the budget without creating chaos." The group, including Nelson Rockefeller, Tom Braden, William Donovan, Allen Dulles, Arnold Wolfers, and Stacy May, concluded that this was unfortunate because it seemed that countries that did the least for themselves, such as France, received the most aid. But they also agreed that "it was impossible to withhold the necessary aid without risking the very danger that the Marshall Plan was particularly designed to prevent." At this meeting many questions were raised about the political considerations upon which counterpart fund policy was based in France. And a considerable number of sarcastic stories circulated about the French, emphasizing their ponderous bureaucracy and inefficient management practices. At least one skeptic, Randolph Burgess of National City Bank, questioned the entire Marshall Plan concept, arguing that "anyone would be thought a fool to make a four year plan for the U.S. so a plan for Europe is just as ridiculous."[48]

On the other hand, the propaganda counterassault against the Soviets was relatively easy to organize and seemed to have no confusing side effects. Radio turned out to be the most flexible media, once the funding was worked out. Since most stations were government operated, the ECA could help fund them without much chance of detection. One of the most popular programs funded by ECA was "The Answer Man," long a favorite in the United States. By funding stations that would carry "The Answer Man," ECA could get its message across. Along with more typical questions sent in by listeners, such as "What is the highest mountain in the world?" ECA might see to it that questions on the Marshall Plan were also submitted. For instance, a typical question might have been, "In addition to military assistance, does Indo-China get any economic aid from America similar to the Marshall Plan for Europe?"

If Harry Bayard Price had answered he might have said that Asian aid "did not develop as a unified undertaking in behalf of a whole group of countries at once. It began with an authorization of aid to China, under the legislation which launched the Marshall Plan."[49] As "The Answer Man," Price might not have explained, but tells us elsewhere, that "as of January 1949 the President transferred from the Department of the Army to the ECA responsibility for administering economic assistance in Korea"; including "nearly 30 million in unexpended Government and Relief in Occupied Areas funds."[50] Additionally, once China had "fallen," residual funds in China Aid—about $100 million—were used by ECA in the "general area of China."[51]

ECA-sponsored programs were heard over the Austrian network Red-White-Red, AVRO in the Netherlands, RIAS in Germany, Radio Luxembourg, the Armed Forces Network in Germany, and Radio Lille in France, which broadcast in Polish. Broadcasts aimed at countries like Poland were very successful; 90 percent of the questions were political. For instance, one listener purportedly asked, "Who was responsible for the Katyn Woods murders?" The answer: Russia. Radio also allowed programming for specific listeners such as women. On shows such as "The Women's Program," politics and homemaking shared equal time.

As with the use of counterpart funds for purposes of balancing trade deficits, controversy arose over the use of counterpart funds for radio stations. Usually William Foster, of the Office of the Special Representative in Paris, handled the problem deftly. In the case of RIAS, the German radio station, the initial suggestion came from the Office of the Military Government of the U.S. (OMGUS) in Berlin. The economic advisor for OMGUS in Berlin contacted Ambassador Foster regarding use of the 5 percent counterpart funds for the operation of RIAS.[52] ECA had turned down a request through regular channels. Foster told OMGUS representatives that "according to the strict letter of the law, operation costs of the station could not be charged against the counterpart funds as administrative expenses, but he would be glad to have the proper people in ECA have another look at the case."

Foster was also the top man in Europe with authority to make payments from confidential funds for special emergency projects. Justifications for expenditures, as well as receipts for the money, went to him, to be kept in his personal files. The vouchers were eventually signed by

Hoffman when they found their way to Washington "in the normal course of events," but on-the-spot approval was given by Foster in Paris. ECA personnel justified these types of expenditures as a buttress to the overt agenda of the Marshall Plan. The ECA mission chief wore two hats. He was the conduit for economic assistance and defense mobilization, as well as for psychological and economic warfare components provided by the OPC.

Was the threat they were responding to real? There seems little room for doubt that Communism, or at least leftist leanings, were prevalent in French labor before the war. During the war much of this spirit was marshalled against the Germans in resistance activity, making heroes of leftist figures after the war. And living conditions were terrible in France. One frequent correspondent of Allen Dulles's wrote: "It's always the same, not enough bread for the working class." The French were hungry, dispirited, and restless.

But some credit has to be given the French for efforts toward their own postwar economic recovery. In addition to previously mentioned efforts to reinstitute trade with their territories, the French pursued a plan, called the Monnet Plan, to modernize their own industrial complex. In fact, American policymakers noted that it was unheard of for the French to support a domestic policy with such unanimous enthusiasm. The plan called for modernization to increase productivity. French labor pitched in, extending their work week to forty-eight hours in order to make up for worker shortages caused by the war. Later, even ECA officials in Washington had to admit that the French had been almost entirely responsible for the spectacular success in rebuilding French railroads within only a year.

But policymakers were still worried. Although postwar European policy favored the formation of left-leaning governments, policymakers hoped these governments would tilt toward the United States, not the Soviet Union. With so many French laborers in Communist unions, an outcome favorable to the West could not be assured. And they clearly were not willing to leave the matter to chance. That the Communist party was active in Paris is unquestionable. The Soviets had a huge gold reserve and were using it politically. Paris was organized by district, with a Communist headquarters in each. There were daily or weekly fliers printed in each district, mimeographed handbills with local news by district, news of Communist party activities, reports from Moscow, invitations to "soirées" and rallies. They were not glossy or sophisticated, but they were plentiful and appealing: "La Voix de Montparnasse vous invite" for a New Year's celebration. Such invitations mixed celebration and politics: "The year which ends encourages us to pursue and intensify the struggle. For 1952, which saw the arrival of Pinay in power, has also seen the decline and defeat of these attempts: . . . the military service has not been extended two years, the accords at Bonn have not been signed, social security has not been sabotaged, . . . thanks to the capture of the growing consciousness of the laboring classes to their true interests."[53] The gatherings offered a free buffet, music, and dancing. One could get further information by contacting the deputy of the sector, who was named. The invitations were signed by the cell: La Cellule Montparnasse du Parti Communiste Français, for example.

Newsletters stressed politics with a Communist interpretation. For instance, in 1953 all local handouts called for "Sauvons les Rosenberg" with instructions for sending telegrams to Truman.[54] By 1954 it was Dien Bien Phu: "Assez de Sang en Indo-Chine" cried one local Communist publication, *Jacob-Malaquais*, on 23 May 1954. French labor in the quarters was clearly informed regarding the Communist point of view.

Yet in some sense it was a small-time effort, especially when compared to the Marshall Plan with its massive dollar resources and its glittery extravaganzas. Marshall Plan officials pumped great resources into sophisticated propaganda, including a poster war in Paris. One Marshall Plan piece showed a meeting of top level Allied leaders after the war, with Stalin in uniform. The poster made a good deal of the fact that the peace-loving nations of the East are shown in the dress of war while the supposedly warmongering Western leaders are in civilian clothes.

It is hard to assess the effect of this type of propaganda on the French laborer or how he responded to the daily Communist handouts with local gossip and party invitations. But policymakers were concerned because they held an almost mythical view of the ordinary laborer; indeed the image had some similarity to Thomas Jefferson's yeoman farmer, exalted for his "honest industry, independence and frank spirit of equality."[55] Somehow the notion that "land is the common stock of society to which every man has a right" became the notion that a job and the fruits of the burgeoning industrial society were the rights of the new laborer. As such, like his agricultural ancestor, the laborer had "a special claim to be fostered and protected by the state."[56] Protection meant ensuring that the commercial entity did well so the benefits of prosperity were numerous and cheap, therefore easily attainable by the worker.

As with the Jeffersonian myth, there was a political agenda as well. The agrarian laborer was seen as important to the victory over the British empire in revolutionary times, becoming a "symbol of the new nation."[57] Similarly, the postwar European industrial laborer would be key to defeating totalitarianism. But there was some cynicism involved as well. The industrial laborer was a numerically significant class. Appeals like those to the common man in the Jacksonian era were proferred from necessity as much as anything else. What policymakers, and certainly the cohort of determined interventionists, believed was that the European laborer was the key to the success of the American plan for European democracy. If he became a U.S. ally, governments would follow. The laborer would become an ally when production facilities were modernized and brought into the new Western world trading scheme. Success, complete with a rising standard of living based on the American model, would garner the support of this mythical laborer for a democratic form of government. The shallowness of the Soviet system would be revealed.

French management, seen as an outmoded class, was also crucial to the success of the Marshall Plan. French industrial strategy put a priority on family-owned and operated companies. Many were passed down from generation to generation. The French felt strongly about local reputation; a plant owner and his family wanted to be respected by their workers and their community because the firm was equated with family name. Modernization and efficiency were less important than tradition. Little thought was given to expansion and none to price competition. French firms tended to hold high reserves and "equated going to a bank with getting a doctor."[58] Marshall Plan people thought this was a problem. Without competition there were extensive overlaps in industry, too many people making the same things, little diversity. They thought open competition would trim the market, making it lean and tough. They encountered considerable resistance, however. In order to exert influence, they enlisted the support of American labor.

American labor activists worked hard on French management and labor alike. A variety of methods were employed, chiefly personal contact. The OPC, acting as a conduit for Marshall Plan funds, financed visits to the United States for scores of French managers and laborers. The French had an opportunity to visit their American counterparts, inspect plants in operation, and otherwise learn the American way. Greeted warmly, they received invitations to speak before the Council on Foreign Relations and other prestigious groups. In return hundreds of American labor activists who went abroad attended labor rallies, visited workers in their homes, and helped to get American funds transferred to French union coffers. There was even a suggestion that Ford Motor Company set up a model American plant in France so that French labor would have an opportunity to work and manage it, thereby learning modern American methods.

American labor activists worked closely with Marshall Plan personnel, but under strict cover. Dick Kelly, a labor consultant at the Marshall Plan Paris office, reported to a supervisor at the American Newscasters Bureau, which happened to be in the Marshall Plan building. His supervisor, Harry Martin, worked for the OSR as labor information officer and advisor to the special representative.[59] A typical week for Kelly in the early months of the Marshall Plan was very hectic. In the week of 16 December 1949, Kelly reported to Martin that he had put out the bulletin *Syndical* and organized and attended a Trade Union evening with Irving Brown, the primary labor conduit for OPC funding. The Trade Union evening featured films on the American Federation of Teachers and a documentary on the TVA. In the same week Kelly sponsored a second labor exhibit with more films and arranged for a meeting between United Automobile Workers President Walter Reuther and the French Socialists.

Kelly was working on a pamphlet called "Joe Smith, American Worker," which he apparently believed would be a particularly successful handout. But he clearly favored the meetings between Socialist laborers and men like Reuther. Kelly called it a "good bull session" because Reuther shared many of the views of the French unionists, and the French responded well to him. He advised ECA to listen to Reuther and the Socialists if they wanted to be successful with them. Key American labor leaders serving conduit functions for OPC funding were always present at these meetings: Jay Lovestone and Irving Brown, as well as Milton Katz, of the Office of the Special Representative on the Marshall Plan in Paris.

American labor leaders worked well as OPC/ECA conduits. Their sense of patriotism and loyalty to union concerns meshed well with Washington's need to influence European labor. One of their top priorities was funding a relatively new union called Force Ouvrière, which had been part of the Communist union CGT but split off in 1947. It was socialistic and anti-Communist. Policymakers saw it as a possible rival to the strength of the CGT and poured considerable money into it.

The results were mixed. Often Force Ouvrière was forced to join strikes sponsored by the CGT because the issue had popular appeal. Such was a strike on the French-Belgian border in December of 1949. The argument was over currency convertibility clauses for laborers working in a border area. These workers—called the "Frontaliers"—could be paid in either currency, depending on the nationality of the industry employing them. The worker, if he were living in one country and paid by another, had to defray the cost of converting his paycheck. Labor leaders wanted the government and employers, rather than the worker, to finance the exchange rates for currency. Force Ouvrière leaders saw no way to argue.[60] But occasionally Force Ouvrière leadership could hold firm, as in a strike at the Michelin plant at Clermont-Ferrand. Force Ouvrière opposed the strike but still won an upset victory, perhaps because the bulk of Michelin's thirteen thousand workers was not in any union.[61]

Force Ouvrière leadership also took the lead in criticizing French capitalism for its outdated methods. By this method, as well as OPC funding and direction of Force Ouvrière, Marshall Plan thinking was brought to bear on French manufacturers. French labor called for new tools and increased productivity, claiming that only Marshall Plan money could bring needed modernization. American labor leaders such as William Bellanger of the CIO Textile Workers in Massachusetts, Harold Gibbons of Local 688 of the Teamsters in St. Louis, and Carmen Lucia of the AFL Hatters Union in the southeastern United States agreed. Visiting French plants in 1950, they did not like what they saw, at least as compared with the position of American labor. They complained that the Marshall Plan was not working, labor was divided, and the collective bargaining mechanism was inadequate in France. Workers were organized by industry only, not by individual plant, which made it more difficult to negotiate. American labor thought the French needed full-time American unionists in France to help them organize and as much money as possible. They clearly believed they had a big stake in, and substantial responsibility for, the success of the Marshall Plan. In March 1951 the AFL magazine, the *American Federationist*, carried a headline "ECA: Labor on the Inside." The subtitle was "Plain People Take Part at Top Level, So Marshall Plan Projects a Success." American labor believed in the myth of the yeoman worker too and saw it as crucial to winning over French labor for the West.

Force Ouvrière leaders were also useful in propagandizing French labor problems in the United States. When Italian and French labor leaders visited the United States in April 1949, Andre LaFond of Force Ouvrière was among them. LaFond was considered an ally by the ECA. Jay Lovestone arranged for the group to speak to the CFR on 6 April. LaFond told the group that the Communist CGT favored Interim Aid to France and the Monnet Plan, but not the Marshall Plan, which LaFond characterized as "the oxygen tank of the Monnet Plan."[62] He then explained that the Communist refusal to support the Marshall Plan had caused the split in CGT that triggered the founding of Force Ouvrière.

The OPC was also used for problems requiring urgent attention rather than long-range planning. Giving aid to friendly publications and writers, as well as setting up consultants for specific projects such as East-West trade relations were typical short-term ventures. For that purpose the ECA Appropriations Act provided for a confidential fund of $200,000, which could be authorized only by the administrator and the deputy administrator, Paul Hoffman and Richard M. Bissell, Jr.[63] Congressional sources were aware that Marshall Plan money was being skimmed off the top to fund propaganda and in fact encouraged Marshall Plan personnel to do so. But the lines of authority soon blurred. What transpired in a closed hearing room in Washington was one thing, bureaucratic safeguards another. Marshall Plan personnel, needing flexibility in the field, were adept at following the spirit rather than the letter of the regulation. As Leland Barrows, the executive assistant to Milton Katz, wrote: "We have gotten around this obvious administrative difficulty (approval by only the Administrator and the Deputy Administrator) through the device of an allotment to OSR against which vouchers can be paid, but nonetheless the administrative approval of such vouchers is still obtained by forwarding the original to Washington for Hoffman's signature after the fact."[64]

It was a difficult problem. Marshall Plan personnel had to act fast in some situations, but they had a duty to report as well. Barrows and Katz explored a number of possible ways to handle the reporting problem. Barrows outlined three alternatives. They could routinely report to Washington, transmitting supporting vouchers; they could report to Katz for clearance; or they could send "a polite letter to Washington stating that the security implications of some of the payments here make inadvisable the transmitting of these vouchers to Washington (this last point was considered to be true at least with regard to the CIA expenditures)."[65] Barrows recommended that an explanation of each payment be sent to Washington, directed to Foster or Hoffman rather than to the controller, and that they work to get control of the confidential funds in the Paris office.

Yet Washington policymakers had greater aspirations than just a pro-American France; they wanted an absorption of American culture and values. As such, the small emergency handouts under the confidential funding system were insignificant compared with efforts at managing labor's politics or controlling acculturation devices, such as the film industry. Former OSS agent and filmmaker Gerald Mayer spearheaded the drive to corner the French market for U.S. films. It was a lucrative and cutthroat business. Negotiations were held at the highest level. Dean Acheson spoke to Jean Monnet about it as early as September of 1945. Monnet agreed to try to straighten out any problems at once. Max Milliken and Will Clayton continued the negotiations. Mayer's consortium wanted 100 percent of the monopoly and complained about receiving only 75 percent, even though the French indicated that although the film industry should be open to free competition, the French preferred American films. Eventually Léon Blum and James Byrnes signed a film accord in 1946. Apparently, it was a politically sensitive issue. Ambassador Caffery cabled the secretary in 1946 that "the current political situation in France has undoubtedly reinforced the opposition to the Blum-Byrnes film accord and strengthened the Communist elements in the government."[66] The French argued that their observance of the American plan would hurt their balance of payments.

In June 1947 George Marshall became involved in the negotiations, by this time an eleven million dollar deal. Agreement was finally reached on 14 June 1947, with Gerald Mayer and Robert Lovett flying to Paris to finalize it. In the end the U.S. companies won, showing 108 films in 1948 alone. Mayer had double the number of films of any other company exporting to France. Italian films also did well. Walt Disney, one of the losers, was squeezed out by Mayer and complained heatedly. Some films had value as propaganda as well as acculturation devices, but it was hard to get them shown. The French refused to show *The Iron Curtain* in 1949 because they were afraid of Communist uprisings. Italian officials watched to see what France would do and followed suit.

How did the French react to all this attention? The reception was mixed. First of all, French "peasants" seem to have been largely outside the propaganda effort.[67] Policymakers were aware of this oversight and tried to correct it by sending groups of American laborers into the country villages where John Bross had seen the Russian flags flying. Speaking at the CFR, Richard

M. Bissell, Jr., said that "the elimination of injustice as between the peasants and workers is more important than the absolute standard of living. . . . It is an immensely subtle problem."[68] How successful American industrial labor was in relating to French agricultural workers can only be surmised. Perhaps, as Franklin Lindsay said of the Yugoslav peasants, "their support of any government, left or right, will be determined primarily by the extent to which that government lets them alone. . . . They will oppose any government which requisitions crops, takes sons for the army, taxes them, and provides no stable currency."[69]

French city dwellers reacted with violent protests in the Marseilles region and skepticism in Paris. Marseilles was the scene of disruptions directed at Allied military personnel stationed there. In Paris the ECA funded a 1950 Gallup poll, which found that about 40 percent of Parisians were opposed to the Marshall Plan, deeming it an encroachment on French decisionmaking. Clearly the Parisian Communist press agreed, finding excellent propaganda ammunition in wounded French pride. *Cahiers du Communisme* contained articles excoriating Harriman and the Marshall Plan people for imperialism in Paris. Communist posters traded on that line of reasoning, showing the United States as an octopus about to tighten its tentacles around France. Counterpropaganda funded by OPC through a conduit called Paix et Liberté showed the Eiffel Tower with a hammer and sickle on top and the inscription "Jamais Ça."[70] American posters also sought to make the connection between various forms of totalitarianism. One featured cartoons of Kaiser Wilhelm, Hitler, and Stalin with the inscription, "La Barbe."[71] Paris became a propaganda battlefield. This was even more the case in 1950 after the outbreak of the Korean War. The war intensified the propaganda barrage because it was the cheapest way to win the minds of the French. Even though the war shifted resources to Southeast Asia, policymakers could not afford to ignore France, where Communist propaganda scored heavily on the metropole's involvement with the Bao Dai regime in Vietnam. By the summer of 1952, however, the acting U.S. Special Representative to Europe, Paul Porter, wrote Bissell that the ECA "missions should bring to the attention of the [recipient] governments the prospect that a portion of the counterpart [funds] will most probably have to be earmarked for military purposes."[72] Scaling down in Europe to increase funding for Korea did not mean the complete abandonment of traditional ECA projects. But Porter warned that "in France and Italy we should concentrate on only major objectives, i.e., military purposes and one or two high-priority social objectives such as low cost housing."[73]

The model of coordinated intervention developed for France through the complementary relationship of the Marshall Plan and the OPC was relatively benign. Keeping in mind U.S. goals for France, policymakers demurred to French pride, seldom taking a heavy-handed approach. Before we conclude that this pattern prevailed throughout "Marshall Plan" Europe, however, we must examine other models. The plan for each country approached its target both as a unique nation and as part of an American global strategy for continued, and perhaps even greater, influence. Therefore, models for each country developed according to the perception of Marshall Plan personnel as to each nation's postwar problems, potential, and use to the United States. Furthermore, Marshall Plan/OPC strategy for each country took into consideration the ways in which success in one country would ensure American dominance in another, perhaps more pivotal state. As we will see in the models for Italy and Iran, when one country was deemed essential to securing another, the themes for each country were fully coordinated.

SIX

ITALY-IRAN: INTERLOCKING THEMES
FOR GLOBAL INTERVENTION

rance and Italy are often discussed in the same breath, as it were, in agency and departmental reports for the post–World War II period. They were the countries that seemed most vulnerable to Communism, having the largest Communist parties and significant Communist labor movements. But it would be a mistake to think that policymakers viewed them similarly or as equals. American goals and aspirations for Italy were considerably different than for France. Refashioning Italy posed an entirely different set of problems and suggested solutions not conceived of for France. What the United States wanted in Italy was military bases. The security of the Mediterranean was uppermost in the minds of policymakers, and the geographic situation of Italy made it important. All other goals and aspirations flowed from this desire. As Rhodri Jeffreys-Jones put it: "The selection of Italy for special attention . . . was by no means a matter of democratic principle alone. The country was strategically important. The NSC noted that the peninsula flanked the Balkans and dominated the Mediterranean. It was a potential base for eastward air strikes, and it could be used to guarantee—or, in the wrong hands, impair—oil supplied from the Near East."[1] There were, to be sure, ancillary considerations relating to Italy. But they were issues of propaganda value, not the essence of policy. Paramount in the strategy for protection of Italy and the Mediterranean were Iran and its oil fields; hence, a notation on an Organization for European Economic Cooperation report listing the first priority as "Italy-Iran."[2]

It may seem outrageous to think of Italy in that fashion, but the cohort of determined interventionists were economic and political warriors. They thought in terms of the long-term global economic and political position of the United States. Iran was crucial economically, Italy politically, so that U.S. military goals would be secure. The fates of the two countries were intertwined; therefore the covert political schemes for each were interrelated. Italy was to be secured with alacrity so that a massive modernization plan for Iran could be facilitated.

Naturally there were corollary considerations, often issues more familiar to the public. When policymakers sought to engage public empathy, they spoke about the seat of Western culture residing in Italy. Among themselves they worried that the Communists might gain control in Italy by legal means. That would make Italy the "first instance in history of a communist accession to power by popular suffrage and legal procedure." This was not a prospect the West relished because "so unprecedented and portentous an event must produce a profound psychological effect in those countries threatened by the Soviets and . . . striving to retain their freedom." There was also the Catholic question. Policymakers were sure "devout Catholics everywhere would be gravely concerned" if the Holy Sea vanished behind the Iron Curtain.[3] But all of these were side issues—serious considerations, but side issues nevertheless.

Policymakers thought there were two ways to stabilize Italy. The first was modernization and industrialization. But that would not be enough. And creating a climate for influence would not be enough either. Italy had a unique problem—too many people. The primary theme for Italy, before modernization and industrialization would work, was to thin the population. The method selected was emigration. Policymakers assumed that if Italy could be stabilized, the Mediterranean could be protected by an American military presence. Therefore, the CIA reported that "it is of vital strategic importance to prevent Italy from falling under Communist control." Not only would it have a "demoralizing effect throughout Western Europe, the Mediterranean, and the Middle East," but "militarily, the availability to the USSR of bases in Sicily and southern Italy would pose a direct threat to the security of communications through the Mediterranean."[4]

In order to secure American interests in Iran a great deal more than military bases would be necessary. American policymakers were determined not to follow in the footsteps of the British in Iran. Rather than colonize the country, they wanted to refashion it after the American model. Strongly influenced by the New Deal, they idealized that a TVA approach in Iran would help create a new democracy in the Middle East, a strong ally and equal trading partner, particularly in the oil trade. The theme for Iran was modernization.

P olicymakers had strong perceptions of Italy, as they had of France. But in Italy there was a duality of perceptions, some positive, some not very flattering. Allen Dulles closely collaborated with Italian aristocrats and leftist politicians during the final years of the Second World War when he was orchestrating Operation Sunrise. He developed a close affinity for the people he worked with, keeping up correspondence of an affectionate nature with many of them long after the war.[5] The strain of thinking that produced the perception of Italy as the "seat of Western Culture" rested comfortably upon the experience men like Dulles had with upper class Italians. But there was another perception of Italy, as well. In contrast to the sophisticated Italians of Dulles's acquaintance were the masses of illiterate and vulnerable Italians, a group that worried U.S. policymakers. Too many Italians were desperately poor and therefore viewed as targets for Communist propaganda.

Italy had a host of other problems too that were reminiscent of France. The President's Committee on Foreign Aid estimated in 1947 that for the fiscal year April-June 1948 the Italian balance of payments would be minus $186.4 million. For the fiscal year 1948–1949 they expected it to rise to minus $707.5 million.[6] But James D. Zellerbach, the chief of the ECA mission in Italy, told the CFR that the Italian trade deficit had fallen from $801 million in 1947 to $551 million in 1948.[7] ECA Data Books for Italy published in 1950 show that Zellerbach was close; the deficit appears to have been roughly $472 million. But what aggregate figures did not tell was the vast disparity between imports and exports. For the year 1949 Italy exported about one million dollars worth of goods while importing $473 million.[8]

Italy, like France, had a problem with colonies. While the French position in the U.S. scheme for Europe caused Washington to rhetorically support the metropole's efforts in shoring up their colonial position, the Italians' plea fell on deaf ears. American policymakers thought the Italian colonies were not worth much. CIA reports indicate that the significance of the Italian colonies in Africa—Libya, Eritrea, and Somaliland—was their proximity to the Near East "where the accomplishment of U.S. objectives requires administrations which are stable and favorably disposed toward the U.S."[9] Not particularly concerned about the Italians' desire to increase their prestige and create a "better position in foreign relations and popular morale," intelligence reports indicate that the colonies were "economically unimportant except by providing a minor outlet for Italian emigrants."[10] Since intelligence reports indicated that the colonies could not support much more in population than they already had, policymakers did not think it was worth the bother to retain them. Because Italy was "of relatively little direct value to the U.S.," except as a base, the colonies were expendable.[11]

What seemed to be major stumbling blocks in Italy were ignorance and overpopulation. The Italians produced a half million infants each year of the Second World War, a healthy increase for a small country.[12] Policymakers saw the increase as adding to unemployment, which was already hovering around two million, or 10 percent, in 1947.[13] Of particular concern to the CIA was the area north of Rome, the Adriatic coast from Pescara to Bari, the Taranto Naval Base, and Sicily. These were the areas the CIA believed would fall to the Communists if there were a civil war. Although the CIA estimated that the Communists could win a civil war, it was believed that they "would rather not provoke one because they would rather infiltrate and force a take-over by legal means."[14] It was crucial to American policy objectives that these areas be stabilized.

The overt component of stablization policy was the Marshall Plan effort to modernize and industrialize Italy. While that effort must not be minimized, it is important to note American attitudes toward that effort. Perhaps because policymakers had limited goals for Italy and legitimate concerns about Italy's monumental problems, they seem not to have had much hope of success in Italy. Even the usually optimistic ECA was cautious. A 1950 report stated that "the factors which limit Italy's ability to sustain herself at adequate and improving living standards are principally two: (1) the poverty of those natural resources essential to modern industrial production, and (2) the very low ratio of capital to population."[15]

"Scarcity of natural resources," it went on to say, "made the Italian economy heavily dependent on international trade."[16] The result was that Italy could not make any gains or accumulate capital for investment, because "so large a share of her total output must be devoted to satisfying every day consumption needs and maintenance costs of the economy."[17]

In what was perhaps the hardest blow to Italy, the CIA reported to the president that "from the strictly economic point of view, the participation of Italy is not essential to the success of the European Recovery Program. The elimination of Italy from the program would permit increased allocations . . . to the other countries."[18] In some sense CIA reports in the late forties are reminiscent of a view posited by Allen Dulles in 1944. In an address before the CFR entitled "European Affairs as Viewed from Berne," Dulles said that "badly off as the Italians are and may be, the world would nevertheless go on if no immediate solution is found for the Italian problem."[19]

Since the CIA was concerned about the loss or retention of military bases, they paid close attention to Communist party activity in Italy. The CIA thought Italian Communists would "follow a special variant of the Cominform line on European Recovery Program, that Italy is not getting enough." Intelligence reports reaching President Truman indicated that besides countering the European Recovery Program with the use of a "maximum degree of covert obstruction," Communist propaganda attacks in Italy claimed that American aid was actually niggardly. Corollary attacks condemned the Italian government for letting this happen, in hopes of finessing a political takeover. If it appeared the Soviets could not gain control by political means, Italy could expect "strikes, sabotage, incendiarism, disorders, and possibly an insurrection." In short, Moscow would do "all in its power to disrupt the economic rehabilitation and political stabilization of Italy."[20] In a final twist, the agency predicted that if the Communists did take control in Italy, they would manipulate the European Recovery Program into continuing support for Italy while insisting that the United States forgo its controlling administrative function.

Even if Soviet disruption was successful, though, CIA reports indicated that trade between the United States and Italy would continue.

While Italy and the Soviet Union were seen as economically complementary—Italy exported equipment and the Soviet Union exported grain, coal, and lumber—Italy would still need the United States for scrap iron, steel, and fertilizers. Since the Soviets could not provide those items, another component of their special policy in Italy would be to allow continued trade with the United States. Essentially what the Soviets aimed for was to reap the benefits of American aid and trade in Italy.[21]

The stakes were high for the superpowers in Italy; the reward was control of the Mediterranean. For the United States the overt strategy was to add strength to the army and embark on a modernization program. The covert theme for Italy was emigration. The plan was to relocate Italians from troubled areas to South America, easing the unemployment strain and thinning a population that might be subject to propaganda assaults. There was little belief that Italians could be won over from errant ways, as with the French. That is, there was no myth of the yeoman laborer in Italy, although Count Carlo Sforza tried to create one, telling the CFR that there were "millions of small landowners in Italy and they form a strong bulwark against Communism."[22] American policymakers had little affinity with the Italian working man and little confidence that he could be a bulwark of democracy.

Italian labor was not really all that different from French, despite policymakers' perceptions. Enormous trade unions, largely Communist, operated in the northern region around Milan. In that city the CIA estimated that of the 343,176 workers employed, 229,176 were members of Communist unions. Nonunion workers numbered 114,000. Milan was also a focal point for disruptive tactics planned in Moscow. Agency reports indicated that Partito Comunista Italiano (PCI) "on order of Moscow and Cominform leaders" and in union with the French Communist party, "has allegedly prepared a vast plan of sabotage in Italian and French ports when United States vessels with war materials are to arrive."[23] Soviet officers reportedly paid substantial sums to obtain the schedules of American ships, particularly in the Taranto region.[24]

Things were not much better in Genoa, where the CIA feared PCI members were organizing to enable themselves to carry out directives from the Cominform. The PCI was creating a strong capability in case the party was outlawed. If that happened, members would be prepared to carry out paramilitary operations and guerrilla warfare. To do so they streamlined the party, replacing "older leaders" with "prepared and decisive young men."[25] Similar to the Paris plan, the PCI organized by city, province, and territory, with political coordinators to integrate the sections. Its aim was "the eventual absorption and full control of the labor movement . . . to prepare steps which can be directed against defense production, i.e., sabotage, slow downs, etc."[26] Other targets of the party were the Atlantic Pact and the Italian armed forces, which the CIA believed had been infiltrated by PCI "military cells." To facilitate these and other goals "many activists were trained in offensive roles, such as occupying factories, throwing up road blocks."[27]

U.S. army intelligence reported much the same type of activity. In Florence, a Communist party rally in September 1949 drew 500,000 for a parade and speeches by various Communist officeholders and party members, including the city's Communist mayor, Mario Fabiani. There was at least one representative of the Eastern bloc speaking, Peter Georghiev, from the Bulgarian Communist party. Italian army intelligence agreed that 500,000 was a number "not believed greatly exaggerated," although they thought the large attendance could be explained by the fact that Florence was a railway center and therefore easily accessible.[28]

There is one significant difference between French and Italian labor activity in the postwar period. In Italy there were not as many strikes, but there was real violence, and many people died. In Modena in January 1950 the Communist Confederazione Generale Italiano del LaVoro (CGIL) occupied four foundaries and six workers died.[29] Italian Communists, like the French, were politically savvy, using their resistance reputations to purge hated industrial leaders by charging them with Fascist collaboration. In the south there was little labor organization. There the laboring classes were agriculturalists, very poor and apolitical, much like the French "peasants," but far more numerous.

American labor policy in Italy tended to follow that in France. New labor unions, such as the Free Italian General Confederation of Labor (LCGIL), were encouraged; they were left-leaning but not Communist.

But they encountered the same problems as Force Ouvrière in France. In order to retain their integrity, they found themselves supporting strikes also supported by the Communists, because the causes were popular. For instance, before the Modena strike, the Communist CGIL had been in strength until the formation, with the help of ECA, of the pro-Western LCGIL. When employers realized they had a rival union to bargain with, they got tough. CGIL called for a strike. Once the strike was settled the employers cut back workers, giving preference to the LCGIL. The non-Communist labor union had also struck the foundaries but ordered no demonstrations and no civil disobedience, instead ordering workers to stay home. That is when CGIL ordered the occupation of the foundaries. In the end LCGIL also proposed a two-hour strike, to mourn the dead CGIL workers.[30]

Italian management did not escape attention either. But in Italy there was a difference in approach, largely because of two beliefs held by policymakers. They feared that if a solution was not found quickly, the enormous numbers of impoverished Italians would revolt. Accordingly, something had to be done to force a cohesive policy agreed upon by Italian industrial management and the Italian government. Policymakers' desire for a quick industrial remedy and government coordination led to arguments over tactics. For instance, a plan to build a hydroelectric development project on the Tiber met with resistance because it called for importing the equipment rather than letting the Italians contribute the materials. On one side was the argument that the ECA should rebuild each industry in Italy vertically so that all levels of a project would be Italian and a variety of Italian industries could be developed. On the other was the belief that vertical rebuilding would take too much time, that bringing in American products would get the job done and provide instant modernization to assuage Italian discontent.[31]

ECA planners exerted influence on the Italian government to coordinate efforts in consumer industries as well. Fiat, for instance, asked for $5,850,000 to build a new plant with the resources to allow them to develop a new model. The ECA replied, to the Italian government rather than Fiat, that it would give the auto company $14.8 million, but ECA insisted the government embark on an extensive roadbuilding project and remove gasoline and horsepower taxes as part of the bargain. They also insisted that Fiat build a small, cheap car.[32] Consumer possibilities for the average Italian was a high priority. Hopeless as Italy was seen to be, there was still a glimmer of hope that the government could be convinced to take the steps necessary to provide a reasonably high standard of living.

The European Recovery Program scheme for Italy was to thin the population, modernize Italian industry as much as possible, get the government to cooperate with the modernization plan, strengthen democratic labor, and propagandize. Some of the plan was overt: the modernization and efforts to gain governmental support. Some was covert: the propaganda, the labor effort, and the solution for overpopulation.

Encouraging massive emigration was a touchy issue. Yet CIA reports, President Truman's files, and State Department reports from Rome indicate that American policymakers were serious about emigration as a solution for Italy's population problem. Italian officials agreed as well, although at least one, Amintore Fanfani, thought that the numbers of Italians who were being relocated in 1948 "were not large enough to indicate that emigration can solve the problem of unemployment, even though increased emigration possibilities would naturally help the situation."[33]

Though emigration had been settled on as a possible solution, significant problems remained. The first was transportation. The Italian merchant marine was in poor shape after the war. Early ECA efforts promoted the modernization and rebuilding of the merchant marine fleet. By October of 1947 the Italian merchant marine had been "restored to about 67 percent of its prewar tonnage." But, as the report indicated, "this measure of recovery has been possible . . . only by reason of very substantial financial and material aid from the United States."[34]

But the aim was not to help them transport goods as much as people. ECA records showed considerable enthusiasm for the emigration theme. The 1950 Data Book said that "the Government is actively pursuing measures to assist emigration, as another means of attacking the problem of unemployment and over-population."[35] James D. Zellerbach, the chief of the ECA mission in Italy, told the CFR that Marshall Plan money was being used to rebuild the Italian merchant marine to "double the number of Italian emigrants who can be carried overseas each year."[36] State Department reports from Rome indicated that "emigration as a means of reducing unemployment was arranged for with other countries by means of agreements, beginning in a very small way in 1945 and continuing in 1946."[37] By "a very small way" Ambassador James Clement Dunn meant 75,761 workers and 10,267 members of their families in 1947. ECA reports showed 54,000 workers emigrating in 1947 but stated that the figure climbed to 150,000 in 1949.[38] Ambassador Dunn states it this way: "During the first 8 months of 1948, 39,464 workers and 12,154 members of their families emigrated. The weekly average during the last few weeks has been 1800 units."[39]

Emigration was also a costly solution. As ECA admitted, "Considerable capital is required to finance the cost of settling emigrants and to provide them with necessary job opportunities."[40] ECA reports said that the Italian government was "addressing itself to this problem," but the primary sponsors were the American government, through ECA, and some international agencies.

The ECA had some difficulty locating a place to settle Italian emigrants. Intelligence reports indicated that many countries were reluctant to accept them. The French, for instance, felt threatened by unemployment in Italy, especially "if the movement of labor were uncontrolled."[41] Emigration of Italians to France was discussed by a Franco-Italian commission but would be acceptable "only under strict control . . . on the basis of quarterly requests for specific jobs to be filled."[42] James Zellerbach told the CFR that Marshall Plan money was being used to retrain workers "thereby making them more acceptable to other countries."[43] The ECA finally decided on South America because it contained some "relatively less developed areas," which presumably would be cheaper, and there were already large pre-existing Italian communities that might more readily accept the emigrants. The State Department decided in January 1950 that "subject to the necessary economic and financial limitations, and subject to the obviously necessary coordination of our policies in this field with the U.S. foreign policy goals in Latin America and Africa, the US Government should try to facilitate Italian emigration in all possible ways."[44]

Because the sensitivity of this solution made secrecy necessary, those advocating it scrambled for mechanisms already in place that could be used as cover. Congress had already made a good start by authorizing the refitting of up to ten vessels for the "purpose of transporting emigrants from Italy to parts of the world other than the United States."[45] The second mechanism was to tap the counterpart funds or the technical assistance provisions.[46] The third was international banking, and ECA suggested that "sympathetic consideration" be given to Italian requests for loans from Export-Import Bank or the International Bank "for specific projects of economic development in Latin America which could absorb large numbers of Italian emigrants."[47]

In mid 1950 ECA began to negotiate with six South American countries to discover whether they would be receptive to new immigrants—specifically, if they would help locate the Italian immigrants.[48] Under the ECA technical assistance program an emigration survey was funded for $425,000. The first authorization covered "certain expenses . . . of technical missions . . . to locate specific lands suitable for Italian settlement" and "to formulate specific plans and . . . give technical advice during the initial stages of development of such lands for settlement."[49] At first it was a relatively small effort, but it grew. The first money allocated for emigration went to Brazil in August 1950. It was funded with counterpart funds from Italy.

The ECA and the State Department did not advocate emigration without careful consideration. The Rockefeller Foundation's American International Association (AIA) was asked to advise ECA on the economic and social ramifications of this type of emigration plan.[50] William Foster of the Office of the Special Representative—W. Averell Harriman's Marshall Plan command post in Paris—hired AIA as a consultant in August 1950. But the Italians were not privy to the report. In fact Foster specified that it be kept secret from the Italian representative on the project.[51] The ECA also received advice and help from the "foreign sector" of the U.S. Department of Agriculture—the intelligence unit of USDA.[52]

Propaganda to stabilize the remaining Italians was equally important.

In Italy the campaign was developed and coordinated by Waldemar Nielsen. It was a sophisticated campaign relying heavily on radio broadcasts geared to specific audiences. Again, as in France, women were a primary target. ECA personnel were concerned because Italian women did not seem to go out to labor rallies and could not be reached through normal channels. Specific broadcasts were aimed at that population, as at other discrete populations. Italy was also the prime recipient of the showboat ECA propaganda efforts, extravaganzas of the Hollywood type, which were thought to be particularly attractive to the Italian audience.

The European Recovery Program's propaganda effort in Europe relied heavily on "card-carrying American trade unionists" who were stationed in the field missions under the Labor Information Program.[53] Since the "basic structure of the recovery program demanded the support of industrial workers," and since European labor played a "significant political role" in each country, ERP thought they needed special attention. Policymakers believed that the American trade unionists could "speak as workers" to their European counterparts, that they had a "fundamental identity of interest."[54] In other words they were counting on American labor to convince European labor that the Marshall Plan was a benefit. American trade unionists would use the European labor press, radio, films, pamphlets, posters, lectures, and informal social gatherings to help get across the message.

In Italy the mission "early determined that it was advantageous to speak to Italians through organizations or entities that were identifiably Italian."[55] In other words they used indigenous organizations rather than blatantly American-identified sources to get the message across. ERP realized that Italians, like anyone else, would object to the "intrusion upon their moral and intellectual privacy" that a "fullscale, out-in-the-open propaganda campaign" would represent. What they were aiming for was indirection.

Among the more successful efforts at indirection was the Confederazione Italiana Femminile (CIF), a women's organization that produced wall newspapers carrying the Marshall Plan story. The posters were distributed by and attributable to CIF, not the ECA. Organizzazione Epoca operated the ECA Mission's mobile units, carrying a sound message from town to town, using Italian crews and a program "that is purely Italian in character." Women and children were also targeted by Organizzazione Bambi, which had its own mobile unit featuring women's and children's programming. The ECA was enthusiastic about Bambi and recommended its expansion to six units. Atlante, S.A., published pamphlets and booklets for the mission without identifying ECA as the source. And finally, Radio Epoca produced the mission's radio programs, "including a regular half-hour weekly documentary." The programs produced by Radio Epoca were "used by the Italian radio broadcasting system as Italian-produced shows."[56]

As in France, commercial film distribution was a large part of the influence program, and films were distributed through unattributable channels such as trade unions, factories, industrial groups, schools, and universities. In these cases private agency efforts to assist the Marshall Plan were "aided by providing advice, personnel, or financial help." And of course, governments receiving assistance from the Marshall Plan were obligated by bilateral agreement to assist in publicizing the program. Sometimes ECA films were not detected by Communist propagandists and were reviewed favorably by their publications. Sometimes the artistic merit of the enterprise won it a place in a Communist-sponsored exhibition, even when the source was known. And, as in France, "The Answer Man" was a favorite in Italy.

Lest all of this seem somewhat cynical, Communist propaganda in Italy reached a level unheard of in France; it was blatant and openly inciting to riot. In Milan groups of Communists set up tents in a square and attracted, by barker methods, a small crowd. After angering them with all-too-true rhetoric about the sorry state of affairs in Italy, they organized ad hoc schools to teach methods of insurrection against the "Fascist-inspired, American-backed reactionary government" in power. This scene was repeated all over Italy. Communist propaganda in Italy was not a poster war with seductive parties. Party workers simply gathered hungry, angry, out-of-work people in each town and taught them how to fight.[57] The irony is that ECA fought back in the way it did and was successful.

The commitment of American labor helped the ECA effort in Italy and made Nielsen's propaganda effort successful. In Italy the ubiquitous Irving Brown had plenty of help. Substantial segments of organized labor—particularly in the New York City area—were Italian Americans. They adopted the project with gusto. Following the same scheme developed for France, labor leaders exchanged visits with Italian labor, visited plants, and received help and financial support from American labor counterparts. Jay Lovestone and David Dubinsky sponsored a group of Italian labor leaders who visited the United States in April 1949. Among their speaking engagements was the CFR. The group included Enrico Parri of the Italian Confederation of Labor and also a member of Parliament, Renato Cappugi of the Agricultural Workers Union and a member of Parliament, Vasco Cesari of the Electrical Workers Union, Giovanni Pasqualini of the Welfare Office and the Italian Republican party.[58]

The State Department coordinated labor activities through Irving Brown, whom they called the AFL European representative. Brown, who filled a similar role at the CIA, reportedly "ran around Europe organizing things."[59] At State, Brown worked closely with Paul Nitze, who was responsible for the Technical Assistance Program.[60] And the Department of Labor provided labor attachés, who acted as "shirt-sleeve diplomats," representing the "ordinary American man in the streets to the ordinary man in the streets of foreign capitals." The job of the shirt-sleeve diplomat was to "develop intimate and close contacts with key foreign trade union, management and government labor ministry officials as a basis for gathering and evaluating information on foreign labor developments, act as advisors, and promote understanding."[61]

ECA officials also received help from American businessmen on these sponsored labor trips. Charles F. H. Johnson, president of Botany Hills, Inc., in Passaic, New Jersey, was told by Dick Bissell that "these visits have been notably successful in directly reducing the strength of the Communists in Europe." Bissell told Johnson that one labor leader, after a trip to the United States "to study our free enterprise production system," switched his allegiance, taking his 500,000 union members out of the Italian General Conference of Workers to set up a "rival conference which has since become a powerful factor in reducing the strength of the Communist Party in Italy."[62]

Sometimes there were funny twists to the Italian labor visits that showed the handicaps the Italians were working under in Washington. When an Italian labor group was scheduled to set sail in April 1948, Dean Acheson suddenly worried about bringing them over first class. Acheson thought it would not look good to their left-leaning European labor counterparts if they traveled in luxury aboard the *Queen Mary*. He fussed a good deal about it until finally it was agreed that the Italians would sail cabin class. Acheson sent the bill to Lovestone.[63]

Visiting labor groups were sometimes frustrated by State Department requirements. James Carey complained to the CFR on 8 April 1948 that the State Department refused to give visas to anyone whom immigration laws excluded from this country. Carey wanted an upcoming international meeting of the World Federation of Trade Unions to be held in Chicago but was frustrated because State would not allow Communists entry. Carey tried for approval to have the meeting in New York City but was offered only a two week pass for use in limited geographic areas of the city. When France got the bid for the meeting, Carey complained that "our democracy could not be so weak that we cannot allow labor leaders to come in for a few weeks." He said it made it hard to campaign against the Iron Curtain, especially in light of the growing Red scare in the United States. He told the CFR that European labor would come to one of two conclusions: either the Communists would take over the government within the next few weeks, or American labor was as reactionary as the Communists had led them to believe.[64]

American policy in Italy had an equal mixture of the overt and the covert. Italy, however, provides a glimpse of an unusual example of covert economic warfare in the emigration plan to remove some of the troublesome numbers of Italians from critical areas in the peninsula. It is true that in Italy, as in France, there were the usual confidential expenditures to individuals presumed useful.[65] They, too, were paid from the 5 percent administration fund supervised by William Foster in the Paris office. But, as in France, it would be a mistake to miss the larger agenda by concentrating on these small adventures.

Determined interventionists were concerned that the oil-rich Middle East would fall into the hands of the Soviet Union. To prevent that from happening they devised a multifocal development plan for Iran based on the Tennessee Valley Authority (TVA) replete with all its attendant mythology. The planners believed, as had their New Deal counterparts, that U.S. assistance in planning and implementing the necessary components for a modern industrial-age nation would have the effect of drawing Iranian society out of its "economically retarded" condition, provide education, jobs, and a higher standard of living, thereby developing loyalty among its citizens, forestalling Soviet influence, and setting Iran permanently on a course of modernization and affiliation with the West.[66]

This bold and aggressive policy drew on the belief that the economically comfortable do not turn to Communism. Writ large as global strategy, this theory evolved into the idea that developing nations receiving adequate assistance from the West in the form of planning and technology would aspire to emulate Western ideas and would be less vulnerable to Communist agendas. In fact this notion guided American policy toward the so-called Third World for at least another decade and would only be called to question when Lyndon Johnson declared that he would create a TVA in the Mekong Delta.

Perhaps because Marshall Plan–era strategists had no intention of backing up ideology with bombing raids, they relied on more sophisticated mechanisms to safeguard their plans. Knowing that a Communist Italy would provide military and naval bases for the Soviets, obviating Western plans for Iran, they moved to secure Italy politically in order to maintain U.S. military options there. As such they were linking countries through regional planning. They could not move armies into Iran, but they could create conditions amenable to Western influence. They could secure navy bases in Italy, given the West's postwar position in the peninsula. Geographically that plan was more attractive than military forces in Iran, because Italian bases allowed control of the Mediterranean. The only threat was a Communist takeover.

T he scheme for Iran began in 1948 when Overseas Consultants, Inc., an "association of US engineers," represented by Allen Dulles, "made surveys . . . and reported that a large-scale development program, properly administered, was practical in Iran."[67] As noted earlier, Americans had a tradition of involvement on a professional planning level in Iran. But what Overseas Consultants presented was more than a stopgap. It was a "comprehensive economic-development program."[68] Inspired by the TVA, this Seven-Year Plan, as approved by the Iranian parliament, called the Majlis, included

> housing and municipal improvements, public health measures, expanded educational facilities, and the construction of government buildings; agricultural projects, and the importation of agricultural machinery and fertilizers; expansion and improvement of railroads, roads, ports and airports; improvement and expansion of industry and mining, formation of a government petroleum company to develop the oil resources in areas outside the Anglo-Iranian Oil Company concession; and the reequipment of the post and telegraph systems.[69]

Calling the plan comprehensive was an understatement. Overseas Consultants intended to bring Iran into the modern world in seven years. It also aimed to develop the oil not controlled by the Anglo-Iranian Oil Company (AIOC). When the plan was stymied because of political problems in Iran, it turned to the OPC, providing an excellent example of the way in which OPC acted to complement foreign assistance programs, particularly in situations where the ERP needed help but did not have the mechanisms.

Kermit Roosevelt was the man called upon to make things right in Iran. He began by training himself in the language, culture, and customs of Iran, studying with Ralph Bunche. He then traveled through the region, relying on old friends, school acquaintances, and Millspaugh Mission leftovers to provide housing, transportation, and information about Iranian society. Knowing the shah personally gave him an extra edge, which came in handy later when the political scene heated up.

Roosevelt's goal was to strengthen the shah's hand against the insurgency of Mohammed Mossadegh, the prime minister of Iran. Mossadegh was a pragmatist—flirting with East and West, looking for the most generous ally. Part of his political appeal in Iran was his critique of Britain's oil dealings with Iran. The British had acted in a cavalier fashion with the Iranians, or at least had acted unwisely in an anticolonial era. As John Sherman of the PSB noted, "AIOC sitting while liberalization elsewhere in world."[70] The Iranians had a list of legitimate complaints about AIOC. They had constructed oil removal facilities in Iran and charged the Iranians heftily by demanding 80 percent of the profits. They sold oil to Iran at world market prices; no special deals for the country of the oil's origin. About seventy thousand Iranians were employed by the AIOC, but none at upper levels. Added to that, Iranians were not allowed to audit the company's accounts, so government officials could not document the magnitude of their losses. Mossadegh was suspicious though, and he used British exploitation as a rallying cry in his speeches. American political activists were aware of the anti-British sentiment. John Sherman said that "anti-British and nationalist feeling is basic to Iran." The British disagreed, saying all that was necessary was to "get rid of M and a few [to] solve the problem."[71]

The Americans did not believe it. What they did believe, however, was that the situation in Iran was deteriorating. Although the Seven Year Plan was three years old, nothing had been done to implement it. The crisis between the shah and Mossadegh, a crisis aided and abetted by British truculence, was delivering a knock-out punch to the modernization scheme. The British were clearly slipping from ally to albatross status in the Middle East. Not only would Mossadegh have to go but so would the British.

It was a classic covert operation, using political and economic warfare methods. While Mossadegh and the British raged at each other, Kermit Roosevelt and George V. Allen, a longtime friend of the Sauds, cut a deal with the Saudis to develop their oil resources, giving them a fifty-fifty split. Since the Iranians had an eighty-twenty deal with the British, the Saudi-American agreement threw Mossadegh into a frenzy and strengthened his hand against the shah. Since an enraged Mossadegh usually blackmailed the West by threatening to accept aid from the Soviets, the

Americans were given a pretext for aiding the shah. When the British were ousted from Iran by Mossadegh, a slightly dissembling Dean Acheson observed, "Never had so few lost so much so stupidly and so fast."[72] He might have added, and with such interesting help.

The covert battle for Iran was in full swing. Kermit Roosevelt was to orchestrate Project Ajax, the plan to reinforce the shah. George Allen was appointed Ambassador to Iran and then superseded by Loy Henderson. Both men were considered experts on psychological warfare and were often called to advise the PPS at the State Department.[73] And the Soviets were in gear as well, assigning Anatol Lavrentiev ambassador to Iran. Lavrentiev had engineered the 1948 coup in Czechoslovakia that brought the Communists to power.

Roosevelt's Project Ajax aimed to discredit Mossadegh by showing that his allegiance to Moscow thwarted his ability to serve the shah. Key to the plan was the allegiance of the Iranian "tribes," large bands of people orbiting around powerful chieftains operating autonomously beyond Teheran's influence. The tribes had no particular reason to be allies of the shah, especially since the shah's plan for modernization, the one written by Overseas Consultants, would surely lead to a diminution of their power. They correctly surmised that a modern state's tendency to supply social services and daily occupations outside of the tribal society would wean tribesmen away from their traditional fealty. In one of the more bizarre stories of personal contact as a method of unorthodox diplomacy, Roosevelt recounted his visits to tribal leaders. Living in splendor in a Nebuchadnezzar-style ancient tribal castle, one Brooks Brothers-clad, European-educated tribal leader treated Roosevelt to the joys of *Arabian Nights* in his feudal world while the two tried to come to an agreement on tribal support for the shah.

The political action that finally ousted Mossadegh was practically bloodless. The shah left Teheran feigning a *hegira*. Once safe outside the capital he signed orders replacing Mossadegh with Gen. Fazlollah Zahedi. Roosevelt had carefully propagandized the Iranians for months with stories of Mossadegh's allegiance to the Russians and lack of loyalty to the shah. What Roosevelt counted on was the support of the Iranian people for the shah as their religious, as well as secular leader. But he was also counting on the tribes for at least the threat of military support. He succeeded in two ways. Not only did the tribes back the shah, but the requirements for a successful covert operation were met. The power behind the operation was not the United States, but the tribes that had been enlisted by Roosevelt. An indigenous group provided the strength by threatening to send military reinforcements to the shah.

For any reader who enjoys these accounts, Roosevelt's *Countercoup* is lively and detailed.[74] The coup was successful, the shah in place with strength. But Roosevelt left out the rest of the story. Once the shah was in place, the plan developed by Overseas Consultants could be adopted, and it was. The shah was free to concentrate on the enormous modernization plan developed by Overseas Consultants in 1948. The plan was begun during the Marshall Plan years, but not until the shah was secure was the plan secure. Creating a climate favorable to the shah, which allowed the plan to develop and justified the expenditure of American aid, had been the work of Kermit Roosevelt of OPC.

What is perhaps most important to say about it, however, is that despite massive coordination and effort, Project Ajax was, at least to date, a failure. What can be said at this time could not have been said twenty years ago; this failure was not a product of the evil design of covert operators but of an optimistic idealism. The reasoning behind the plan was this: If you give a "backward" country a top flight modernization plan, the money to fund it, an adequate and stable chief of state, and internal political stability, that country will evolve toward democracy. That was the thinking behind the coordination provided by OPC. Iran is a good example of a well organized, initially successful, covert operation. It was, to be sure, in the interest of the United States to have close trade relations with Iran. But the United States marries self-interest with aid and modernization plans and tries to change things. As George V. Allen said of earlier aid plans, it is first necessary to create the desire for change in a country, make the people aspire to more. That is the American role: to make them want more and then provide it.[75] What the United States did not count on in Iran was the personal factor. How would the shah use his power? As Roosevelt so poignantly analyzed it in hindsight, the United States could provide the means to open the society socially and economically, but it could not force an opening of the political system without showing its hand. The reason the men of the OPC era did not do so was not because they favored dictators, but because they believed in the natural evolution of democracy in a society with a rising standard of living. The shah fooled them by not opening up the political system. In fact he repressed every party except his own.

There are some strange outcomes to the Italy-Iran story. Iran, which received so much sophisticated attention from Roosevelt, is perhaps one of the nations most estranged from the United States today. Italy, for which the United States had little hope, will play a leading role in the European Community of the 1990s.

The bitter irony in Iran is that Roosevelt, despite his extensive research, ignored political and religious movements in Iran's history. What Roosevelt believed was that the mullah, the official clerical class in Iran, would fade away as modernization took place. Roosevelt saw them as an outdated, quarrelsome bunch and decided not to bother to recruit them in his efforts on behalf of the shah. This was a belief totally consistent with the modernization scheme for Iran. One of the things that seemed expendable to the determined interventionists was outdated, superstitious religious groups.

What Roosevelt did not know or did not take into account was that throughout modern Iranian history, when the Iranians become determined to oust a concessioner—in earlier cases Russia or Britain—a temporary alliance forms between the mullah and the bazaari to accomplish that goal.[76] The bazaari of Iran is a group we might describe as shopkeepers, but they have additional functions. They act as religious ward heelers in that they also organize their assigned neighborhoods for religious festivals, processions, and obligations. They are, if you will, entrepreneurs and religious barkers. The marriage between the mullah and the bazaari is a strange one, and it never lasts. But it is quite effective on a temporary basis.

This unusual affiliation is usually instigated by the bazaari when they feel threatened economically. In the time of the shah the problem was very simply a new highway system that diverted traffic from traditional shopping areas in Teheran. The mullah were easily enlisted because they despise foreign intrusion, seeing it as a threat to traditional religious mores. It is a formidable combination since the bazaari know how to bring out the crowd and the mullah know how to proselytize them. It ousted the Russians, the British and, in 1979, brought the Ayatollah Khomeini to power.

SEVEN

INTERVENTIONISM AND PRESIDENTIAL TRANSITIONS

H aving "adopted" covert political activism in 1948, Harry Truman became responsible for managing it. It turned out to be a challenging task. Truman, who initially recruited for the CIA through his appointments secretary, Matthew Connelly, began to fret about CIA coordination with other departments and agencies by 1950.[1] In later years Truman attributed his 1947 support for an intelligence agency on the failure of the State Department to cooperate with the executive, particularly regarding Iran. "There were a large number of people in the State Department when I took over," he claimed, "who were certain I did not know what was going on in the world and they tried to keep me from finding out."[2]

Truman created the new intelligence agency, in part to get around the State Department. The CIA was to coordinate information because the president felt he could not rely on State. He believed the State Department was too muscular bureaucratically because its employees outlasted administrations and therefore did not feel compelled to cooperate. Besides, the president opined, "the Army . . . had intelligence in really every country in the world. The Department of Agriculture, Commerce, Labor, also had such organizations, but the president had no way of finding out what those agencies were doing behind his back."[3]

All of this cannot easily be dismissed as the rantings of an elder statesman because in 1951 and 1952 the president took steps to achieve the coordination of intelligence and cooperation by the State Department. Truman created a new board to coordinate covert operations but was never able to do much about the State Department.

On 4 April 1951, Truman established, by secret directive, the Psychological Strategy Board, "for the more effective planning, coordination and conduct within the framework of approved national policy, of psychological operations."[4] The new board would "develop and promulgate 'as guidance' and as directives, the national psychological objectives, policy and programs and also actively coordinate and evaluate the national psychological effort."[5] The PSB was a "National Security Council subcommittee" whose members were Under-secretary of State James Webb, Deputy Secretary of Defense Robert Lovett, and CIA Director Walter Bedell Smith.[6]

Early correspondence in the board's files indicates that the agency and department the president most wanted coordinated were the Economic Cooperation Administration and the State Department. PSB reports show they did considerable investigation to determine how many ECA and State Department employees were engaged in psychological warfare. They found that among personnel stationed in the United States, ECA had 69 working on propaganda while the State Department had 2,724.

The president evidently believed that the new board would be useful in coordinating ECA activities with those of the OPC. The justifying argument for this move was that ECA's persuasion leaned more toward publicity than propaganda. Additionally, it was argued that because ECA programs had as their objective the publicizing or advertising of Marshall Plan aid, their recruitment policies tended to draw individuals with skills in publicizing and advertising. Perhaps because this simply was not the case with the ECA, or perhaps because OPC was so firmly embedded, it proved impossible for PSB to get a footing.

Nonetheless, in defense of their efforts and because they were aware that cooperation was mandated by the president, ECA began to brief the PSB staff on the overseas psychological operations of ECA. ECA informed the board that in addition to ECA personnel working on propaganda from the Washington office, there were 180 Americans working on propaganda in the Paris Office of the Special Representative.

The PSB was informed that ECA "does engage in some gray and black propaganda" but that "these programs represent a very small percentage of the total effort and are coordinated with CIA."[7] The PSB defined gray propaganda as meaning "that the United States Government connection is not acknowledged but is concealed and attribution is made to some other source within or outside the United States (other than a hostile source) or no attribution of the source is made," while black propa-

ganda "means that the United States Government connection is not acknowledged but is concealed and attribution is made to Soviet,
Communist or other hostile sources, or to sources dominated by or
known as sympathetic with such sources."[8] However, ECA admitted that
there was "less control (by CIA) than in the case of the State Department
because ECA works much more on a decentralized basis."[9] They might
have added that they had a special relationship with the CIA. But then
that should rapidly have become apparent to members of the PSB.

The State Department proved to be overtly uncooperative. Gordon
Gray, having left his post as president of the University of North Carolina, Chapel Hill, to become the director of the PSB, set up his office in
space lent by the CIA. He had no money, although he was supposed to
be financed out of the budgets of the Defense Department and the CIA.
He put a staff together and found "some buildings" on Jackson Place,
around the corner from Blair House, where his friend Harry S. Truman
was residing while the White House was being refurbished. Gray was
outmaneuvered by State, and later by the CIA. He thought his charter
was "to draw a plan for the Cold War." Not surprisingly he found that
"the State Department felt that this was an invasion of their job" as did
"some other departments." Typical of the treatment Gray had to live
with was his encounter with Paul Nitze, by then head of the State Department's Policy Planning Staff. "I went in to see him about something and
he said 'look, you just forget about policy, that is not your job; we'll
make the policy and then you can put it on your damn radio.'"[10] Nitze
was straightforward; others were more sophisticated in accomplishing
their mission. Although Gray was a close confident of the president and
"could any evening just walk around the corner . . . to talk to Truman,"
the board was not established with enough power to maintain itself. It
had bureaucratic enemies from its inception and was excluded from actually carrying out operations, including psychological operations.

In a discussion of George Frost Kennan's role in endorsing covert
action "as one of the means available to implement containment," John
Lewis Gaddis noted that "propaganda and psychological warfare techniques attracted increasing attention and funding as time went on."[11]
Gaddis added that, "Still, the administration's primary emphasis be-

tween 1947-1949 was much as Kennan said it should be—on the economic instrument as the cheapest and most effective way to achieve containment."[12] That is certainly true, but the "economic instrument" was not outside the realm of covert action and was itself attracting increased attention throughout the Marshall Plan years. Kennan probably had economic warfare in mind as much as propaganda and psychological efforts. The asymmetrical response to the Soviet threat was designed to consider the reality of limited resources in countering Soviet subversion.[13] In the years of the European Recovery Program the economic instrument was perceived to be the strongest suit.

Early on, the board lost any opportunity to engage in the economic sphere. At the first meeting Director Gray encountered NSC subcommittee members Walter Bedell Smith and Robert Lovett, who informed him that the task of the PSB should be to develop a master plan. By the second meeting developments had limited the range of PSB options. PSB guidelines provided that the board act as a go-between for agencies seeking policy guidelines from the NSC. This part of the directive would have cut off the agencies from the president, not a pleasant prospect for the CIA. Smith convinced Gray to agree not to engage in economic warfare, retaining the CIA's options with the NSC and the president. Additionally, since economic warfare was so integral a part of covert political activism, particularly as associated with foreign aid programs, Gray was signing his own death warrant.

It is difficult to tell when Gray realized he was out of the picture. The CIA appeared to cooperate with the PSB by lending a deputy director and a planner. The OPC War Room was regularly used as a briefing station for PSB members. Top OPC field specialist Frank Lindsay was usually present to describe the status of current operations. Additionally, Bedell Smith filled Gray with ideas about succeeding him as director of the CIA. If Gray believed this he might have gone along with things longer than one might have expected. But by the time of his oral testimony he admitted that the PSB was "largely . . . abortive . . . because most of the agencies didn't cooperate."[14] It seems that those most uncooperative were agencies with members on the NSC subcommittee overseeing the PSB.

That is not to say that no attempts at coordination came out of the temporary OPC-PSB collaboration. A panel on political activism in Western Europe was formed, strongly supported by ECA, the CIA, and the Defense Department, but strongly opposed by the State Department. It came to nothing, however, because the PSB members wanted to have each local ambassador approve plans for covert political operations, while the OPC was looking for an avenue to avoid the State Department altogether.[15]

There is some evidence that consideration was given to centralizing paramilitary activity. PSB, through its deputy director, Tracy Barnes, an old OPC hand, participated in forming a committee on covert political activism, which produced a report later incorporated as part of NSC 10/5. Robert Joyce, the OPC liaison with the State Department, assisted in this effort as well.[16]

The OPC-PSB collaboration resulted in coordinated recruiting efforts for a while. Potential recruits were listed according to their affiliation, i.e., ECA coordinator or Harvard Russian Research Program. Their abilities were categorized, such as outstanding in psychological warfare. They were then referred to someone for use—OPC, etc. It was not unusual to find prominent names on these lists. George Gallup assisted the recruitment effort as did Edward R. Murrow. Frank Lindsay contacted Gray about recruiting Barry Farber, stating that Farber appeared "to be a very unusual individual and I hope we can use him. We are starting a security check on him."[17]

By far the most important result of the OPC-PSB interaction was that it allowed an OPC specialist the upper hand in lobbying for covert political activism at a very important time—the first presidential transition since the institutionalized acceptance of the covert method. Since the OPC had created an aura of cooperation with PSB, and since Lindsay was an acknowledged expert in field operations, he assumed the task of providing a detailed analysis of covert political action to be approved and used by both groups. This report was eventually transmitted by Lindsay to the Adlai Stevenson campaign. In this way presidential candidates began to be informed of a policy option that they might not have considered, on which they certainly would have had little information, from those who had the expertise to deliver the option.[18]

The American public was less informed than presidential candidates. Gray wanted to publish a report about the PSB and sent a copy to Arthur Krock of the *New York Times* Washington bureau. By March 1952 Gray was requesting that Krock not publish it, however, and Krock agreed. Gray and Krock probably believed at that time that the State Department had been responsible for the early demise of the PSB. Krock received mail from a friend who condemned the State Department in the PSB matter in language that surely would have pleased Truman. Krock's correspondent labeled State "lame-brained," its inhabitants "highly-placed chowder heads" or "fancypants."

That is not to say that the American public was completely in the dark. While official reports were not forthcoming, the *Saturday Evening Post* carried a story by Donald Robinson in 1948 entitled "They Fight the Cold War under Cover." Robinson certainly had the story right: "Though little is being said about it, CIA is known to be making wide use of the same spectacular techniques which OSS employed to rally resistance movements against Hitler. Both in front of and behind the Iron Curtain, CIA men are assisting democratic forces to resist Red excesses. Anti-communist political leaders, editors, labor-union chiefs, clergymen and others are getting support in their struggles to retain or regain democracy."[19]

The State Department had no great affection for Gordon Gray and the PSB, but there were other reasons why PSB could not last. It seemed unable to carve out operational authority and was talked out of economic warfare. Gray had no position at the CIA until after the demise of the board, and the agency was firmly entrenched in Cold War bureaucracy and did not welcome competitors. Gray was a personal friend of Truman's and could not survive the transition without friends in the bureaucracy. And last, as soon as Eisenhower became president he completely reorganized the Cold War effort after an intensive war games session known as the Solarium Studies. The PSB was a lame duck, was partisan, and by the time of the transition seemed to know it. Members turned weekly meetings into occasions for cocktails and a fine lunch.

B y the time of the Nixon-Humphrey election in 1968, the transition team approach was perfected. Frank Lindsay acted with at least three different teams on topics important to presidential transitions: a study on covert activities, a task force on reorganization of the executive branch, and a team for "dealing with the old administration." Lindsay's reports showed the usual mix of themes— efficiency in government and covert operations.

The team on covert operations centered around a study group at Harvard's Institute of Politics. The final report was sent to Nixon on 1 December 1968. The Harvard group advertised itself to Nixon as "entirely private"; no publicity on its existence or its findings. The memo presented was for the private use of the new administration. A "next to final draft" of the memo was reviewed by John Bross, a senior officer at the CIA, and "the findings have been discussed with him." Appended were separate reports on clandestine operations and biographies of several key operatives prepared for the Johnson administration. Lindsay sent the entire package to H. R. "Bob" Haldeman who replied directly to Lindsay.[20]

The task force also concerned itself with presidential powers it thought Congress should give the president or should be taken by the president. They recommended the formation of an "Office of Special Studies" with "a small staff of career personnel and authority . . . to provide long range planning and in depth studies of problems on which the president . . . needs advance thought." This office "would provide studies which are responsible to the president's needs and . . . are much less subject to the risks of irresponsible action inherent in public commissions." To strengthen the president's hand the team also recommended that the congressional veto be made more difficult—by concurrent resolution or constitutional majority—but doubted it was worth the fight to get this goal accomplished.[21]

What the team believed was that the president needed "freedom from any further encroachment, through added statutory limitations . . . increased flexibility . . . an increased capability for 'quick reaction' responses to urgent problems." While team members worked to establish this flexibility, they urged the president, in the interim, to use a small cabinet or "NSC committee" as "flexible instruments for executing programs which cut across departmental and agency boundaries."[22] They also suggested that the president needed access to increased executive funds, and if he was denied these, the way to get them within the system was to use the NSC and Special Projects Funds without transferring them—"Just give them a second hat."[23]

M y aim in this book has been to explain how the United States institutionalized covert actions. A group of men, determined to intervene in global politics in the Cold War years, actually began their evolution toward covert activism in their college days. There they were well educated in areas necessary to capitalist industry, finance, government, and academia. They were also taught that it was progressive to apply their expertise, in other words, that it was positive, patriotic, useful, their duty, and mutually beneficial.

During their educational years they also had social relations that connected them to their peers and to older men who served as models. Most of their peers shared their views, and often as the years went by they found themselves in the same board rooms, faculty lounges, government agencies, business associations, foundations, and social sets. Together these individuals experienced the scare of the Depression. In particular they heard from their models and learned from their professors that it was a danger to the capitalist system, that Americans deserved and expected a continuously rising standard of living. They, like others, began to believe that bereft of that expectation, Americans would deal harshly with the power structure and those who represented it.

The New Deal provided an electrifying experience for some of the determined interventionists, a time when expertise could be applied to prevent the worst of all possible outcomes, the demise of capitalist democracy in the United States. Soon they graduated to wartime agencies and continued to apply their expertise, this time without the constraints of the New Deal in the form of ideological meanderings about laissez-faire economics, long-range planning, and government regulation.

As they applied their expertise in government, they also went forward in their professional lives in the private sector. Their networks increased as did their ability to "get the job done." They learned how to manipulate power in Washington, whom to call when they needed help, who were the powerful men and who had access to them, and who could come on at the working level and be relied upon to produce.

After the war some returned to the private sector for a while and others remained in government. But so rapidly did the new threat appear that networks were still strong and willingness to act had not faded. That new threat, in the form of covert political subversion of European political institutions, brought them in direct contact with the president who personally took on the challenge of preventing Soviet subversion.

The president and his top policymakers were determined, because of political events in 1948, to take the initiative. As they groped for a method to counter Soviet subversion, they leaned on the experience and expertise of the determined interventionists, who not only had the skills but a belief system that included global activism. At first the steps were tentative, but the covert method was rapidly institutionalized by NSC directive.

During the next three or four critical years determined interventionists swarmed the CIA, helping to establish it as a bureaucratic apparatus for covert political activism. At the same time they explored private foundations in the hope that they might be useful in the new interventionism. When foundation charters proved restrictive, they applied themselves even more diligently to the task of absorbing the CIA, overwhelming the agency's intelligence experts.

Having established a bureaucratic apparatus to carry out covert political activism, the determined interventionists ensured that it would survive. They achieved this by skillful application of their bureaucratic skills, particularly in times of presidential transition. Since presidential candidates did not and could not know the extent and importance of covert operations, they provided information, through proper channels, to inform and convince potential chief executives. In more common language, they lobbied, as do other special interests. Alongside farm groups, fishing rights groups, orthodox defense interests, and probably other intelligence groups, the covert political activists of the CIA angled for the opportunity to make their voice heard.

Because the determined interventionists could point to many examples of Soviet influence around the world, there were few who doubted the need for the expertise they had to offer. Since the 1960s—a time when "Kennedy got himself killed," Vietnam prompted reexamination of American foreign policy, and the Church Committee revealed a great deal about covert operations in the Cold War—Americans have begun to ask a great many questions.[24] Those questions have prompted congressional intrusion in the field of foreign policy, creating occasional conflict between the executive and legislative branches. Loch Johnson commented that "the Chief result of the Church Committee . . . has been to draw Congress more deeply into the making of intelligence policy through the detailed review of budgets, the offering of policy suggestions . . . and even votes on sensitive operations."[25] Johnson added that while there have been only "two rare secret sessions" in which "Congress voted to prohibit covert operations, in Angola in 1976 and Nicaragua in 1982," and that although "votes on covert actions have been only a show of 'advice', they sometimes represent powerful political signals about what is permissible from the legislative view-point and have given the executive branch pause."[26] As the Iran-Contra hearings indicated, however, Ronald Reagan was immune to the signals.[27] In fact Loch Johnson has suggested that Reagan's director of Central Intelligence, William J. Casey, may have used "elements of the regular NSC staff . . . as a kind of surrogate CIA," in order to avoid what Johnson has termed the "legal restrictions placed upon the intelligence agencies."[28]

We might wonder why there are still covert operations. Clearly someone is still convinced that capability is needed. That someone has to be the president. The NSC directive establishing the OPC vested the power to regulate covert operations in the president, except in times of war when that duty falls to the Joint Chiefs of Staff. Because the United States has had no declared wars since 1948, covert operations have remained the province of the executive. No president has been willing to re-linquish covert political activism as a complement to orthodox foreign policy procedures. We can only conclude that they have all agreed with the determined interventionists.

APPENDIX

A ll that you have read began at a tailgate picnic in a parking lot at Lehigh University Chapel during an intermission in Bach's Mass in B Minor. There is a Bach choir in Bethlehem, Pennsylvania, funded by subscription. It performs twice a year, on the second and third weekends of May. The routine has been the same for about one hundred years—on Friday afternoon and evening there are cantatas, on Saturday, the Mass in B Minor. The only deviation, and that about every eight years, is that the Friday cantatas may be replaced by the St. John or the St. Matthew Passion. For years I attended on both weekends.

There is a good deal of ritual at the Bach Festival. Attendance is multi-generational, people in their seventies, their kids, and as time goes on, their grandchildren. They come from all over the country, the same people, year after year. I have been going with the same crowd for years.

Part of the ritual at the Bach Festival is the intermission tailgate picnic—the planning, the preparation, the overproduction, who is to eat whose food, and how it is all to be eaten before the intermission ends. The ritual begins with all cars assembling at the parking lot slightly uphill from the chapel, before the Mass begins. At the intermission everyone dashes for the parking lot, trunks fly open, gourmet snacks emerge—homemade bread, country pâtés, cheeses, and most importantly Moose Juice, a sly concoction of rum, pineapple, and grapefruit juices. All of this has nothing whatsoever to do with covert operations except that Richard M. Bissell, Jr., is part of the crowd at the tailgate picnics.

No one has ever made much of a fuss over Dick Bissell. But it was made clear, early on, that there were "certain topics" you just did not broach with him. Nevertheless on 23 May 1983, fortified by Moose Juice and spinning off considerable energy generated by a required readings course in the Rutgers University graduate history program, I approached

Dick Bissell and asserted: "I want to learn to think like a national security person."

The targeted Bissell adeptly covered his amusement. I babbled about George Kennan, Daniel Yergin's theory of the National Security State, anything to sound worthy of his time. We were rapidly joined by two of his former Yale schoolmates, Edmund G. (Ted) Thomas and Andrews Wanning. The encounter between the five-foot-two, middle-aged lady graduate student and the six-foot-three or so retired CIA deputy director of plans promised some amusement, not that I could see it at the time, standing there, hands on my hips, fighting. But finally, the magic words, "Well, you'd better come see me in Farmington."

Of course the interview process had already started. Over that weekend, as with every other occasion when we have been together, we talked about the "interesting topic" of national security. On the first weekend we explored possible areas of future discussion. Bissell spent considerable time ruminating on presidential transitions and the particular problem of maintaining a cohesive national security policy through changing administrations. I went home to read Lauren Henry, Hammond and Snyder, and everything I could find on the CIA, Harry Truman, and Dwight Eisenhower. My basement office in Van Dyke Hall acquired a huge peg board that rapidly gathered tiny sheets of paper representing incidents and personnel in the early Cold War chronology. Fellow graduate students John Rossi and Dave Schmitz dumped "relevant" books on my desk and dragged me to Lloyd Gardner, who assured me that this was a prospect worth following. With prescience I did not recognize at the time, my advisor David Oshinsky quipped that I would be "flying off the seat of my pants on this one."

In July 1983 I went to Farmington for my first interview. A man who claims he would be just as glad if nothing had ever changed, except perhaps the addition of some modern conveniences such as telephones, Bissell keeps an interesting office. The small suite is located in an enormous wood frame and glass structure that resembles in some odd way an old sailing ship. The building allows restaurants, retail establishments, and professional offices to cohabit, a veritable symbol of modernity.

It was clear from the first interview that Dick Bissell was a pragmatist, a man who liked to find out how things work by locating the realities of power. Describing himself as an America Firster before the Second World War, he recounted his "conversion to anti-isolationism" and his subsequent wartime work in Washington. Comparing the wartime years with his later experience as deputy administrator of the ECA, he described the earlier years as a time when they were all "largely unreconstructed." He meant that it took years for the new men in Washington to learn where to exert pressure to get things done. Clearly he believed this formative experience gave him skills he would use later.

While the majority of the first interview was given to various angles on the transition story, particularly the Truman to Eisenhower transition and its effect on the NSC, there was some mention of intelligence. Even then it was a pragmatic approach, how it worked at the station level, where the fault lines were in the bureaucracy, and a brief mention of something called psy-warriors. He also talked a lot about the Marshall Plan and what he thought its aims were.

I still didn't know where I was going but went home and worked more on my Cold War chronology and read a lot of George Kennan and material on the Marshall Plan. I mailed Bissell a copy of my chronology and asked some questions about Kennan and about the concept of massive retaliation—had there been other options? In the meantime in my reading I had come across occasional brief statements, sometimes only one line, about something called the Office of Policy Coordination. I made a date to see Bissell in September.

This time we talked more about Kennan, Germany, massive retaliation, and the fear of the Soviets in the late forties. We also began to talk about the OPC. I knew we were zeroing in on the origins of covert operations. This time when I went home I made up, literally, an outline of what I thought the OPC looked like organizationally. The outline suggested the organization as a complement to Marshall Plan activity in Europe. I mailed it off to Bissell.

My next interview was in November. This time I repeat his exact words. He said, "You certainly have been reading a lot since last time." I said, "Yes, and I've also been thinking a lot." He asked where I got this, meaning the outline. I said from thinking about what he had told me.

There was a pause and then he said, "A lot of what you say in here rings true." He then went on to indicate where he thought my emphasis was off. For instance, he said it was wrong to call the OPC a "covert arm" of the Marshall Plan. He said this was a misrepresentation because Paul Hoffman was a pacifist and would turn in his grave. He added that Hoffman had always thought of economic health first and did not want the Marshall Plan involved with rearmament, and that he probably didn't know much about OPC. Subsequent interviews largely followed this pattern; I put together pieces of the story, he confirmed them or suggested where he thought the emphasis was off.

The November interview marked a substantial change. From that point on we talked about the OPC. It was in November 1983 that he confirmed the breadth of the organization and described the funding mechanism of which he was a part. He also described in some detail, and with considerable delight, the bureaucratic rivalry. I knew at this point that I wanted to explain not only the origins of this unique organization, but also its fight to gain a position in the bureaucracy. Later there would be other questions.

The second most important event of the November interview was that he directed me to John A. Bross of McLean, Virginia, and Franklin A. Lindsay, then of Lincoln, Massachusetts. I contacted Bross by mail. Nothing happened. After about three weeks I received a letter from Bross saying that since my letter had arrived, he had had a visit from Dick and Anne Bissell. Dick had described my project in more depth, and as a result of that conversation, he would be interested in seeing me. This time I called.

On 13 December 1983, I went to Washington to see John Bross. While I had called him at the CIA where he was employed, the interview took place at his home in McLean, Virginia. There were three general areas of discussion that day: Bross's personal history, OPC, and possible alternatives to the CIA.

Bross, a former Wall Street attorney, was an OSS officer stationed in London during the war. Certain experiences in the immediate postwar period had made him strongly suspicious of the Soviets and sent him into a long and influential career in the CIA. He spoke with some passion about having the OPC story done in context. Indicating that he had spent a good deal of time with other authors, he noted his chagrin at having each one turn out just another tale of the boys and their dirty tricks.

His complaint with my thesis at this time was that he felt the OPC-Marshall Plan connection was not planned, that it had evolved. He also talked about a book by John Loftus, entitled *The Belarus Secret,* which claimed that the OPC was used to bring large numbers of former Nazis to the United States. Bross thought that Nazis had been brought to the United States but not in the numbers Loftus claimed and not under the CIA 100 Persons Act, which allows the agency to bring in one hundred people a year without much scrutiny. He claimed that Loftus had lied about the files he saw, and later in a letter to me he stated that no one he had talked to thought Loftus was telling the truth.

In answer to my questions about the applicability of OPC methods today he noted that Western European governments exerted influence through quasi-private organizations funded by the government. He mentioned specifically the British and West German organizations and noted that similar proposals had been defeated here after the scandals revealing CIA funding of student organizations in the 1960s. He favored the quasi-private organization, economically and politically focused, and expressed some doubt about the applicability of OPC methods in areas like Latin America where there was no heritage of democracy to be restored, as had been the case in postwar Europe.

Bross indicated that he would be willing to see me through this project and in fact read successive drafts of seminar papers sending lengthy comments on each, clarifying his views, arguing with my interpretations, and suggesting other points. Since the interview in 1983, however, my communication with him has been by telephone and mail.

Bross made several suggestions at the close of the December 1983 interview. First that I read Anne Karalekas's brief history of the OPC in the Senate Report on Intelligence. He thought I should see CIA General Counsel Lawrence Houston and former operative Kermit Roosevelt. He also strongly recommended that I see Cord Meyer, whom Dick Bissell called the "creative genius" behind covert operations. I telephoned all three. Houston and Roosevelt agreed to see me; Meyer would not.

On 20 and 21 March 1984, I interviewed Houston and Roosevelt at their homes in Georgetown. My discussions with Houston dealt almost entirely with the legal aspects of establishing the OPC. My notes consistently indicate that Houston's concern was control, which he claimed "got dicey." But he insisted that the NSC was always in charge and had to approve anything with a budget over $25,000. Yet he spoke enthusiastically about the entrepreneurial drive of OPC personnel in designing projects that funded themselves while aiding the national security effort. He also talked at some length about Walter Bedell Smith's successful integration of the OPC into the CIA, again stressing the control theme.

Houston also thought I should see Cord Meyer as well as Walter Pforzheimer, the CIA archivist and legislative liaison during the time when the agency was being established. He also agreed to see the project through and critiqued, often with acerbity, annual drafts of seminar papers. In general his criticism goes to my assertion that reliance on individuals with past experience to get something done in a hurry led to a blurring of the line between policymaker and operative in the flurry of activity surrounding the events of 1948. My contact with him has been entirely by mail since the interview.

Roosevelt was not physically well when I saw him. While he was mentally keen, he was obviously in some physical discomfort and under his wife's careful scrutiny. His driver, who took me to a taxi stand after the interview, informed me that no one ever stayed more than twenty minutes with Roosevelt. Nevertheless, he had talked for almost two hours.

Unlike Houston, Roosevelt did not emphasize control; rather he spoke of inconsistency of personnel, blind spots in personnel selection, the ease of acquiring funding in the field, the erosion of what he called Achesonian elitism, and the impossibility of conducting covert operations in a media age. Roosevelt clearly believed the key was expert field operatives.

Obviously I had a contradiction. Houston, a desk man, insisted that there was control through various "murder" boards—committees and groups with the power to supervise and abort covert actions. Roosevelt, a field man, insisted that the power resided in the field and emphasized the importance of having the right man do the job. It seemed obvious that in addition to my questions regarding the origins of the organization and its fight to establish itself in the bureaucracy, I would have to locate the power, whether in Washington or in the field, or if both, show how dual responsibility worked.

Roosevelt also agreed to continue with the project and read yearly seminar drafts, usually commenting briefly to correct small points, and urge me on. I have not seen him since the 1984 interview.

The fifth person interviewed was Franklin A. Lindsay, head of paramilitary operations for the OPC. Lindsay was hard to get to. After a series of phone calls and aborted meetings, I was finally able to meet with him at the Committee for Economic Development in Manhattan, an organization Michael Hogan has described as peopled with progressive business leaders, with an agenda combining Keynesian economics with those of the associative state.[1] Lindsay had a busy schedule as evidenced by constant phone calls asking him to switch his calendar, be in Washington at this moment, somewhere else later.

An enormous man, Lindsay conducted most of the interview seated in a chair precisely placed so that when tipped back it would hit the wall just short of the point where it would fall backward altogether. He punctuated the interview in this manner, noting with considerable delight my attention to this detail.

Lindsay did not comment on drafts of my paper until the fall of 1986. At that time I interviewed him in Cambridge, Massachusetts. He argued with some points and emphases and discussed further his view of Tito. He recommended that I see Irving Brown of the AFL-CIO as a good source on the early Cold War effort in France. Attempts to catch up with Brown proved futile.

I have written this appendix to inform the reader of the circumstances and general content of the interviews. Recently John Lewis Gaddis wrote that "we need to begin systematically to interview . . . retired intelligence officials . . . and to cross check what they say."[2] Gaddis, calling for a balance between the study of individuals and their institutions, said that "it may well be that in this field, as in most others, what particular individuals do to, within, and apart from bureaucracies is generally more important than the structure of the bureaucracies themselves."[3] Accordingly, I have used the interviews as a roadmap to the facts and a guide to the nuances. The facts I have substantiated as much as possible through archival research. The nuances I could only get from the activists themselves. I owe them all a great debt for the time they spent helping me come to an understanding of the issues and ideas surrounding the formation of America's first institutionalized covert capability.

NOTES

ABBREVIATIONS

FFA   Ford Foundation Archives
FRC   Federal Records Center
HIW   Hoover Institute on War, Revolution and Peace
HSTLI   Harry S. Truman Library Institute
SGMML   Seeley G. Mudd Manuscript Library

CHAPTER ONE. INTRODUCTION

1. Gaddis Smith, *Morality, Reason and Power* (New York: Hill and Wang, 1986), p. 16. Smith was referring to what he calls the ghost of Woodrow Wilson, his World War I determination to see that "men everywhere . . . choose their way of life" (p. 15). But in applying it to Jimmy Carter's efforts on human rights, he rightly connects it to the earlier, broader view, including self-determination.

2. Harry Howe Ransom, *Central Intelligence and National Security* (Cambridge, Mass.: Harvard University Press, 1958), p. 201.

3. Ibid., p. 203.

4. Ibid., p. 84.

5. Ibid., p. 204.

6. Ibid., p. 203.

7. Peter Wyden, *Bay of Pigs: The Untold Story* (London: Jonathan Cape, 1979), Richard H. Immerman, *The CIA in Guatemala: The Foreign Policy of Intervention* (Austin: University of Texas Press, 1982); Stephen Schlesinger and Stephen Kinzer, *Bitter Fruit: The Untold Story of the American Coup in Guatemala* (New York: Doubleday, 1982).

8. Frank Snepp, *Decent Interval: An Insider's Account of Saigon's Indecent End Told by the CIA's Chief Strategy Analyst in Vietnam* (New York: Random House, 1977).

9. Arturo Cruz, Jr., *Memoirs of a Counterrevolutionary* (New York: Doubleday, 1989).

10. Morton H. Halperin et al., *The Lawless State: The Crimes of the U.S. Intelligence Agencies* (New York: Penguin Books, 1976); Harry Rositzke,

The KGB: The Eyes of Russia (New York: Reader's Digest Press, 1981), p. 276; Jonathan Kwitny, *The Crimes of Patriots: A True Tale of Dope, Dirty Money, and the CIA* (New York: W.W. Norton, 1987).

11. John Prados, *President's Secret Wars: CIA and Pentagon Covert Operations since World War II* (New York: William Morrow, 1986), p. 10.

12. Ibid.

CHAPTER TWO. A GROUNDING
IN AMERICAN INTERVENTIONISM

1. Interview, Franklin A. Lindsay, 9 Apr. 1984.

2. Perry Miller, *Errand into the Wilderness* (Cambridge, Mass.: Belknap Press, 1956), p. 1–15.

3. Robert H. Ferrell, *American Diplomacy: A History* (New York: W.W. Norton, 1959), p. 97.

4. Ibid., p. 233.

5. Ibid., p. 200.

6. Ibid., pp. 343–4.

7. Ibid.

8. Ernest May, *From Imperialism to Isolationism, 1898–1919* (New York: Macmillan, 1964), p. 18.

9. Howard Beale, *Theodore Roosevelt and the Rise of America to World Power* (Baltimore: Johns Hopkins University Press, 1956), p. 81.

10. Ferrell, *American Diplomacy*, p. 404.

11. Daniel M. Smith, *The American Diplomatic Experience* (Boston: Houghton Mifflin, 1972), p. 242. Roosevelt had help on the "dago" question. Robert Ferrell reports that one of his cabinet members wrote a limerick entitled "Lines for the Inspiration of the State Department in dealing with Dago Nations":

> There was a young lady named Tucker,
> Who went up to her mother and struck her.
> Her mother said "Damn! Do you know who I am?
> You act like you was a mucker!"

See Ferrell, *American Diplomacy*, p. 401. So much for the notion of uplifting, civilizing, and christianizing "our little brown brothers."

12. *The Shaping of American Diplomacy*, ed. William A. Williams (Chicago: Rand McNally, 1956), p. 494.

13. Ibid., p. 495.

14. John Morton Blum, *The Republican Roosevelt* (Cambridge, Mass.: Harvard University Press, 1965), p. 141.

15. Arthur S. Link and Richard L. McCormick, *Progressivism* (Arlington Heights: Harlan Davidson, 1983).

16. John W. Chambers III, *The Tyranny of Change* (New York: St. Martin's Press, 1980), Chapter 6.

17. Arthur S. Link, *Wilson: The New Freedom* (Princeton, N.J.: Princeton University Press, 1956), p. 478.

18. Albert C. Ganley, *The Progressive Movement, Traditional Reform* (New York: Macmillan, 1964), p. 28.

19. George E. Mowry, *The Era of Theodore Roosevelt and the Birth of Modern America* (New York: Harper, 1958), p. 88.

20. Papers of Allen Welsh Dulles, Box 21, letter from Walter Pforzheimer, 1 Jan. 1965, Seeley G. Mudd Manuscript Library (SGMML), Princeton University, Princeton, N.J.

21. Thomas F. Troy, *Donovan and the CIA: A History of the Establishment of the Central Intelligence Agency* (Washington, D.C.: Central Intelligence Agency, Center for the Study of Intelligence, 1981), pp. 3-5.

22. Ibid., p. 6.

23. Ibid.

24. Ibid., p. 7.

25. Leonard Moseley, *Dulles: A Biography of Eleanor, Allen, and John Foster Dulles and Their Family Network* (New York: Dial Press, 1978), p. 61. And see Papers of Charles Seymour, Sterling Library, Yale University.

26. Walter Isaacson and Evan Thomas, *The Wise Men* (New York: Simon & Schuster, 1986), pp. 42, 43.

27. Daniel Yergin, *Shattered Peace: The Origins of the Cold War and the National Security State* (Boston: Houghton Mifflin, 1977), p. 27.

28. Joan Hoff Wilson, *American Business and Foreign Policy 1920-1933* (Boston: Beacon Press, 1971), p. 2.

29. Ibid., p. 3.

30. Ibid, p. 6.

31. Ibid.

32. Ibid., pp. 7, 9.

33. Ibid., p. 3.

34. Gordon S. Wood, *The Creation of the American Republic, 1776-1787* (New York: Norton, 1969), p. 68.

35. Lewis V. Thomas and Richard N. Frye, *The United States and Turkey and Iran* (Cambridge, Mass.: Harvard University Press, 1951), pp. 247-49.

36. Julian Bharier, *Economic Development in Iran, 1900-1970* (New York: Oxford University Press, 1971), p. 63.

37. Ibid.

38. Ibid.

39. George B. Baldwin, *Planning and Development in Iran* (Baltimore: Johns Hopkins University Press, 1967), p. 10; and Thomas and Frye, *United States and Turkey and Iran*, p. 248. See also Arthur C. Millspaugh, *Americans in Persia*

(Washington, D.C.: Brookings, 1946). Millspaugh, like the determined interventionists, was a devotee of efficiency in government. Two of his books on the subject link efficiency and democracy. They are *Democracy, Efficiency, and Stability,* (Washington, D.C.: Brookings, 1942), and *Toward Efficient Democracy* (Washington, D.C.: Brookings,1949). See also Emily Rosenberg, *Spreading the American Dream: American Economic and Cultural Expansion, 1890–1945* (New York: Hill and Wang, 1982), pp. 119, 129, 155–56.

40. Michael J. Hogan, *The Marshall Plan: America, Britain and the Reconstruction of Western Europe, 1947–52* (Cambridge, England: Cambridge University Press, 1987), p. 13. Hogan mentions Harriman and Paul Hoffman as examples of the "spokesmen."

41. John Lewis Gaddis, "The Corporatist Synthesis: A Skeptical View," *Diplomatic History* 10, 4 (Fall 1986):361.

42. Interview, Richard M. Bissell, Jr., 12 Jan. 1987, at Farmington, Conn.

43. Yale University Catalogues, 1927–33; Papers of James R. Angell, president of Yale, Box 91, Folder 921, Sterling Library, Yale University.

44. Wilson, p. 240.

45. Hogan, p. 3.

46. Council on Foreign Relations (CFR), Records of Meetings, Vol. 22, "Overseas Development: The Role of American Firms and Foundations," 16 May 1956, speaker: J. G. Harrar, director of Latin American Agricultural Programs, Rockefeller Foundation, and "Overseas Operations of IBEC" (International Basic Economy Corporation), 5 Mar. 1956, speaker: Robert Fulton. IBEC was largely a business investment and management group.

47. Ford Foundation, interview with John McCloy, 26 June 1972, p. 28; CFR, Records of Meetings, Vol. 22, "Overseas Development: The Role of American Firms and Foundations," "Overseas Operations of IBEC"; John P. Quirk, *CIA: A Photographic History* (Guilford, Conn.: Foreign Intelligence Press, 1986), p. 62.

48. Bissell interview, 8 July 1983.

49. Walter Isaacson and Evan Thomas, *The Wise Men* (New York: Simon & Schuster, 1986), p. 484.

50. Ibid.

51. Bradley F. Smith, *The Shadow Warriors: OSS and the Origins of the CIA* (New York: Basic Books, 1983), p. xiii.

52. Ibid., p. 11.

53. Ibid., p. 39.

54. Supplementary Detailed Staff Reports on Foreign and Military Intelligence, Box IV, Final Report of the Select Committee to Study Governmental Operations with Respect to Intelligence Activities, United States Senate, 1976, pp. 4, 5. And see Smith, *Shadow Warriors*, chapters 3 and 4.

55. Interview, Kermit Roosevelt, 21 Mar. 1984.

56. Ibid.

57. Bissell interview, 8 July 1983.

58. Isaacson and Thomas, *Wise Men*, p. 407–8. The authors are speaking of their subjects, the older determined interventionists, Lovett, McCloy, Harriman, Bohlen, Kennan, and Acheson. But the description also fits the later generation.

CHAPTER THREE. UNCOORDINATED INTERVENTION

1. Thomas G. Paterson, *On Every Front: The Making of the Cold War* (New York: W.W. Norton, 1979), pp. 1–3.

2. Ibid., p. 2, from Charles M. W. Moran, *Churchill: Taken from the Diaries of Lord Moran* (Boston: Houghton Mifflin, 1966), p. 289.

3. Ibid., p. 3.

4. "Came to believe" is a phrase often used by Dick Bissell. In usage it seemed to mean more than changing one's opinion, but rather indicated changing a long-standing, strong conviction and replacing it with an equally strong conviction. In usage there was also an implication that this process took time and was the result of persuasion by one's peers.

5. Thomas K. Finletter, *Can Representative Government Do the Job?* (New York: Reynal & Hitchcock, 1945), pp. 9, 19, 20.

6. Ibid.

7. While Meyer's agenda in 1945, 1946, and 1947 may have been as set forth in this chapter, it is clear from his own writing that by 1948 he was more concerned with "Centralized and autocratic control of the economy . . . so long as the nation must be continuously prepared to resist an atomic attack." Because of this threat Meyer believed that "the right to strike is not likely to survive the urgency of such defense plans. Either the labor unions will voluntarily restrict their strike actions or they will be denied that basic freedom in the name of preparedness." Concern about subversion doubtless prompted him to reflect that "citizens of the United States will have to accustom themselves to the ubiquitous presence of the powerful secret police needed for protection against sabotage and espionage." Cord Meyer, Jr., *Peace or Anarchy* (Boston: Little, Brown, 1948), pp. 55, 56.

8. Bissell interview, 10 Nov. 1986; Francis H. Heller, ed., *The Truman White House: The Administration of the President, 1945–53*, (Lawrence: University Press of Kansas, 1980), p. 66.

9. Bissell interview, 10 Nov. 1986. This penchant for order may have lead Bissell and a group at ECA known as the "Planning Group" to argue, unsuccessfully, for "economic integration" of Europe into one of two "economic units." The planning group, certainly prescient of the EEC, included Theodore Geiger, Harold B. and Harlan Cleveland, and John Hully. See Alan S. Milward, *The Reconstruction of Western Europe, 1945–51* (Berkeley: University of California Press, 1984), at pp. 283–84. Allen Welsh Dulles probably sympathized with the planning group. In an unpublished book on the Marshall Plan written in 1948, Dulles stated that "the principle of self-determination . . . has dangerous impli-

cations in the economic field." Dulles papers, Box 205. Dulles argued in this manuscript that the redrawing of the European map after the First World War, with such strong emphasis on nationalism, may have done a disservice to the economic health of the continent.

10. Milward, *Reconstruction of Western Europe*, p. 2.

11. Alonzo L. Hamby, *Beyond the New Deal: Harry S. Truman and American Liberalism* (New York: Columbia University Press, 1973), pp. 57, 62.

12. Ibid., p. 62.

13. Heller, *Truman White House*, p. 66.

14. Ibid. The director was John Steelman.

15. Ibid., p. 96.

16. Bissell interview, 10 Nov. 1986. But see Harry S. Truman Library Institute (HSTLI), Independence, Mo., oral history of Richard M. Bissell, Jr., interview, 9 July 1971, by Theodore A. Wilson and Richard D. McKinzie, pp. 16–18, where Bissell said he left OWMR because they were not interested in converting the office into a semipermanent part of the White House staff and weren't particularly interested in long range policy issues. He also indicated disagreements with Snyder who apparently thought Bissell was too activist.

17. Bissell interview, 10 Nov. 1986. Bissell believed that Murray had a "card-carrying" Communist on his executive board.

18. Donald R. McCoy, *The Presidency of Harry S. Truman* (Lawrence: University Press of Kansas, 1984), pp. 50, 57, 291–92.

19. Ibid.

20. Ibid.

21. Ibid.

22. Bissell was also working for the Department of Commerce at this time. It is instructive to see his files, which clearly demonstrate the interaction of War Reconversion, Commerce, major academic institutions, and the major industries. The cooperative effort developed during World War II assisted their plans for the reconversion process.

23. Richard M. Bissell, Jr., personal files, Marshall Plan, copy of memo from Murray to Truman, 14 Nov. 1947.

24. In fact, a cynic might conclude that the whole OPC operation was some sort of re-creation of a Marxist society, with the laborers of Europe and the United States as the proletariat and the OPC as the vanguard.

25. Interviews.

26. The council declined to do so.

27. CFR, Records of Groups, Vols. 30, 31, "Aid to Europe," Part I and II, 1948–51. The group included Allen Dulles, David Lilienthal, Dwight Eisenhower, McGeorge Bundy, Jim Carey, Will Clayton, George Kennan, Richard M. Bissell, Franklin A. Lindsay. Meeting 7 Mar. 1949.

28. John Ranelagh, *The Agency: The Rise and Decline of the CIA* (New York: Simon & Schuster, 1986), p. 123–24, 131; Joseph Jones, *The Fifteen Weeks: February 21–June 5, 1947* (New York: Harcourt, Brace & World, 1955).

29. See Foreign Relations of the United States, 1948, Vol. IV, p. 1, et. seq., for cables on the Greek crisis and Griswold's part in it.

30. Bissell claims that the Marshall Plan was never "cut in" in OPC activities, meaning they never knew. Please refer to later chapters for evidence to the contrary.

31. See Michael Wala, "Selling the Marshall Plan at Home: The Committee for the Marshall Plan to Aid European Recovery," *Diplomatic History*, 10, 3 (Summer 1986):247–65.

32. Dulles Papers, Box 36, "What the Marshall Plan Means to the American Exporter," speech given before the Export Managers Club of New York City, 6 Jan. 1948.

33. *Report of the Thirty-Fifth National Foreign Trade Convention*, New York, 8, 9, 10 Nov. 1948, address of Paul G. Hoffman, administrator for the ECA, pp. 336, 337.

34. Seymour Papers, Box 102, File 2 on the Marshall Plan, letters dated 15 Mar. 1948 and 13 Mar. 1948. See also Box 102, National Citizens Committee for the Marshall Plan.

35. Bissell interview, 9 July 1986; Papers of Franklin A. Lindsay, Hoover Institute on War, Revolution and Peace (HIW), Stanford University, Stanford, Calif., files on American consultants in Paris at beginning of ECA, Box 1.

36. President's Committee on Foreign Aid, Boxes 11, 20, HSTLI. Also Bissell's personal files, letter to Fred Roe of Stein, Roe and Farnham, Chicago, on the membership of the committee, 10 Mar. 1948.

37. Ford Foundation Archives (FFA), New York City, oral histories, Milton Katz, p. 6.

38. Ibid., p. 8.

39. Ibid., pp. 12–14.

40. Ibid.

41. RG 59, National Archives, Diplomatic Branch, Minutes of the PPS meetings, 15 June 1948. John McCloy, who had experience with both the Ford and Rockefeller foundations, thought the Rockefeller people were more effective, less ivory tower, more able to deal with emergencies in the field, or as he said, "off campus." Oral history, John McCloy, p. 28, FFA.

42. Oral history, John McCloy, p. 31, FFA. Eberstadt's report is the report on intelligence for the Hoover Commission, officially known as the U.S. Committee for the Organization of the Executive Branch.

43. Oral history, W. H. Ferry, p. 33, taken by Ronald Crele and Charles Morrissey, FFA. This interview was taken in 1972, at which time Ferry was still seething. The interview fairly bristles with the hate Ferry felt toward Bissell.

44. Oral history, Edwin H. Land, p. 2, FFA.

45. Papers of the Office of the President H. Rowan Gaither, Area One—Establishment of Peace—CIA, Box 1, Group 21, Series 1, Folder 1, handwritten notes of a meeting, FFA.

46. Ibid.

47. Ibid.

48. Gaither Papers, Folder 3, Group 21, Box 1, Series 1. I have paraphrased this request.

49. Ibid., Folder 4.

50. Ibid.

51. Ibid., Program 1, The Establishment of Peace—CIA, Folder 4. I am assuming the note is from Dyke Brown.

52. Ibid. At the National Archives, Diplomatic Branch, there are entry cards regarding this project. When I called for the files I received a note that they had been destroyed at the State Department before being sent to the archives.

Ron Grele of the Columbia University Oral History Project, who took the Ford oral histories, informed me that in his recollection the Joseph McDaniels oral history at the FFA is key to this conflict. Unfortunately it is closed until well into the next century. Ford Archivist Anne Newhall informed me that many Ford papers are closed for the long term to protect the lives of those who gave testimony or Third World political figures who are mentioned in the files.

There was a suggestion made by John McCloy that the entire project be transferred out of Ford Foundation over to the CFR, but I was unable to find anything on it at the council.

53. Gaither Papers, Area Three, Group 21, Box 4, Series 3, Folder 44. Bissell was working for Harvard's Project Troy when Ford Foundation hired him.

54. Ibid.

55. Records of the Psychological Strategy Board (PSB), Box 4, 080 Ford Foundation, HSTLI.

56. Ibid., memo written by Arthur Cox of the Office of Coordination.

57. Dulles papers, Box 117, letter from Harry S. Truman to Dulles, 6 Nov. 1963.

58. Senate Report on Intelligence, Vol. IV, pp. 33–38.

CHAPTER FOUR. COORDINATED INTERVENTION

1. Rhodri Jeffreys-Jones, *The CIA and American Democracy* (New Haven, Conn.: Yale University Press, 1989), p. 30.

2. Papers of Harry S. Truman, Post-Presidential Files, Box 4, in a letter from Truman to William B. Arthur of *Look Magazine*, 10 June 1964, HSTLI.

3. Truman Papers, President's Secretary's Files, NSC meetings, Box 203, 7th meeting, NSC, 11 Mar. 1948, HSTLI.

4. PSB, File 1290D, letter from Truman to Gordon Gray, 31 May 1951, HSTLI.

5. Dulles Papers, Box 24, Box 33, reports from George K. Bowden to Everett Dirksen, 10 Aug. 1948.

6. Found in Daniel M. Smith, *The American Diplomatic Experience* (Boston: Houghton Mifflin, 1972), p. 403.

7. Bissell interview, 9 July 1986.

8. Jones, *The Fifteen Weeks*, pp. 34–35. Alan S. Milward, in *Reconstruction of Western Europe*, has argued that the postwar European boom precipitated a dollar-sterling convertibility crisis that precipitated Marshall Plan aid.

9. I am paraphrasing Bissell.

10. Bissell interviews, 8 July 1983, 9 July 1986. The committee included Owen D. Young, retired board of directors member of General Electric, Robert Sproul, Chester Davis, Paul Hoffman, E. Masson, Robert LaFollette, Calvin Hoover, Jim Carey of the CIO, and George Meaney. Meaney attended only one or two meetings. Carey attended regularly, according to Bissell.

11. Interview, Franklin A. Lindsay, 20 Sept. 1986. In the Lindsay Papers, State Department memos indicate that Lindsay was accompanied to Florina by Richard M. Nixon, James F. Richards, Arthur Parsons of the American Consulate at Salonika, correspondents from the *New York Times*, the *Philadelphia Bulletin*, and the *Chicago Tribune*, and First Secretary Horace Smith from the American Embassy at Athens. The trip took place 24 Sept. 1947; its purpose was "to investigate the Refugee and Guerilla Problem on the Spot." Memo dated 24 Oct. 1947. Initially Lindsay was to be accompanied by Congressmen Thomas Jenkins and George Mahon, but they were sent instead to Kilkis.

12. Dulles Papers, Box 32, Brown Alumni, Commencement 16 June 1947.

13. Bissell interview, 15 Sept. 1983.

14. Public Law 472, Foreign Assistance Act of 1948, p. 1356, Point E.

15. Dulles Papers, Box 289, copy of Final Report on Foreign Aid, House Select Committee on Foreign Aid, May 1948, HR 296, Dulles and Lindsay consultants.

16. Among the regular correspondents were Eric Warburg and Wolf von Eckhardt, on Germany, Dulles Papers, Box 32; Herman Phleger, Box 31; Robert Murphy, Box 31; from Paris, Raymond A. Schuhl, Box 32; from Italy, Alfredo Pizzoni, Box 36. It is also clear that Dulles had mixed feelings about reintegration into everyday life after the thrill of the OSS days. See Box 22, Royall Tyler; Box 22, Rino de Nobili; and Box 26, 630 Group (Veterans of the OSS).

17. Dulles Papers, Box 21, file on William J. Donovan. Donovan is an important example of those whose Cold War ideology stemmed from the Russian Revolution and its ideological implications rather than from post–World War II political concerns. On this theme see David M. Oshinsky, *A Conspiracy So Immense* (New York: Free Press, 1983), Chapter Six, "The Red Bogey in America, 1917–1950."

18. Dulles Papers, Box 25, Foreign Policy Association.

19. Ibid., Box 24. I have paraphrased his speech.

20. Ibid., Box 32, notebook.

21. He also proposed determined interventionists such as Admiral Thomas C. Kinkaid, Gerald M. Mayer, McGeorge Bundy, Robert Bowie. Bissell and Lindsay already were members. From Dulles Papers, Box 24, file on CFR. See also Box 34, letter from Dulles to Knight Woolley of Brown Bros. Harriman on how to get into the council.

22. Lindsay interview, 9 Apr. 1984. The Czechs managed to coexist with East and West even though tied to the Soviets by treaty. By 1947, even though the Communist party held 38 percent of the vote after the 1946 elections, Czechoslovakia was pulling away from the Soviets. Walter LaFeber, *America, Russia, and the Cold War, 1945–75*, 3rd ed. (New York: Knopf, 1967), p. 73. See the "popular" version of the Long Telegram "The Sources of Soviet Conduct," *Foreign Affairs* (July 1947), pp. 566–82, signed Mr. X. James Forrestal, secretary of defense, was particularly impressed and had about one thousand copies distributed in the capital. Kennan's view was not new, however. It found an audience because it was a scholarly rendering of what was already accepted in the capital.

23. Bissell interview, 15 Sept. 1983.

24. Robert A. Divine, "The Cold War and the Election of 1948," *Journal of American History* 59 (June 1972):95; LaFeber, *Cold War*, p. 73.

25. Divine, "Cold War and the Election of 1948," p. 95; Daniel Yergin, *Shattered Peace: Origins of the Cold War* (Boston: Houghton Mifflin, 1977), pp. 343–53, presents a different version. Yergin believes that the coalition government in Czechoslovakia was built on a "modus vivendi between the Soviet Union and the United States," that Czechoslovakia could "look both east and west" as long as the two agreed, but that the Czechs followed the Soviet foreign policy line. In Yergin's view, the United States missed an opportunity to use economic power effectively and created an impression that "the west was abandoning" the Czechs. Since the harvest of the previous summer had been bad, the Czechs were desperate. The Soviets "with great fanfare" delivered. Yergin therefore concluded that the Munich analogy worked both ways, reminding the Czechs, as well, of the debacle of the Second World War.

26. John Lewis Gaddis, *The U.S. and the Origins of the Cold War 1941–47* (New York: Columbia University Press, 1972), p. 317.

27. Ibid.

28. Divine, pp. 95–96. Eisenhower clearly still had Czechoslovakia on his mind in 1952 when he wrote John Foster Dulles: "There is only one point that bothered me. . . . It is this: What should we do if Soviet *political* aggression, as in Czechoslovakia, successively chips away exposed positions of the free world? So far as our resulting economic situation is concerned, such an eventuality would be just as bad for us as if the area had been captured by force." Quoted in John Lewis Gaddis, *Strategies of Containment* (New York: Oxford University Press, 1982), p. 128.

29. James V. Forrestal Diaries, Vols. 9–10, Nov. 1947–Apr. 1948, SGMML, meeting on 16 Feb. 1948, 3 p.m., p. 2080, attended by Admiral Hillenkoetter of CIA, Maj. Gen. Chamberlin of G-2, Admiral Inglis, and Brig. Gen. Chas. Cabell. The report is Forrestal's paraphrase of the Hughes report.

30. CFR, Discussion Groups, Vol. 19B, U.S. Foreign Policy.

31. All found in Vol. 24D, CFR Groups, 1947–1948. The meeting at which McKeever proposed propaganda within the Marshall Plan was 16 Feb. 1948; Wood's letter to Armstrong was 5 Mar. 1948, handwritten. The notes between

Armstrong and his colleague on the staff at CFR were 8 Mar. 1948; and Wood's proposal was 10 Mar. 1948. The sources for "East Coast Money" may have been found at the CFR. It is my proposition that at certain times the council has been far more influential in providing coordination for foreign policy objectives than was thought to be the case by Robert Schulzinger in his book on the council. See Robert D. Schulzinger, *The Wise Men of Foreign Affairs: The History of the Council on Foreign Relations* (New York: Columbia University Press, 1984).

32. Bissell interview, 15 Sept. 1983.

33. Interview with John A. Bross, 13 Dec. 1983, for discussion of areas where activity was deemed necessary by Forrestal. Interview with Lawrence Houston, 20 Mar. 1984, legal problems of creating a covert capability under the National Security Act.

34. Supplementary Detailed Staff Reports on Foreign and Military Intelligence, Book 4, Final Report of the Select Committee to Study Government Operations with Respect to Intelligence Activities, prepared by Anne Karalekas, Staff Member, 1976, pp. 25-31, commonly known as the Church Committee Report.

35. PPS Meetings, RG 59, Box 32, 9 Apr. 1948, National Archives, Diplomatic Branch. In 1948 PPS members were Kennan, George Butler, John Davies, Bernard Gufler, Carlton Savage, and Henry Villard. See State Department Biographical Registries for each year.

36. All senior State Department officials, with extensive field experience in ambassadorial service.

37. The memo is not available.

38. The description of Kennan is from an interview with Bissell, 15 Sept. 1983. The quote is from a letter from Kennan, 4 Jan. 1985, to the author. Kennan was not willing to be interviewed.

39. Truman Papers, President's Secretary's Files, NSC meetings, Box 203, 7th meeting NSC 11 Mar. 1948, from NSC 1/2.

40. Church Committee Report, Vol. IV, section on OPC, names legislators who shared the confidence of the early covert political activists, p. 39; Carl Vinson, Clarence Cannon, Chan Gurney, Millard Tydings, Richard Russell, and Leverett Saltonstall. On 16 Feb. 1948, the afternoon that Forrestal met with Emmet Hughes at 3 p.m., he met with Senators Gurney and Saltonstall at 3:30 p.m. Forrestal Diaries, Vols. 9-10, p. 2081.

41. Truman Papers, President's Secretary's Files, NSC Meetings, Box 203, 13th meeting, 17 June 1948.

42. Oral history of Gen. William H. Draper, Jr., 11 Jan. 1972, pp. 63-67, HSTLI. See also RG 59, Diplomatic Branch, National Archives, 093.41D4/1-145 to 103.512/12-3147, Box 27.

43. Truman Papers, President's Secretary's Files, NSC Meetings, Box 220, minutes of meetings 48-53, meeting of 20 Aug. 1948. The minutes show that NSC 10/2 was also discussed on 21 May 1948.

44. RG 59, National Archives, Diplomatic Branch, Box 3023, item 700.00116/6-3049, 30 June 1949, from Joyce to Kennan.

45. Despite the fact that Joyce was a member of the PS, there are no entries on him in the subject or lot files at the Diplomatic Branch, National Archives.

46. Bissell interviews, 8 July 1983, 9 July 1986.

47. Church Committee Report, Vol. IV, pp. 31–34; Houston interview, 20 March 1984; Bissell interview, 9 July 1986.

48. Lindsay interview, 9 Apr. 1984; Church Committee Report, Vol. IV, section on OPC.

49. W. Averell Harriman, the special representative to Europe, held ambassadorial status; William Foster was his deputy in Paris at the Office of the Special Representative; Milton Katz was also a deputy at the OSR in Paris.

50. It is also known as "wearing two hats." Oliver North spoke of it in the Iran-Contra hearings. See last chapter, *Interventionism and Presidential Transitions*, p. 135.

51. Frank Wisner was director of OPC.

52. Paul Hoffman was the administrator of the CA.

53. Bissell interview, 2 Nov. 1983. In retrospect some perceive covert operations as a "fad." See Roger Hilsman in *Armed Forces and Society* 8, 1 (Fall 1981):129–43, "On Intelligence."

54. Bissell interview, 18 May 1985.

55. Bissell interview, 2 Nov. 1983. Bissell says the key psy-warriors were Wisner, C. D. Jackson, Nelson Rockefeller, and Allen Welsh Dulles.

56. Lindsay interview, 9 Apr. 1984.

57. Bross interview, 13 Dec. 1983.

58. Lindsay interview, 9 Apr. 1984.

59. Church Committee Report, Vol. IV, p. 33.

60. Roosevelt interview, 21 Mar. 1984.

61. Church Committee Report, Vol. IV., pp. 33–34.

62. Ibid; Bissell interview, 9 July 1986.

63. Church Committee Report, Vol. IV, p. 33.

64. Bissell interview, 9 July 1986. Dulles built a great reputation based on his service in Bern during the Second World War. In 1948 he coauthored the Dulles-Jackson-Corea Report on intelligence. In 1950 he was appointed deputy director of Plans, the term used for covert operations. He rose quickly to become director of the agency in 1953. He was what agency people call a "planner," one who conceptualizes covert operations.

65. Stewart Alsop, *The Center: People and Power in Political Washington* (New York: Harper and Row, 1968), p. 229.

66. Lawrence Houston took strong exception to my claim that the distinction between policymaker and operative became blurred. Letter to the author, 15 July 1985.

67. Harold Macmillan, *War Diaries: Politics and War in the Mediterranean, January 1943–May 1945* (New York: St. Martin's Press, 1984), p. 753. See also pp. 517–763. I am indebted to Roy Domenico of Upsala University for bringing the Macmillan-Offie connection to my attention.

68. RG 59, National Archives, Diplomatic Branch, Box 123, Carmel Offie, from Kirk to secretary of state 21 Sept. 1945, and see also telegram of 3 Sept. 1945.

69. Ibid., letter from E. Paul Tenney, Chief, Division of Foreign Service Administration, 24 June 1946, to U.S. Political Advisor, Tokyo, George Atcheson, Jr., and other correspondence on the subject of Offie's buying sprees, plus Offie's letter disclaiming any knowledge of an automobile, 18 July 1946.

70. Roosevelt interview, 21 Mar. 1984; Houston interview, 20 Mar. 1984.

71. Harry Howe Ransom, *The Intelligence Establishment* (Cambridge, Mass.: Harvard University Press, 1970), p. 247.

72. Roosevelt interview, 21 Mar. 1984.

73. Houston interview, 20 Mar. 1984; a detailed account of the OPC air arm is found in William M. Leary and William Stueck, "The Chennault Plan to Save China: U.S. Containment in Asia and the Origins of the CIAs Aerial Empire, 1949–1950," *Diplomatic History* 8 (Fall 1984):349–64.

74. Church Committee Report, Vol. IV, pp. 36–38; Houston interview, 20 Mar. 1984; Bissell interviews, 2 Nov. 1983, 9 July 1986. At some point Wisner had asked Bissell to speak to Harriman about Hillenkoetter, who Wisner said "was more a nuisance than anything." Wisner was operating with representatives from State and Defense and saw Hillenkoetter as a stumbling block. Harriman told Bissell that the situation would be cleared up. Shortly after that, Smith came in as director.

75. Church Committee Report, Vol. IV, pp. 36–38, section on merger; interviews with Lindsay and Bissell.

76. Bissell interview, 2 Nov. 1983, 9 July 1986. Bissell said that the Allies and the Nazis both suffered from this kind of split in World War II, causing competition for agents.

77. Church Committee Report, Vol. IV, pp. 36–38.

78. Dulles Papers, Box 117.

79. Truman Papers, Official File—1289 (1951)–1295 (1948), Box 1656. And see also Central Files, Box 9.

80. Truman Papers, Post-Presidential Files, Box 4, Truman to Wayne Morse 11 Apr. 1963, on the problem of congressional intrusion in the matter of intelligence. For more on the subject of the president's aims in establishing OPC see chapter six.

CHAPTER FIVE. FRANCE:
FULLY FUNCTIONING INTERVENTION

1. Transcript, Eric Sevareid's "A Conversation with Dean Acheson," CBS Television Network, 28 Sept. 1969, quoted in Thomas G. Paterson, *On Every Front: The Making of the Cold War* (New York: W. W. Norton, 1979), p. 69.

2. Ibid.

3. Foreign Assistance Act of 1948, known as Public Law 472, Title I, Findings and Declaration of Policy, p. 145.

4. J. R. Frears, *Political Parties and Elections in the French Fifth Republic* (New York: St. Martin's Press, 1977), p. 131.

5. Dulles Papers, Box 32, file on Brown Alumni speech, 16 June 1947.

6. RG 59, National Archives, Diplomatic Branch, 851.00 Political Affairs, France, Box 581, Report MA 177 from SANA (Valentine), 22 Apr. 1949.

7. CFR, Study Group, Vol. 28B, "Western European Cooperation," 1948, Langbourne M. Williams, Jr., ECA Industry Division, Paris. The group included Nelson Rockefeller, Ray Bastedo, Tom Braden, Bill Donovan, Allen Dulles, Arnold Wolfers, Stacy May.

8. Records of the OSS, RG 226, Entry 108, Box 23, France, F2200–2299, report F-2236, 22 May 1945, National Archives, Military Reference.

9. CFR Study Group, Vol. 36B, 1950, "France Today," discussion group led by Raymond Aron of *Figaro*, 31 Oct. 1950.

10. Ibid. Arnold Wolfers told another discussion group at CFR that "the surprising aspect about the communist party in western Europe has been its weakness in all countries except France." CFR Study Group, Vol. 20A, "Reconstruction in Western Europe 1946."

11. CFR Study Group, Vol. 20A, "Reconstruction in Western Europe 1946."

12. Bissell interview, 12 Jan. 1987. Bissell also expressed these sentiments before the Senate Foreign Relations Committee, in executive session in 1949, p. 265: "Our belief very emphatically is that they [the European nations] should balance their accounts before their standard of living recovers to the 1939 level."

13. Research and Analysis Reports of the OSS, RG 226, ORI 3491, French Economic Outlook and Commodities Trade, 15 Mar. 1946, National Archives, Diplomatic Branch. For the importance of Africa as a supplier in the Second World War see Raymond Dumett, "Africa's Strategic Minerals During the Second World War," *Journal of African History* 26 (1985):381–408.

14. Lindsay Papers, Accession Number XX258-8.29, Box 1, memos from Tom Geiger and Franklin A. Lindsay to Richard M. Bissell, Jr., 30 Apr. 1948, "Intra-European Balance of Payments," p. 2. In 1948 Lindsay was an American representative to the OEEC in Paris.

15. Report by Geiger and Lindsay 24 Mar. 1948, "Intra-European Clearing System," Lindsay Papers. Another OEEC/ECA memo, dated 30 Apr. 1948, said, "U.S. aid should be neither a supply operation . . . or cover balance of payments deficits." Lindsay Papers, File 17, report by Lindsay and Geiger entitled "Programming."

16. RG 59, National Archives, Diplomatic Branch, 851.00 Political Affairs, France, Box 581, MA 242, 20 May 1949.

17. Hearings held in executive session before the CFR United States Senate, Eighty-first Congress, First Session on S 833, to Amend the Economic Cooperation Act of 1948. Hearings held in February and March of 1949, made public September 1974. The Civil Administration Committee is the administrative

branch of the U.S. military government, OMGUS, Germany. These files are located in the Military Reference Branch of the National Archives but do not reveal the recommendation mentioned by Henderson. The controversy continued at least through 1951 when, in a hearing of the Foreign Aid Appropriations committee, Dick Bissell was questioned by Congressman Wigglesworth about the use of counterpart funds for debt retirement. Bissell claimed the European nations stopped that practice in November 1949 but under heavy pressure from Wigglesworth admitted that they might start the practice again, at least in Britain. Foreign Aid Appropriations for 1951, Eighty-first Congress, Second Session, p. 84.

18. Research and Analysis Reports, RG 226, ORI 3491, French Economic Outlook and Commodities Trade, 15 Mar. 1946, National Archives, Diplomatic Branch.

19. Harry Bayard Price, *The Marshall Plan and Its Meaning* (Ithaca, N.Y.: Cornell University Press, 1955), p. 384.

20. Ibid., p. 385.

21. Records of the OSS, RG 226, F3400–3499, Box 24, National Archives, Military Reference. May 1945 the OSS reported that the French believed the United States was agitating in North Africa, trying to get colonies by dumping goods or selling them cheaply.

22. Ibid., p. 169.

23. Records of the OSS, RG 226, Entry 108, Box 21, France, F1200–1299, National Archives, Military Reference.

24. Records of the OSS, RG 226, Entry 108, Box 21, France F100–1099, report F-1038, 14 Feb. 1945, National Archives, Military Reference.

25. Records of the OSS, RG 226, Entry 108, Box 21, France, F1400–1499, report F-1421, 15 Mar. 1945, National Archives, Military Reference.

26. One such was a Monsieur Joufflot, a former executive of Citroen. See Records of the OSS, RG 226, Entry 108, Box 22, F2100–2199, National Archives, Military Reference. Ibid., Box 24, F300–3099.

27. CFR, Study Group, Vol. 36B, 1950, "France Today," second meeting, 19 Dec. 1950, speaker Andre Istel of Neuflize, Schlumberger et Cie.

28. Records of the OSS, RG 226, Entry 108, Box 21, F100–1099, National Archives, Military Reference.

29. Ibid., Box 25, F5600, report F-5609, Nov. 1945.

30. Alexandre Parodi, Permanent Representative of France to the UN, at the CFR meeting, 15 Dec. 1947. M. Parodi was a former Resistance member.

31. Records of the OSS, RG 226, Entry 108, Box 22, F1650–1699, report F-1671, Apr. 1945, National Archives, Military Reference.

32. Ibid., Box 23, France, F2200–2299, report F-2217, 10 Apr. 1945.

33. Ibid., Box 24, F3300–3399.

34. Ibid., Boxes 22–24.

35. Ibid., Box 24, F3300–3399.

36. Ibid., Box 23, report F-2218, 18 May 1945, from Antibes.

37. John Ranelagh quoted Tom Braden as saying even the attention to Marseilles was by AFL-CIO order because the unions had an "interest in protecting the docks." Ranelagh, p. 248.

38. Records of the OSS, RG 226, Entry 108, Box 25, F-3900, 27 Aug. 1945.

39. Ibid., Box 25, report F-5600, 10 Dec. 1945.

40. Ranelagh, p. 248. Ranelagh, again quoting Braden: "The secret funding of the AFL and CIO by the CIA I have always thought predated the agency. I suspect it was done by the OSS or the army or State Department."

41. Senate Foreign Relations Hearings, Feb. and Mar. 1949, pp. 44, 45.

42. Ibid.

43. Barry Bingham, chief of the ECA Mission in Paris, to Congressional Foreign Aid Appropriations Committee, 1950, Foreign Aid Appropriations Committee, hearing for 1951, Eighty-first Congress, Second Session, p. 200.

44. Ibid.

45. Ibid.

46. Things sometimes got extremely dangerous for ECA personnel nonetheless. Irving Ross, the ECA trade negotiator with the Soviets, was murdered in Vienna on 30 Oct. 1948. He had taken up with a female Soviet agent who lured him to a wooded area where he was bludgeoned to death by unknown assailants. National Archives, Diplomatic Branch, RG 59, Box 234, 103ECA02/10-148 to 103.1/12-3049.

47. Records of U.S. Foreign Assistance Agencies, 1948–61, RG 469, Box 9, European Program Division, Mediterranean Branch, France, Papers of ECA, letter from Harlan Cleveland to Paul G. Hoffman, 13 Dec. 1949, Federal Records Center, Suitland, Md.

48. CFR, Study Groups, Vol. 28B, "Western European Cooperation," 1948. In attendance were Nelson Rockefeller, Raymond Bastedo, Tom Braden, Bill Donovan, Allen Dulles, Arnold Wolfers, Stacy May.

49. Price, *The Marshall Plan*, p. 179. Price was referring specifically to Title IV of Public Law 472.

50. Ibid., p. 172.

51. Ibid.

52. Political and economic advisors are often in charge of indirection for the State Department.

53. "La Voix de Montparnasse," publication of La Cellule Montparnasse du Parti Communiste Français, for New Year's party, Jan. 1952. An excellent collection of these publications is at HIW.

54. From La Voix de St. Germain des Près, 17 Jan. 1953, and Seine-Visconti, 11 Jan. 1953.

55. Richard Hofstadter, *The Age of Reform: From Bryan to FDR* (New York: Knopf, 1955), p. 23.

56. Ibid., p. 27.

57. Ibid., p. 28.

58. CFR Study Group, Vol. 36B, 1950, "France Today," second meeting, 19 Dec. 1950, led by Andre Istel of Neuflize, Schlumberger et Cie.

59. Records of U.S. Foreign Assistance Agencies, 1948–61, RG 469, FRC. Organization Directory of the ECA-OSR in Paris. Harry Martin's boss was Alfred Friendly, chief of the Information Division.

60. Records of U.S. Foreign Assistance Agencies, 1948–61, RG 469, Papers of ECA, Box 5, Labor Information Division, Office of Economic Advisor, France D-L. See files on strikes, 1949–50.

61. Ibid.

62. Ibid.; CFR meetings, Vol. 14, "Italian and French Labor Leaders," 6 Apr. 1949.

63. Records of U.S. Foreign Assistance Agencies, 1948–61, RG 469, Box 1, Special Rep. to Europe, Central Secretariat, memos and letters sent 1948–1949, from Leland Barrows to Milton Katz, 22 June 1949. There is no claim made here that this was the total amount available for confidential fund expenditures.

64. Ibid.

65. Ibid.

66. RG 59, National Archives, Diplomatic Branch, General Records, Decimal File 1945–49, Box C-584, 851.24/1-147 to 851.48 RCO 12-3149.

67. That is not to say that nothing was done to counter Soviet moves among the "paysans, agriculteurs et cultivateurs." Jean-Paul David directed Paix et Liberté, mentioned herein. The *New York Herald Tribune* identified him, in positive terms, as a radical Socialist, an ex–tank commander, ex-dairy farmer, who served in 1952 as a deputy from Seine-et-Oise and was mayor of Nantes. Seeley G. Mudd Manuscript Library houses an excellent collection of posters produced by Paix et Liberté aimed at the agricultural peasants. These posters emphasized quotes from Stalin on the fact that the Soviet state had rejected private property for farmers and peasants on the land. There are also posters that drew on the Nazi-Communist connection, as there were in Paris. One shows three pictures: Stalin with Von Ribbentrop, Molotov in Berlin on 12 Nov. 1940, Molotov and Goering in Berlin. The heading on the poster is Swastikas, the bottom hammer and sickles. The caption reads "Souvenirs des rendez-vous cimentés par le sang." See Paix et Liberté, AM 14591, one box.

68. CFR, Records of Groups, Vols. 30, 31, "Aid to Europe," Parts I, II, 1948–51, meeting of 10 Jan. 1951.

69. Lindsay Papers, Box 9, file 23, "Developments in Yugoslavia March-August 1945," written by Lindsay and presented to Stanford 6 Sept. 1946, found at HIW.

70. Cà, with an accent, means here. Ça, without an accent, is a contraction of the pronoun çela which means this or that.

71. *La barbe* means beard, but can also mean a thorn or to enjoy a joke at someone else's expense. Kathy Hjele of Brookdale Community College tells me it is also a slang expression meaning "what a pain!"

72. Records of U.S. Foreign Assistance Agencies, 1948–61, RG 469, Box 3,

Productivity and Technical Assistance Division, from Paul Porter, Acting U.S. Special Representative to Europe, to Richard M. Bissell, Jr., 25 Aug. 1951, at FRC.

73. Ibid.

CHAPTER SIX. ITALY-IRAN: INTERLOCKING THEMES FOR GLOBAL INTERVENTION

1. Rhodri Jeffreys-Jones, *The CIA and American Democracy* (New Haven, Conn.: Yale University Press, 1989), p. 51. For other strategic implications see Melvin Loeffler, "The United States and the Strategic Dimensions of the Marshall Plan," *Diplomatic History* 12, 3 (Summer 1988): 277-306.

2. Papers of Joseph Jones, Box 1, notes on SWNCC Special Ad Hoc Committee Report on Economic Aid, 5231, 9 Apr. 1947, in Jones's hand, listing of priorities: "1.priority Italy-Iran," HSTLI.

3. Truman Papers, President's Secretary's Files—Intelligence, Box 254, CIA report, ORE 47, 10 Oct. 1947, "The Current Situation in Italy."

4. Ibid., p. 1.

5. Dulles Papers, Boxes 22, 32, 36, 148, 201, 203, files on Sunrise, Secret Surrender, and individual names associated therewith. Dulles kept up correspondence with individuals who had helped him during his OSS years.

6. President's Committee on Foreign Aid, Box 8, report of 19 Nov. 1947, HSTLI.

7. CFR meetings, Vol. 14, "Italy and the ERP," speech given by James D. Zellerbach, 27 Jan. 49.

8. ECA Data Book for Italy, 1950, tables II-2a, II-5.

9. CIA report 39, 25 July 1947, "Significant considerations regarding the disposition of the Italian African Colonies," HSTLI

10. Ibid.

11. CIA report, ORE 47, HSTLI.

12. House Reports, Eightieth Congress, First Session, 3 Jan.-19 Dec. 1947, report 1145, "The Italian Crisis and Interim Aid; Preliminary Report One, Subcommittee on Italy, Greece and Trieste," p. 9.

13. Ibid.; RG 59, 865.504/9-2348, airgram from Ambassador Dunn in Italy to Secretary of State, p. 2, National Archives, Diplomatic Branch; and see ECA Data Book for Italy, 1950.

14. CIA report, ORE 6-48, "Consequences of Communist Accession to Power in Italy by Legal Means," 5 Mar. 1948, HSTLI.

15. ECA Data Book for Italy, 1950, p. 4.

16. Ibid.

17. Ibid., p. 5.

18. CIA report, ORE 6-48, p. 5.

19. CFR meetings, Vol. 11, Tab B, 1944-45.

20. CIA report, ORE 21/1, 5 Aug. 1947, "Probable Soviet Reactions to a U.S. Aid Program for Italy"; CIA report, ORE 47.

21. CIA report, ORE 6-48. But note that the ECA, according to James Zellerbach, had approved a bilateral trade agreement between the Italians and the Soviet Union.

22. CFR meetings, 9 Sept. 1946, Count Carlo Sforza, "Italian Republic: Politics and Portents."

23. CIA report 35610, 4 Jan. 1950. A letter to the CIA describing my project elicited copies of reports from Lee S. Strickland, Information and Privacy Coordinator, on 29 Apr. 1987.

24. Ibid.

25. CIA report 80262, Nov. 1951.

26. Ibid., p. 2

27. Ibid., p. 3.

28. RG 59, 865.00 (W)/9-3049 from Rome to Secretary of State, MAR 829, Department of the Army memo 1 Oct. 1949, National Archives, Diplomatic Branch, p. 5.

29. RG 469, Records of U.S. Foreign Assistance Agencies 1948–61, FRC, Labor Information Division Office of Economic Advisor, Italy, Boxes 11, 12.

30. Ibid.

31. Ibid. The argument for bringing in the products from the United States was made by James Zellerbach, the ECA station chief in Rome.

32. Ibid.

33. RG 59, National Archives, Diplomatic Branch, Italy, 865.504/9-2348.

34. CIA report, ORE, 47.

35. ECA Data Book for Italy, 1950, p. 10.

36. CFR meetings, "Italy and the ERP," James D. Zellerbach, 27 Jan. 1949.

37. RG 59, National Archives, Diplomatic Branch, Italy 865.504/9-2348.

38. ECA Data Book for Italy, 1950, p. 10.

39. State Department Report, A-1002, 23 Sept. 1948, National Archives, Diplomatic Branch, RG 59, Italy, 865.504/9-2348.

40. ECA Data Book for Italy, 1950, p. 10.

41. Milward, *Reconstruction of Western Europe*, p. 253.

42. Ibid., p. 254.

43. CFR meetings, "Italy and the ERP."

44. Records of U.S. Foreign Assistance Agencies 1948–61, RG 469, FRC, Labor Information Division, Office of Economic Advisor, Boxes 11, 12, Italy, Memo from Department of State on Italian Emigration, 26 Jan. 1950.

45. Section 117(e), Foreign Assistance Act of 1948. And Ibid.

46. Ibid.

47. Ibid.

48. The countries were Brazil, Uruguay, Chile, Paraguay, Bolivia, and Peru. Records of U.S. Foreign Assistance Agencies 1948–61, RG 469, FRC, Boxes 11, 12.

49. Ibid., "Emigration Surveys in South America," 1 July 1950.

50. Annual reports for the Rockefeller Foundation do not mention any funding for this study.

51. Ibid.

52. By 1951 at least 24 agencies of the U.S. government had "Facilities and Arrangements . . . for the production of Foreign Economic Intelligence." In the case of the Department of Agriculture, their "chief Components for Economic Intelligence," that is their office in charge of collecting intelligence, was the Office of Foreign Agricultural Relations. Truman papers, President's Secretary's Files, Box 213, meeting 94, 13 June 1951, Economic Intelligence, report of 1 June 1951, Appendix C to Tab A.

53. Records of U.S. Foreign Assistance Agencies 1948–61, RG 469, Labor Information Division, Boxes 11, 12, "A Case Study of Communism in One Country—Italy."

54. Ibid.

55. Ibid.

56. Ibid.

57. Interview, 1 July 1987, Dr. Tristano Guitardi, West Park, N.Y. Guitardi was a doctoral candidate at the University of Milan in 1948.

58. CFR meetings, Vol. 14, "Italian and French Labor Leaders," 6 Apr. 1949.

59. Ranelagh, *The Agency*, p. 248, quote attributed to Tom Braden.

60. RG 59, National Archives, Diplomatic Branch, Box 4829, 811.5043/10-147 to 5047/12-3147.

61. Papers of Philip Raiser, Biographic Register of the U.S. Labor Attachés, 16 Oct. 1953, HSTLI.

62. Records of U.S. Foreign Assistance Agencies 1948–61, RG 469, Box 1, Assistant Administrator for Production, letter from Bissell to Johnson, 1 May 1951.

63. RG 59, Box 4829, document 811.5043/2-2449, 7 Mar. 1949, National Archives, Diplomatic Branch.

64. Almost verbatim from Carey's speech, 8 Apr. 1948, "Labor Movements in Europe," CFR, Vol. 13.

65. Giovanni D'Orlandi, chairman of the Coordinating Committee on East-West Trade controls, was paid thirty thousand francs on 6 May 1970 to help him set up an office. Eventually a location would be found for D'Orlandi in the Embassy. Box 1, Special Representative, Confidential subject files A-C, RG 469, Records of U.S. Foreign Assistance Agencies 1948–61, FRC. D'Orlandi was paid through a conduit, Michael V. Forrestal, son of the secretary of defense.

66. Price, *The Marshall Plan*, p. 368. Marshall planners considered the Middle East and "independent countries in Africa" as among the "economically retarded."

67. CIA report "The Current Situation in Iran," ORE 65–49, published 27

June 1949. A copy of Overseas Consultants's plan can be found at SGMML, Dulles Papers, Box 40.

68. Ibid.

69. Ibid., p.5.

70. There is a handwritten set of notes by Sherman dated September 1951, which he filed under "OPC" on the Iranian problem. They appear to be notes taken at a meeting where he was being briefed. They are found at HSTLI, Records of the PSB, Box 13, 091.411, file marked OPC. This is the only place where I found a file marked OPC.

71. Ibid. M presumably is Mossadegh. From his notes it appears that Sherman did not agree.

72. Dean Acheson, *Present at the Creation* (New York: W.W. Norton, 1969), p. 503.

73. See early cites on PPS. See also CFR meeting, 10 Mar. 1949, where George V. Allen, at that time assistant secretary of state, told the audience that he "has accepted the term 'propagandist' and likes to recall that St. Paul was one of the first propagators."

74. Kermit Roosevelt, *Countercoup: The Struggle for the Control of Iran* (New York: McGraw Hill, 1979).

75. Papers of George V. Allen, Box 1, an unpublished manuscript entitled "Mission to Iran," Chapter II, HSTLI.

76. See Nikki R. Keddie, "The Origins of the Religious-Radical Alliance in Iran," *Past and Present,* 34 (July 1966): 70–80.

CHAPTER SEVEN. INTERVENTIONISM AND PRESIDENTIAL TRANSITIONS

1. Central Files, Box 9, and Official Files, Box 1656, file 1290B, HSTLI. Also involved in the recruitment process was Harry Vaughn, Coordinator, Veterans Affairs and Military Advisor to President Truman. This was not a small effort. There are boxes and boxes of files on recruitment.

2. Truman Papers, Post-Presidential Files, Box 4, correspondence with Wayne Morse, HSTLI.

3. Ibid., letter to Morse dated 14 Mar. 1963.

4. Ed. P. Lilly, "The Psychological Strategy Board and its Predecessors: Foreign Policy Coordination, 1938–1953," from *Studies in Modern History*, ed. Gaetano L. Vincitorio (New York: St. John's University Press, 1968), p. 363.

5. Ibid.

6. Jeffrey-Jones, *The CIA*, pp. 84–85.

7. Records of the PSB, Box 2, memo to PSB staff members from Col. Charles McCarthy of the board, HSTLI, regarding a briefing by a Mr. Mullen of the ECA, 10 Oct. 1951. Also a memo for the record from John Sherman regarding a meeting with ECA people, 8 Oct. 1951.

8. Ibid., Box 040 ECA/PSB, memo dated 9 Feb. 1951, Library No. 969, declassified at author's request, 8 June 1990.

9. Truman Papers, Records of the PSB, Box 2, cited at note 7.

10. Truman Papers, oral history of Gordon Gray, p. 54.

11. John Lewis Gaddis, *Strategies of Containment: A Critical Appraisal of Postwar American National Security Policy* (New York: Oxford University Press, 1982), p. 63.

12. Ibid.

13. Ibid., p. 353.

14. Ibid.

15. Truman Papers, Records of the PSB, files of Tracy Barnes, deputy director, report 5 May 1952.

16. Ibid.

17. Truman Papers, Records of the PSB, Papers of Gordon Gray, Box 1, letter to George Gallup, 5 May 1952; letter from Lindsay on Farber 1 Dec. 1952.

18. Ibid., 20 Sept. 1952. The players surrounding the OPC-PSB coordination by the end of 1952 were Frank Wisner, Frank Lindsay, Tracy Barnes, Richard M. Bissell, Jr., and Gordon Gray.

Gray also served the CIA under a personal service contract numbered P-320–52, 1 Jan. 1952. Gray's history included working for William Jackson as G-2 in Germany under Gen. Edwin L. Sibert, Omar Bradley's chief intelligence officer. Kenneth Royall recruited Gray in 1947 when he was secretary of the army.

19. Cited by Harry Howe Ransom, *Central Intelligence and National Security* (Cambridge, Mass.: Harvard University Press, 1958), pp. 87–88. The story was in the 20 Nov. 1948 edition of the *Saturday Evening Post*, p. 191.

20. Members of this committee were Francis M. Baton, Richard M. Bissell, Jr., Roger D. Fisher, Samuel Huntington, Lyman Kirkpatrick, Henry Loomis, Max Milliken, Lucian W. Pye, Edwin O. Reischauer, Adam Yarmolinsky, and Franklin A. Lindsay. The report is in the possession of the author.

21. HIW, Lindsay papers, accession no. xx2258-8.29, box 10, correspondence with Office of the President Elect. Files do not reveal the full membership of this team, but a memo on National Security Organization, prepared for Richard M. Bissell in Nov. 1968 was signed by Philip Areeda, Ernest May, Henry Kissinger, and Franklin A. Lindsay.

22. Ibid.

23. Ibid.

24. Bross interview, 13 Dec. 1983.

25. Loch K. Johnson, *A Season of Inquiry: The Senate Intelligence Investigation* (Lexington: University Press of Kentucky, 1985), p. 262.

26. Ibid.

27. Ibid., p. 263.

28. Loch K. Johnson, *America's Secret Power: The CIA in a Democratic Society* (New York: Oxford University Press, 1989), p. 282.

APPENDIX

1. Hogan, *The Marshall Plan*, p. 14.
2. John Lewis Gaddis, "Intelligence, Espionage, and Cold War Origins," *Diplomatic History* 13, 2 (Spring 1989): 211.
3. Ibid., p. 212.

BIBLIOGRAPHY

UNPUBLISHED DOCUMENTS

James R. Angell Papers, Sterling Library, Yale University

Richard M. Bissell, Jr., Papers, Farmington, Connecticut

Central Intelligence Agency Reports, in possession of author

Council on Foreign Relations Archives, New York City

Allen Welsh Dulles Papers, Seeley G. Mudd Manuscript Library, Princeton University

Federal Records Center, Suitland, Md., RG 469

Ford Foundation Archives, New York City

James V. Forrestal Diaries, Seeley G. Mudd Manuscript Library, Princeton University

French Communist Propaganda Collection, Hoover Institute on War, Revolution and Peace, Stanford University

Franklin A. Lindsay Papers, Hoover Institute on War, Revolution and Peace, Stanford University

Franklin A. Lindsay Papers, in possession of author

National Archives, Diplomatic Branch, RG 59

_____, Military Reference, RG 226

Paix et Liberté, Seeley G. Mudd Manuscript Library, Princeton University

Paix et Liberté Poster Collection, Hoover Institute on War, Revolution and Peace, Stanford University

Charles Seymour Papers, Sterling Library, Yale University

Harry S. Truman Papers, Harry S. Truman Library Institute

PUBLISHED DOCUMENTS

Economic Cooperation Administration, *Data Books*, 1950-51.

U.S., Congress, House, Foreign Aid Appropriations Committee, *Reports*, 1947-52.

U.S., Congress, Senate. *Supplementary Detailed Staff Reports on Foreign and Military Intelligence, Book IV, Final Report of the Select Committee to Study Governmental Operations with Respect to Intelligence Activities*, 1976.

U.S., Congress, Senate, Committee on Foreign Relations. *Hearings*, 1948-52.

_____. *Hearings in Executive Session*, 1948-52.

U.S., Department of State, *Foreign Relations of the United States*, 1948, vol. 4 (Washington D.C., 1974).

INTERVIEWS

Richard M. Bissell, Jr.
John A. Bross
Tristano Guitardi
Lawrence Houston
Franklin A. Lindsay
Kermit Roosevelt

ARTICLES

Divine, Robert A. "The Cold War and the Election of 1948." *Journal of American History* 59 (June 1972): 90–110.
Dumett, Raymond. "Africa's Strategic Minerals during the Second World War." *Journal of African History* 26 (1985): 381–408.
Gaddis, John Lewis. "The Corporatist Synthesis: A Skeptical View." *Diplomatic History* 10, 4 (Fall 1986): 357–62.
————. "Intelligence, Espionage, and Cold War Origins." *Diplomatic History* 13, 2 (Spring 1989): 191–20.
Hilsman, Roger. "On Intelligence." *Armed Forces and Society* 8, 1 (Fall 1981): 129–43.
Keddie, Nikki R. "The Origins of the Religious-Radical Alliance in Iran." *Past and Present* 34 (July 1966): 70–80.
Leary, William M., and William Stueck. "The Chennault Plan to Save China: U.S. Containment in Asia and the Origins of the CIA's Aerial Empire 1949–1950." *Diplomatic History* 8 (Fall 1984): 349–64.
Loeffler, Melvin. "The United States and the Strategic Dimensions of the Marshall Plan." *Diplomatic History* 12, 3 (Summer 1988): 277–306.
X. "The Sources of Soviet Conduct." *Foreign Affairs* 4 (July 1947): 566–82.

BOOKS

Acheson, Dean. *Present at the Creation*. New York: W. W. Norton, 1969.
Agee, Philip. *Inside the Company: CIA Diary*. Harmondsworth, Eng.: Penguin Books, 1975.

Agee, Philip, and Louis Wolf, eds. *Dirty Work: The CIA in Western Europe.* Secaucus, N.J.: Lyle Stuart, 1978.

Alsop, Stewart. *The Center: People and Power in Political Washington.* New York: Harper and Row, 1968.

Alsop, Stewart, and Thomas Braden. *Sub Rosa: The OSS and American Espionage.* New York: Harvest Books, 1964.

Ambrose, Stephen E. *Eisenhower the President.* New York: Simon & Schuster, 1984.

_____. *Ike's Spies: Eisenhower and the Espionage Establishment.* New York: Doubleday, 1981.

_____. *Rise to Globalism: American Foreign Policy since 1938.* 3d rev. ed. Harmondsworth, Eng.: Penguin Books, 1983.

Baldwin, George B. *Planning and Development in Iran.* Baltimore: Johns Hopkins University Press, 1967.

Bamford, James. *The Puzzle Palace: A Report on America's Most Secret Agency.* Boston: Houghton Mifflin, 1982.

Barnet, Richard J. *The Alliance—America, Europe, Japan: Makers of the Postwar World.* New York: Simon & Schuster, 1983.

Bartlett, C. J. *The Rise and Fall of the Pax Americana: United States Foreign Policy in the Twentieth Century.* London: Paul Elek, 1974.

Beale, Howard K. *Theodore Roosevelt and the Rise of America to World Power.* Baltimore: Johns Hopkins University Press, 1956.

Bharier, Julian. *Economic Development in Iran, 1900–1970.* New York: Oxford University Press, 1971.

Bohlen, Charles E. *Witness to History.* New York: W. W. Norton, 1973.

Braden, Spruille. *Diplomats and Demagogues.* New Rochelle, N.Y.: Arlington House, 1971.

Byrnes, James. *Speaking Frankly.* New York: Harper, 1947.

Cave Brown, Anthony. *The Last Hero: Wild Bill Donovan.* New York: Times Books, 1982.

Chambers, John W. III. *The Tyranny of Change.* New York: St. Martin's Press, 1980.

Cline, Ray S. *The CIA under Reagan, Bush and Casey.* Washington, D.C.: Acropolis Books, 1981.

_____. *Secrets, Spies and Scholars: Blueprint of the Essential CIA.* Washington, D.C.: Acropolis Books, 1976.

Colby, William, and Peter Forbath. *Honorable Men: My Life in the CIA.* New York: Simon & Schuster, 1978.

Colson, Charles W. *Born Again.* London: Hodder and Stoughton, 1977.

Cook, Blanche Wiesen. *The Declassified Eisenhower: A Divided Legacy.* New York: Doubleday, 1981.

Corson, William R. *The Armies of Ignorance: The Rise of the American Intelligence Empire.* New York: Dial Press/James Wade, 1977.

Cruz, Arturo, Jr. *Memoirs of a Counterrevolutionary.* New York: Doubleday, 1989.

DeSilva, Peer. *Sub Rosa: The CIA and the Uses of Intelligence.* New York: Times Books, 1978.

Divine, Robert A. *Eisenhower and the Cold War.* New York: Oxford University Press, 1981.

Djilas, Milan. *Conversations with Stalin.* New York: Harcourt, Brace & World, 1962.

Domhoff, G. William. *The Higher Circles: The Governing Class in America.* New York: Vintage Books, 1971.

Dulles, Allen. *The Craft of Intelligence.* Westport, Conn.: Greenwood Press, 1977.

———. *The Secret Surrender.* New York: Harper and Row, 1966.

Eisenhower, Dwight D. *The White House Years: Mandate for Change, 1953-1956.* New York: Doubleday, 1963.

Ferrell, Robert H., ed. *The Eisenhower Diaries.* New York: W. W. Norton, 1981.

———. *American Diplomacy: A History.* New York: W. W. Norton, 1969.

Finletter, Thomas K. *Can Representative Government Do the Job?* New York: Reynal & Hitchcock, 1945.

Foot, M. R. D. *SOE in France.* London: HMSO, 1966.

Ford, Corey. *Donovan of OSS.* Boston: Little, Brown, 1970.

Forrestal, James. *The Forrestal Diaries.* ed. Walter Millis. New York: Viking, 1951.

Frears, J. R. *Political Parties and Elections in the French Fifth Republic.* New York: St. Martin's Press, 1977.

Gaddis, John Lewis. *The United States and the Origins of the Cold War, 1941-1947.* New York: Columbia University Press, 1972.

———. *Strategies of Containment: Appraisal of Postwar American National Security Policy.* New York: Oxford University Press, 1982.

———. *Russia, The Soviet Union, and the United States: An Interpretive History.* New York: Wiley, 1978.

———. *The Long Peace: Inquiries into the History of the Cold War.* New York: Oxford University Press, 1987.

Ganley, Albert C. *The Progressive Movement, Traditional Reform.* New York: Macmillan, 1964.

Gardner, Lloyd C. *The Architects of Illusion.* Chicago: Quadrangle Books, 1970.

———. *Covenant with Power: American and World Order from Wilson to Reagan.* London: Macmillan, 1984.

Gimbel, John. *The Origins of the Marshall Plan.* Stanford, Calif.: Stanford University Press, 1976.

Halberstam, David. *The Best and the Brightest.* Greenwich, Conn.: Fawcett Crest, 1972.

Halperin, Morton H., et al. *The Lawless State: The Crimes of the U.S. Intelligence Agencies*. Harmondsworth, Eng.: Penguin Books, 1976.

Harper, John Lamberton. *America and the Reconstruction of Italy, 1945–1948*. New York: Cambridge University Press, 1986.

Hawley, Ellis W. *The New Deal and the Problem of Monopoly*. Princeton, N.J.: Princeton University Press, 1966.

Heller, Francis H., ed. *The Truman White House: The Administration of the President, 1945–53*. Lawrence: University Press of Kansas, 1980.

Henry, Lauren L. *Presidential Transitions*. Washington, D.C.: Brookings, 1960.

Hogan, Michael J. *The Marshall Plan: America, Britain and the Reconstruction of Western Europe, 1947–52*. New York: Cambridge University Press, 1987.

Hunt, Michael H. *Ideology and U.S. Foreign Policy*. New Haven, Conn.: Yale University Press, 1987.

Huntington, Samuel P. *Political Order in Changing Societies*. New Haven, Conn.: Yale University Press, 1968.

Immerman, Richard H. *The CIA in Guatemala: The Foreign Policy of Intervention*. Austin: University of Texas Press, 1982.

Isaacson, Walter, and Evan Thomas. *The Wise Men*. New York: Simon & Schuster, 1986.

Jeffreys-Jones, Rhodri. *American Espionage from Secret Service to CIA*. New York: Free Press, 1977.

———. *The CIA and American Democracy*. New Haven, Conn.: Yale University Press, 1989.

Johnson, Loch K. *A Season of Inquiry: The Senate Intelligence Investigation*. Lexington: University Press of Kentucky, 1985.

———. *America's Secret Power: The CIA in a Democratic Society*. New York: Oxford University Press, 1989.

Jones, Joseph. *The Fifteen Weeks: February 21–June 5, 1947*. New York: Harcourt, Brace & World, 1955.

Kennan, George F. *Memoirs*. Vol. 1, 1925–1950: Vol. 2, 1950–1963. Boston: Little, Brown, 1967–72.

———. *Russia and the West under Lenin and Stalin*. New York: Mentor Books, 1960.

Kwitny, Jonathan. *The Crimes of Patriots: A True Tale of Dope, Dirty Money, and the CIA*. (New York: W. W. Norton, 1987).

LaFeber, Walter. *America, Russia, and the Cold War, 1945–1984*. 5th ed. New York: Knopf, 1985.

Leary, William M. *Perilous Missions: Civil Air Transport and CIA Covert Operations in Asia*. Tuscaloosa: University of Alabama Press, 1984.

Ledeen, Michael, and William Lewis. *Debacle: The American Failure in Iran*. New York: Vintage Books, 1982.

Liddy, G. Gordon. *Will: Autobiography*. London: Sphere Books, 1981.

Link, Arthur S. *Woodrow Wilson, Revolution, War and Peace*. Arlington Heights, Ill.: Harlan Davidson, 1979.

Link, Arthur S., and Richard L. McCormick. *Progressivism*. Arlington Heights, Ill.: Harlan Davidson, 1983.

Loftus, John. *The Belarus Secret*. ed. Nathan Miller. New York: Knopf, 1982.

McCoy, Donald R. *The Presidency of Harry S. Truman*. Lawrence: University Press of Kansas, 1984.

Macmillan, Harold. *War Diaries: Politics and War in the Mediterranean, January 1943–May 1945*. New York: St. Martin's Press, 1984.

Marchetti, Victor, and John D. Marks. *The CIA and the Cult of Intelligence*. New York: Laurel, 1980.

May, Ernest. *From Imperialism to Isolationism, 1898–1919*. New York: Macmillan, 1964.

Mee, Charles L., Jr. *The Marshall Plan: The Launching of the Pax Americana*. New York: Simon & Schuster, 1984.

Meyer, Cord. *Facing Reality: From World Federalism to the CIA*. New York: Harper and Row, 1980.

Miller, James Edward. *The United States and Italy, 1940–50: The Politics and Diplomacy of Stabilization*. Chapel Hill: University of North Carolina Press, 1986.

Miller, Perry. *Errand into the Wilderness*. Cambridge, Mass.: Belknap Press of Harvard University Press, 1956.

Millspaugh, Arthur C. *Americans in Persia*. Washington, D.C.: Brookings, 1946.

_____. *Democracy, Efficiency, and Stability*. Washington, D.C.: Brookings, 1942.

_____. *Toward Efficient Democracy*. Washington, D.C.: Brookings, 1949.

Milward, Alan S. *The Reconstruction of Western Europe, 1945–51*. Berkeley: University of California Press, 1984.

Moran, Charles M. W. *Churchill: Taken from the Diaries of Lord Moran*. Boston: Houghton Mifflin, 1966.

Mosher, Frederick C., W. David Clinton, and Daniel G. Lang. *Presidential Transitions and Foreign Affairs*. Baton Rouge: Louisiana State University Press, 1987.

Moseley, Leonard. *Dulles: A Biography of Eleanor, Allen and John Foster Dulles and Their Family Network*. New York: Dial Press/James Wade, 1978.

Mowry, George E. *The Era of Theodore Roosevelt and the Birth of Modern America*. New York: Harper, 1958.

Oshinsky, David M. *A Conspiracy So Immense: The World of Joe McCarthy*. New York: Free Press, 1983.

Paterson, Thomas G. *On Every Front: The Making of the Cold War*. New York: W. W. Norton, 1979.

Patti, Archimedes L. A. *Why Vietnam? Prelude to America's Albatross*. Berkeley: University of California Press, 1980.

Powers, Thomas. *The Man Who Kept the Secrets: Richard Helms and the CIA*. New York: Knopf, 1979.

Prados, John. *The Soviet Estimate: U.S. Intelligence Analysis and Russian Military Strength*. New York: Dial Press, 1982.

Prados, John. *President's Secret Wars: CIA and Pentagon Covert Operations since World War II*. New York: William Morrow, 1986.

Price, Harry. *The Marshall Plan and Its Meaning*. Ithaca, N.Y.: Cornell University Press, 1955.

Prouty, L. Fletcher. *The Secret Team: The CIA and Its Allies in Control of the United States and the World*. Englewood Cliffs, N.J.: Prentice-Hall, 1973.

Radosh, Ronald. *American Labor and U.S. Foreign Policy*. New York: Random House, 1969.

Ranelagh, John. *The Agency: The Rise and Decline of the CIA*. New York: Simon & Schuster, 1986.

Ransom, Harry Howe. *Central Intelligence and National Security*. Cambridge, Mass.: Harvard University Press, 1958.

————. *The Intelligence Establishment*. Cambridge, Mass: Harvard University Press, 1970.

Roosevelt, Kermit. *Countercoup: The Struggle for the Control of Iran*. New York: McGraw-Hill, 1981.

Rosenberg, Emily. *Spreading the American Dream: American Economic and Cultural Expansion, 1890–1945*. New York: Hill and Wang, 1982.

Rositzke, Harry. *The CIA's Secret Operations*. New York: Reader's Digest Press, 1977.

Schlesinger, Arthur M., Jr. *The Crisis of the Old Order, 1919–1933*. Boston: Houghton Mifflin, 1957.

Schlesinger, Stephen, and Stephen Kinzer. *Bitter Fruit: The Untold Story of the American Coup in Guatemala*. New York: Doubleday, 1982.

Schulzinger, Robert D. *The Wise Men of Foreign Affairs: The History of the Council on Foreign Relations*. New York: Columbia University Press, 1984.

Smith, Bradley F. *The Shadow Warriors: OSS and the Origins of the CIA*. New York: Basic Books, 1983.

Smith, Daniel M. *The American Diplomatic Experience*. Boston: Houghton Mifflin, 1972.

Smith, Gaddis. *Morality, Reason and Power*. New York: Hill and Wang, 1986.

Smith, Richard Harris. *OSS: The Secret History of America's First Central Intelligence Agency*. Berkeley: University of California Press, 1972.

Snepp, Frank. *Decent Interval: An Insider's Account of Saigon's Indecent End Told by the CIA's Chief Strategy Analyst in Vietnam*. New York: Random House, 1977.

Taubman, William. *Stalin's American Policy: From Entente to Détente to Cold War*. New York: W. W. Norton, 1982.

Thomas, Lewis V., and Richard N. Frye. *The United States and Turkey and Iran*. Cambridge, Mass.: Harvard University Press, 1951.

Treverton, Gregory F. *Covert Action: The Limits of Intervention in the Postwar World*. New York: Basic Books, 1987.

Troy, Thomas F. *Donovan and the CIA: A History of the Establishment of the Central Intelligence Agency.* Frederick, Md.: University Publications of America, 1981.

Truman, Harry S. *Memoirs. Vol. 1. Year of Decisions; Vol. 2. Years of Trial and Hope.* New York: Doubleday, 1955–56.

Turner, Stansfield. *Secrecy and Democracy: The CIA in Transition.* Boston: Houghton Mifflin, 1985.

U.S. War Department, Strategic Services Unit. *War Report of the OSS. Vols. I and II.* New York: Walker, 1976.

William, William A., ed. *The Shaping of American Diplomacy.* Chicago: Rand McNally, 1956.

Wilson, Joan Hoff. *American Business and Foreign Policy, 1920–1933.* Boston: Beacon Press, 1971.

Winks, Robin W. *Cloak and Gown: Scholars in the Secret War.* New York: Morrow, 1987.

Wise, David and Thomas B. Ross. *The Invisible Government.* New York: Vintage Books, 1974.

Wood, Gordon S. *The Creation of the American Republic, 1776–1787.* New York: Norton, 1969.

Wyden, Peter. *Bay of Pigs: The Untold Story.* London: Jonathan Cape, 1979.

Yergin, Daniel. *Shattered Peace: The Origins of the Cold War and the National Security State.* Boston: Houghton Mifflin, 1977.

ABBREVIATIONS

AFL   American Federation of Labor
AIA   American International Association
AIOC   Anglo-Iranian Oil Company
CFR   Council on Foreign Relations
CGT   Confédération Générale du Travail
CIF   Confederazione Italiana Femminile
CGIL   Confederazione Generale Italiano del Lavoro
COI   Office of Coordinator of Information
ECA   Economic Cooperation Administration
IBEC   International Basic Economy Corporation
LCGIL   Free Italian General Confederation of Labor
NSC   National Security Council
OMGUS Office of the Military Government of the U.S.
ONI   Office of Naval Intelligence
OEEC   Organization for European Economic Cooperation
OPC   Office of Policy Coordination
OSS   Office of Strategic Services
OWMR Office of War Mobilization and Reconversion
PCF   Parti Communiste Française
PCI   Partito Comunista Italiano
PPS   Policy Planning Staff
SWNCC State War-Navy Coordinating Committee
TVA   Tennessee Valley Authority
USDA   United States Department of Agriculture

INDEX

Acheson, Dean, 81, 103, 120, 124, 151n58
Adams, John Quincy, 11
Africa, aid to, 86. *See also* North Africa
Allen, George V., 70, 123, 124, 125, 167n73
Alsop, Joseph, 30, 31
Alsop, Stewart, 76
America Firsters, 28, 141
American Economic Mission to Greece. *See* Griswold Mission
American Federationist (magazine), 101
American International Association (AIA), Italian emigration and, 116
Anglo-Iranian Oil Company (AIOC), 122, 123
"Answer Man, The" (ECA), 94–95, 118
Anti-Communism, 59, 80, 85
Armed Forces Network, 95
Aron, Raymond, 83–84, 160n9
Astor, Jacob, 27
Atlante, S.A., 118
Atlantic Charter, 1, 2, 85
Atlantic Pact, 112
Attaché system, description of, 19–20
AVRO, 95

Balance of power, restructuring, 31
Ball, George, 28
Barnes, Tracey, 31
Barnes, Tracy, 64, 132, 168n18
Barrows, Leland, 102
"Basic Principles Which Must Govern Foreign Aid Programs" (Murray), 39
Bay of Pigs (Wyden), 6
Behavioral sciences, 47
Belarus Secret, The (Loftus), 143
Bellanger, William, 101
Benes, Eduard, 65
Berliet (manufacturer), 88
Beveridge, Albert, 13
Bevin, Ernest, 71
Bidault, Georges, 71
Big Three, cooperation among, 61–62
Bingham, Barry, 91–92
Bissell, Anne, 142
Bissell, Richard M., Jr., 3, 28, 31, 33, 38, 39, 46, 49, 60, 73–76, 79, 85, 102–4, 119, 151n4, 152n14, 152n16, 152n17, 152n22, 152n27, 153n29, 153n43, 154n53, 155n10, 155n21, 158n55, 159n74, 160n12, 161n17, 168n18, 168n20; hiring of, 52; interview with, 139–42; quote of, 25–26, 72–73; recollections of, 78
Bitter Fruit (Schlesinger and Kinzer), 6
"Black Chamber" offices, closing of, 20
Blum, Léon, 83; accord and, 103
Bohlen, Charles, 70, 151n58
Boundary Commission, Dulles and, 20
Bowles, Chester, 38, 39
Braden, Tom, 94, 160n7, 162n37, 162n40, 162n48, 166n59
Brazil, Italian emigration to, 116
British Secret Service, propaganda by, 29
Bross, John A., 3, 25, 30–32, 34, 35, 40–41, 103–4, 134; interview of, 142–43
Brown, Dyke, 51, 154n51
Brown, Irving, 99, 100, 119, 145
Bunche, Ralph, 122
Bundy, McGeorge, 152n27, 155n21
Burgess, Randolph, 94
Byrnes, James: film accord and, 103

Caffery, Jefferson, 87, 103
Cahiers du Communisme, 104
Canal Zone, Roosevelt and, 14
Capitalism, promotion of, 40
Cappugi, Renato, 119
Carey, Jim, 120, 152n27, 155n10
Casey, William J., 137
Castro, Cipriano, 14
Catholics, concerns of, 107
Central Intelligence Agency (CIA), 4, 6–8, 49–51, 56, 130, 132, 133; control of, 57; covert operations and, 55, 68, 70, 79; determined interventionists at, 136; dominance of, 78; establishment of, 53–54, 58, 136; limits on, 69; OPC and, 144; PSB and, 131; Truman and, 128. *See also* Office of Strategic Services
Central Intelligence Group, 54
Cesari, Vasco, 119
CFR. *See* Council on Foreign Relations

CGT. *See* Confédération Générale du Travail
China Aid, 95
Church Committee, 54, 75, 79, 137
Churchill, Winston, 1, 35
CIA. *See* Central Intelligence Agency
CIA in Guatemala, The (Immerman), 6
Civil Administration Committee, 85, 160n17
Clay, Lucius, 35, 66, 71
Clayton, Will, 103, 152n27
Cleveland, Grover, 12
Cleveland, Harlan, 93, 151n9
Cleveland, Harold B., 151n9
Clifford, Clark, 80
Cold War: determined interventionists and, 22, 31–32; Ford Foundation and, 47–48; strategy for, 35, 42; Truman and, 59
Collaboration, 83, 88
Colonialism, 161n21; end of, 85–87; Italian, 108–9
Cominform, 46; ERP and, 93; PCI and, 111–12
Comité de Gestion, 88
Committee on Foreign Aid, 45, 60, 108
Common Sense (Paine), 10
Communism: attraction of, 35, 84; battling, 5, 40–42, 45–47, 57, 63, 78; challenge of, 53; fear of, 36–37, 39, 59–60; French, 81–84, 87–89, 91, 96–97; Italian, 82–84, 106–13
Communist International, 82
Communist National Liberation Front, 42–43
Confédération Générale du Travail (CGT), 88, 89, 100
Confederazione Generale Italiano del Lavoro (CGIL), 112–13
Confederazione Italiana Femminile (CIF), 117
Connelly, Matthew, 80, 128
Coolidge, Calvin: foreign policy of, 19
Cooperation, lack of, 74–75
Coordination, 76, 105, 157n31
Council of Applied Economic Resources, establishment of, 48
Council on Foreign Relations (CFR), 64, 66, 67, 99, 101, 103, 108, 111, 119, 120, 154n52, 157n31; counterpart funds and, 94; Dulles and, 110; role of, 41–42
Countercoup (Roosevelt), 125
Counterespionage (OSS), transfer of, 54
Counterpart funds: debt retirement with,

161n17; Italian emigration and, 116; using, 93–95
Counterpropaganda, OPC and, 104. *See also* Propaganda
Countersubversion, 64, 78, 136; Marshall Plan and, 44. *See also* Subversion
Covert operations, 2–3, 7, 19, 26, 75, 82, 141, 146, 158n64; CIA and, 55, 68, 70, 79; determined interventionists and, 33; evolution of, 59, 135; Dulles and, 62–64; institutionalization of, 69, 135, 136; managing, 128; policy making and, 4; presidential transitions and, 134; shift to, 56–57; using, 4–5
Crimes of Patriots, The (Kwitny), 7
Cruz, Arturo, Jr., 7
Cuba: acquiring, 11–12; interests in, 13
Czechoslovakia, 62, 63, 156n22, 156n25, 156n28; coup in, 43, 59, 64–67, 80

Daily, The (Central Intelligence Group), 55
Dean, Vera M., 63
Decent Interval (Snepp), 6–7
"Defector Program," 49
Defense Department, 78, 132
Deficit financing, 93, 160n15; France and, 85–86; Italy and, 108
de Gaulle, Charles, 83, 90, 92–93
Determined interventionists, 4–6, 9, 13, 17, 36–37, 41, 46, 51–52, 61, 121, 137, 151n58; activism of, 3, 40, 49; at CIA, 136; Cold War and, 31–32; covert operations and, 33; Ford Foundation and, 53; international relations and, 25–26; Marshall Plan and, 62; New Deal and, 135; at OWMR, 38; rhetoric of, 12; as wartime advisors, 30–31
Deutsch-Russische Transport Company, 21, 32
Dillon, Read, 28
Disney, Walt, 103
Division chiefs, role of, 76
Dollar diplomacy, 14, 15, 16, 21
Dominican Republic, intervention in, 15
Donovan, William J., 19, 20, 26–27, 31, 32, 54, 58, 63, 94, 155n16, 160n7, 162n48; appointment of, 29, 30; intelligence interests of, 17–18; internationalism and, 27–28
Draper, William, 71
Dubinsky, David, 119
Dulles, Allen Welsh, 17, 20, 26, 30, 32–33, 45, 49–50, 59, 70, 76, 79, 94, 108, 122, 152n27, 155n16, 158n55, 158n64, 160n7,

162n48, 164n5; covert operations and, 62–64; on France, 83; internationalism and, 27; on NSC directive 10/2, 80; quote of, 61, 96, 110, 151–52n9; role of, 41
Dulles, Eleanor Lansing: determined interventionists and, 64
Dulles-Jackson-Correa Report, 54, 158n64
Dunn, James Clement, 115
Duret, Jean, 89

Eberstadt, Ferdinand, 49, 54, 153n42
Economic Cooperation Administration (ECA), 46, 67, 72, 83, 85, 100, 101, 104, 113, 130, 132, 165n21; covert activities of, 92; de Gaulle and, 93; Italian emigration and, 115–16; Italy and, 109–10; modernization and, 114; propaganda by, 117–19, 129; radio funding by, 94–95; support for, 91
Economic Cooperation Administration (ECA) Appropriations Act, provisions of, 101–2
Economic Cooperation Administration (ECA) Data Book, 108, 114
Economic Recovery Program (ERP), 27; Iran and, 122; Italy and, 117
Economic warfare, 74, 79, 96, 120, 123, 131
Eisenhower, Dwight, 52, 133, 140, 141, 152n27, 156n28
Emigration: ECA and, 115–16; Italian, 107, 109, 111, 114–16, 120; transportation for, 114, 116
"Errand into the Wilderness" (Miller), 9
European Recovery Program (ERP), 41–42, 66, 84–86, 90, 92, 131; Communists and, 93, 110; Italy and, 110, 114; propaganda by, 117
Export-Import Bank, 116

Fabiani, Mario, 112
Fairless, Benjamin, 38, 39
Fanfani, Amintore, 114
Farber, Barry, 132
Fascism, combatting, 82–83
Ferry, W. H., 49, 153n43
Fiat, grant for, 113–14
"Fifth Column Lessons for America" (Donovan), 29
Fillmore, Millard, 11
Film industry: French, 103; Italian, 118
Financial protectorates, 15
Finletter, Thomas K., 37, 66

First World War, impact of, 17
Force Ouvrière, 100, 101, 113
Ford Foundation, 49, 51–52, 153n41, 154n52; Bissell and, 52, 154n53; determined interventionists and, 53; establishment of, 47–48; role of, 48, 50
Ford Motor Company, 99
Forrestal, James V., 28, 56, 59, 66–70, 73, 156n22, 157n31, 157n33, 157n40
Foster, William, 72, 95–96, 102, 116, 120, 158n49
Foundations. See Private foundations
France: Communists in, 81–84, 87–89, 91, 96–97; counterpart funds for, 94; fears of, 36, 102–3; instability in, 87–88; Marshall Plan and, 92–93, 104; revitalization of, 96
Franklin, Benjamin, 10
Franks, Sir Oliver, 46
Freedom Committees, 69
Free Italian General Confederation of Labor (LCGIL), 112–13
"French Crisis, The," 93
French Worker-Management Committee, 88

Gaddis, John Lewis, 65, 130–31, 145
Gade, John A., 19
Gaither, Rowan, 50, 51, 52
Galbraith, John, 28
Gallup, George, 132
Geiger, Thomas, 46, 85
Georghiev, Peter, 112
Germany, dismemberment of, 36
Gibbons, Harold, 101
Gladieux, Bernard, 50–52
Goldberg, Arthur, 91
Gottwald, Clement, 65
Gray, Gordon, 58, 130–33, 168n18
Greece, 60; aid for, 42–45
Greek civil war, 43, 55, 61
Griswold, Dwight P., 43, 44, 50
Griswold Mission, 42–43, 44, 48
Guerrilla warfare, 17, 112. See also Paramilitary operations

Haldeman, H. R. "Bob," 134
Halperin, Morton H., 7
Harding, Warren: foreign policy of, 19
Harriman, E. H., 21
Harriman, W. Averell, 17, 21, 26, 30, 32, 45, 59, 60, 65, 66, 71–73, 82, 104, 116, 150n40, 151n58, 158n49, 159n74

Henderson, Loy, 7, 70, 124
Herter, Christian, 61
Heureaux, Ulises: assassination of, 15
Hillenkoetter, Roscoe H., 56, 68–69, 156n29, 159n74
Hitler, Adolf: subversion by, 29
Hoffman, Paul G., 44, 45, 49, 50, 52, 73, 93, 96, 102, 142, 150n40, 155n10, 158n52
Hogan, Michael, 25, 26, 145
Hoover, Herbert, 155n10; foreign policy of, 19; government intervention and, 25; independent internationalism and, 26
Horton, Philip, 90
Houston, Lawrence, 3, 25, 30, 32, 69, 77, 78, 143, 158n66; interview of, 144
Howard, John, 50
Human rights, 1
Hunt, James, 50

Immerman, Richard, 6
India, aid for, 48
Industrialization, 107, 109; French, 98–99; impact of, 16
Institute of Politics (Harvard), 134
Intelligence gathering, 3, 30, 50, 58, 69
Interdependence, economic, 23
Interim Aid to France, 101
International Bank, 116
International Basic Economy Corporation (IBEC), 27, 150n46
Internationalism, 27–28; independent, 26
Interventionism, 5, 82; Cold War and, 22; commerce and, 20–21; commitment to, 13–14, 16, 31; international relations and, 25–26; negative connotation of, 9; private foundations and, 136; traditional diplomacy and, 20
Iran, 60; ERP and, 122; exploitation of, 123; failure in, 128; Millspaugh Mission to, 23–24; modernization of, 106–8, 121–27; OPC and, 122
Iron Curtain, The (1949), 103
Isolationism, 3, 41, 61
Italian General Conference of Workers, 119
Italy, 91; American influence in, 68, 113, 120–21; capital investment for, 110; Communists in, 66–68, 82–84, 106–13; ECA and, 109–10; elections in, 73; ERP and, 110, 114; European Community and, 126; perceptions of, 108; stabilizing, 107, 109, 110, 121; trade with, 110–11

Jackson, Andrew, 11
Jackson, William H., 64, 168n18
Jacob-Malaquais, 97
Jefferson, Thomas, 10, 11, 98
Jeffreys-Jones, Rhodri, 106
"Joe Smith, American Worker" (pamphlet), 100
Johnson, Charles F. H., 119
Johnson, Loch, 137
Johnson, Lyndon, 121
Joint Chiefs of Staff, 137
Joyce, Robert, 30, 71, 132, 158n45

Katz, Milton, 47, 49, 52, 72, 100, 102, 158n49
Kelly, Dick, 99–100
Kennan, George Frost, 17, 20, 22, 26, 32, 33, 42, 51, 56, 59, 66, 70, 71, 73, 140, 141, 151n58, 152n27, 156n22, 157n34, 157n38; covert activities and, 130–31; Long Telegram of, 64; rise of, 28
"Kennan proposal," 49, 50, 52
Khomeini, Ayatollah, 127
Kinzer, Stephen, 6
Kirk, Alexander C., 77
Knox, Frank, 29
Knox, Philander, 15
Korea, economic assistance for, 95, 105
Korean War, OPC and, 78, 79
Krock, Arthur, 133
Kwitny, Jonathan, 7

Labor: French, 99–101; Italian, 111–13, 120; protection for, 98
Labor Information Program, 117
Labor leaders, U.S.: work of, 99–101, 119
Labor unions, 111–13, 151n7; role of, 117; purging, 38
LaFollette, Robert, 39–40, 155n10
LaFond, Andre, 101
Land, Edwin H., 49
Lansing, Robert, 20
Latin American Agricultural Program, 27
Lavrentiev, Anatol, 124
Lawless State, The (Halperin), 7
Leadership, terms of, 23
Lend-Lease program, 28
Liebert, Herman, 46
Lindsay, Franklin A., 3, 25, 30, 32, 34, 44, 46, 61, 62, 71, 73, 78, 85, 104, 131–32, 134, 152n27, 155n11, 155n21, 168n18, 168n20, 168n21; interview of, 142, 145; role of, 74

Link, Arthur, 16
Loftus, John, 143
Long Telegram, 64, 156n22
Lovestone, Jay, 100, 101, 119, 120
Lovett, Robert, 44, 103, 129, 131, 151n58
Lucia, Carmen, 101

McCloy, John, 151n58, 153n41, 154n52
McDaniels, Joseph, 51, 154n52
McKeever, Porter, 66, 156n31
McKinley, William, 13, 14, 16
Macmillan, Harold, 77, 158n67
Madison, James, 11
Manifest destiny, 12
"March of the Flag" speech (Beveridge), 13
Marquis, Don G., 51
Marshall, George C., 45, 56, 59, 60, 65–66, 68, 70, 73, 103
Marshall Plan, 3, 6–8, 25, 31, 37, 40, 41, 48, 53, 65, 67, 80, 85, 86; benefits of, 44–45, 109; coordination of, 81–82; countersubversive plans in, 44; determined interventionists and, 62; development of, 39, 60–61, 81, 91, 102; France and, 92–93, 104; French Communists and, 97–98; influence of, 92; Italy and, 109; Office of Special Representative and, 82; OPC and, 68, 72–73, 82, 105, 142, 143; promoting, 60, 64; propaganda by, 117–18; Soviet veto of, 62; Truman and, 60; U.S. labor leaders and, 99–101
Martin, Harry, 99, 163n59
Masaryk, Jan: defenestration of, 65
May, Stacy, 94, 160n7, 162n48
Mayer, Gerald M., 103, 155n21
Meany, George, 39–40, 155n10
Memoirs of a Counterrevolutionary (Cruz), 7
Metropole, 85–86, 108
Mexico, stabilizing, 18
Meyer, Cord, 64, 143, 144, 151n7
Michelin, strike against, 100
Miller, Perry: essay by, 9
Milliken, Max, 46, 55, 103, 168n20
Millspaugh, Arthur C., 23–24
Millspaugh Mission, 23–24, 122
Modernization, 24, 40–41, 84, 96, 98, 101, 107–9, 111, 113, 114, 121, 123–27
Monnet, Jean, 103
Monnet Plan, 101; success of, 96
Monroe, James, 11
Monroe Doctrine, 11, 12, 14–15

Moran, Charles M. W., 35
Mossadegh, Mohammed, 123, 124–125, 167n71
Murphy, Robert, 35, 70, 71, 155n16
Murray, Philip, 38, 39, 152n17
Murrow, Edward R., 132

Napoleon, 10
Nationalism, 152n9; economic, 23
Nationalization, 62, 88
National Security Act, 53, 69, 79, 157n33; provisions of, 54; Truman and, 58–59
National Security Council (NSC), 4, 55, 70, 75, 106, 129, 131, 135, 137, 144
National Security Council (NSC) directive 4/A, 56
National Security Council (NSC) directive 10/2, 59, 70, 71, 80
National Security Council (NSC) directive 10/5, 132
National Security Council (NSC) directive 68, 79
National Security State, theory of, 140
Nazi-Soviet Non-Aggression Pact (1939), French Communists and, 83
"Negro in American Life, The" (ERP), 90
Neustadt, Richard E., 38
New Deal, 25; determined interventionists and, 135
Newsweek, poll by, 65
Nielsen, Waldemar: propaganda by, 117, 119
Nitze, Paul, 25, 28, 33, 49, 119, 130
Nixon, Richard M., 61, 134, 155n11
North Africa, 86–87, 161n21. See also Africa

Office for Special Operations (CIA), 55
Office of Coordinator of Information (OCI), creation of, 29
Office of Military Government of the U.S. (OMGUS), 95, 161n17
Office of Naval Intelligence (ONI), 29; attaché system of, 19
Office of Policy Coordination (OPC), 3, 6, 7, 30, 31, 59, 67, 96, 99, 125, 129, 137, 141, 152n24; aid from, 101; CIA and, 144; conflict at, 76; cooperation at, 75; counterpropaganda by, 104; covert activities of, 72, 142; dominance of, 78, 79; establishment of, 70, 159n74; Iran and, 122; Korean War and, 78, 79; Marshall Plan and, 68, 72–73, 82, 105,

Office of Policy Coordination *(continued)* 142, 143; operations of, 32, 39; organization of, 75–76; PSB and, 132; Truman and, 80
Office of Special Operations (CIA), 56
Office of Special Representative (OSR), 82, 99, 100, 129
Office of Strategic Services (OSS), 28, 31, 32, 34, 43, 53, 88, 89; disbandment of, 54, 58; expansion of, 29–30. *See also* Central Intelligence Agency
Office of War Mobilization and Reconversion (OWMR), work of, 37–39
Offie, Carmel, 158n67, 159n69; problems with, 76–78
Oil, 123; protecting, 106
Olney, Richard, 12, 13
100 Persons Act (CIA), 143
ONI. *See* Office of Naval Intelligence
OPC. *See* Office of Policy Coordination
Operation Sunrise, 108
Organization for European Economic Cooperation, 46, 106
Organizzazione Bambi, 118
Organizzazione Epoca, 117–18
OSS. *See* Office of Strategic Services
Ostend Manifesto, 12
O'Sullivan, John L., 12
Overpopulation, Italian, 107, 109, 114
Overseas Consultants, Inc., 122, 124, 125
OWMR. *See* Office of War Mobilization and Reconversion

Pahlavi, Reza Shah, 24
Paine, Thomas, 10
Paix et Liberté, 104
Panama, revolution in, 14
Paramilitary operations, 7, 8, 17, 32, 74, 75, 79, 92, 112, 132. *See also* Guerrilla warfare
Paris Committee of Liberation, 87–88
Parri, Enrico, 119
Parti Communiste Français (PCF), 82, 97, 162n53
Partito Comunista Italiano (PCI), 111–12
Pasqualini, Giovanni, 119
Patterson, Robert, 55
Perry, Matthew C., 11
Pershing, John "Blackjack," 18
Philippines, 13, 17
Pierce, Franklin, 11–12
Pinay, 97
PL 472 (1948), 72
Poland, 62

Policy Planning Staff (PPS), 42, 48–49, 56, 67, 124, 130
"Policy toward France" (ERP), 92
Political warfare, 70, 73, 79, 123
Polk, James Knox, 11
Popular Front (France), 82
Porter, Paul, 104–5
PPS. *See* Policy Planning Staff
Prados, John, 7
President's Secret Wars (Prados), 7
Presidential transitions, covert activities and, 134
Price, Harry Bayard, 86, 94–95
Princeton University Bicentennial Conference on Development of International Society, Dulles speech to, 63
Private foundations, 27, 49, 51–52, 153n41, 154n52, 154n53, 166n50; interventionism and, 53, 136; role of, 47–48, 50, 116
Progressivism, 16; foreign aid and, 24
Project Ajax, 124; failure of, 125
Project orientation, 75, 78
Propaganda, 29, 95, 116–19, 129; anti-Stalin, 97–98, 104, 163n67; Communist, 104, 118. *See also* Counterpropaganda
Prud'homme, Hector, 46
Psychological Strategy Board (PSB): CIA and, 131; establishment of, 128–31; demise of, 133; OPC and, 132
Psychological warfare, 56, 58, 73–74, 79, 91, 96, 124, 128–30, 132, 141, 158n55
Public virtue, 23
Puerto Rico, 13
Puritans, interventionism of, 9–10

Radio: funding for, 94–95; propaganda on, 117–18
Radio Epoca, 118
Radio Lille, 95
Radio Luxembourg, 95
Ransom, Harry Howe, 4, 77
Reagan, Ronald, 137
Red scare, 120
Red-White-Red, 95
Remington, William, 46
Renault, nationalization of, 88
Reparations, 35–36
Resistance, 83, 89
Retardation, description of, 74
Reuther, Walter, 99–100
Revitalization, 84, 92, 96; economic, 81

Reza, Shah Mohammad, 24
RIAS, 95
Riga School, 26; description of, 22
Robinson, Donald, 133
Rockefeller, John D., III, 48
Rockefeller, Nelson, 27, 74, 94, 158n55,
  160n7, 162n48
Rockefeller Foundation, 27, 48, 153n41,
  166n50; Italian emigration and, 116
Roosevelt, Franklin, 1, 26–27, 35;
  government intervention and, 25;
  wartime advisors for, 28–31
Roosevelt, Kermit, 3, 25, 30, 32, 75, 76,
  124–26; goal of, 122–23; interview of,
  143–45; Offie and, 77–78
Roosevelt, Theodore, 14, 16, 30
Rositzke, Harry, 7
Royall, Kenneth, 44, 168n18
Russian Revolution, impact of, 17

Saturday Evening Post, 133
Schlesinger, Stephen, 6
Secret Intelligence (OSS), transfer of, 54
Self-determination, 1–3, 11–13, 22, 147n1,
  151–52n9
Seven-Year Plan (Iran), 123; description of,
  122
Seymour, Charles, 20, 45
Sforza, Count Carlo, 111
Shadow warfare, description of, 28–29
Sherman, John, 123, 167n7, 167n70,
  167n71
Shirt-sleeve diplomats, job of, 119. *See
  also* Labor leaders
Silent Six, role of, 28
Smith, Bradley, 28
Smith, Gaddis, 1, 25
Smith, Walter Bedell, 49, 78, 129, 131,
  144, 159n74
Snepp, Frank, 6
Snyder, John W., 37, 38, 152n16
Socialists, French, 87–88, 99–100
Souers, Sidney, 71
South America, Italian emigration to,
  115–16
Soviet Union: importance of, 22;
  reparations for, 35–36; self-
  determination and, 2
Spanish-American War, 12, 13, 14
Special Operations (OSS), 54
Special Procedures Group (CIA),
  establishment of, 56
Special Projects Funds, 135

Special Services Unit, description of, 55
Speier, Hans, 50, 51
Stabilization, 18, 107, 109, 110, 116–17,
  121
Stalin, Josef, 35, 83, 90; propaganda
  about, 97–98, 104, 163n67
Standard of living, rising, 98, 126, 135
Standing mechanisms, 75
State Department, 27, 42, 54, 67, 69, 70,
  73, 78, 119, 130, 132, 133; France and,
  83; Italian emigration and, 116;
  psychological warfare and, 56; Soviet
  studies by, 22; Truman and, 128
State-War-Navy Coordinating Committee
  (SWNCC), 56
Station chiefs, role of, 76
Steelman, John, 38, 152n14
Stephenson, William, 29
Stevens, Francis, 70
Stevenson, Adlai, 132
Stimson, Henry, 19, 20
Strikes, 100, 113
Subversion, 57, 63, 68, 80; concerns about,
  151n7; importance of, 29. *See also*
  Countersubversion
Syndical (bulletin), 99

Tactics, disagreement about, 73–74
Taft, William Howard: dollar diplomacy
  of, 14, 15, 16, 21
Temporary Controls, 38
Tennessee Valley Authority (TVA), as
  development model, 121
Thompson, Llewelyn, 70
Thorez, Maurice, 82, 83
Tito, Jesip Broz, 43, 61, 145
Traditional diplomacy, interventionists and,
  20
Treasury Department, attaché system of,
  19
Treaty of Versailles, impact of, 17
Truman, Harry S., 32, 35, 37–39, 52, 56,
  66, 110, 130, 133, 140, 141; CIA and,
  53, 58; Cold War and, 59; covert
  activities management by, 68, 128;
  Italian emigration and, 114; Marshall
  Plan and, 60; OPC and, 80; OSS and,
  54; quote of, 59
Truman Doctrine, 43, 44, 80; development
  of, 60
Turkey, 60; aid for, 44
Tuthill, John, 46

Unemployment, 109, 114, 115
Unions. *See* Labor unions
United States: assistance from, 93;
    dominance of, 102–3, 105; French fear
    of, 89–90; influence of, 92; racism in, 90
United States Department of Agriculture
    (USDA), foreign sector of, 116
United States Steel, plans for, 39
Universal Military Training, Truman and,
    66

Vandenberg, Arthur, 54, 60
Vandenberg, Hoyt: CIA and, 54–56
Van Hyning, Samuel, 46
Vietnam, impact of, 137
Vinson, Fred, 37

War Department, 54
War of 1812, 11
War Shipping Administration, 28
Wartime advisors, appointment of, 28–30
War with Mexico, 11
Webb, James, 129
Westernization, 24, 102–3

Wiley, Alexander, 85, 87, 91
Williams, Langbourne, 94
Wilson, Joan Hoff, 22, 26
Wilson, Woodrow, 14, 16–18;
    self-determination and, 1
Wisner, Frank, 25, 30, 64, 71–74, 76, 78,
    158n51, 158n55, 159n74, 168n18
Wolfers, Arnold, 84, 94, 160n7, 160n10,
    162n48
Women, propaganda efforts toward, 95,
    117–18
"Women's Program, The," 95
Wood, Bryce, 66–67
Wood, Gordon, 23
World Federation of Trade Unions, 120
Wyden, Peter, 6

Yale University, 26
Yeaton, Ivan D., 71
"Young America" movement, 11

Zahedi, Fazlollah, 124
Zellerbach, James D., 108, 114, 115,
    165n21, 165n31